THE UNITED STATES, GREAT BRITAIN, AND
THE SOVIETIZATION OF HUNGARY,
1945-1948

Stanley M. Max

EAST EUROPEAN MONOGRAPHS, BOULDER
DISTRIBUTED BY COLUMBIA UNIVERSITY PRESS, NEW YORK

1985

EAST EUROPEAN MONOGRAPHS, NO. CLXXVII

TABLE OF CONTENTS

PREFACE

One of the most important consequences of the Second World War was the extension of Soviet control to Eastern Europe and the establishment there of pro-Soviet governments. The present study examines the response of the British and American governments to that phenomenon of sovietization. I used Hungary as a case history, since that country offers an opportunity to examine the sovietization process over a comparatively prolonged period. Of the various East European countries that became sovietized, Hungary was particularly resistant to the establishment of a Communist government, and was the last to adopt the constitutional form of a People's Republic.

To study the Western reaction to sovietization one necessarily must study the reaction of the United States, which by the end of the war was clearly stronger than any combination of Western powers. But an analysis of British policy is an important if not crucial ingredient for achieving a more thorough understanding of the overall Western position toward Eastern Europe. Even in its postwar decline Britain played a prominent role in that region, as it continued to do elsewhere. The British along with the Americans sat on the Allied Control Commissions for Hungary as well as Rumania and Bulgaria. Both Western powers signed armistice agreements and peace treaties with those Southeast European countries, and they closely monitored—although they had increasing trouble influencing—events in the Balkans. Britain of course could never forget its powerful American partner, especially after 1947. On the other hand the United States found itself obliged to deal with Britain, sometimes with discord, while simultaneously confronting the Soviet Union over the East European problem. Thus, the question of the Anglo-American response to the sovietization of Hungary was both a bipolar issue between East and West, and a triangular one among the powers of the former Grand Alliance.

The British and Americans became involved with Hungarian affairs in the last month of 1944, when a Soviet-sponsored, anti-German government in Hungary opened armistice negotiations with the Soviet Union and the Western Allies. Hungary remained a subject of Western diplomatic meetings, the foreign ministerial discussions of 1945, and the 1946 Paris Peace Conference. Washington and London also paid close attention to important political developments in Hungary and became involved in matters pertaining to economic assistance for the country. Throughout this period, the major challenge facing the British and Americans, as well as pro-Western forces within Hungary, was the growing influence of Hungary's Communist Party, supported politically, economically, and militarily by the Kremlin. Beginning late in 1946, the Communists, allied with the Social Democrats, carried out a sweeping purge of all non-leftist forces. This purge culminated in mid-1947 with the ouster of the centrist prime minister and the establishment of a left-wing government in which the Communists and the Social Democrats shared power. In ensuing months, the Communists enhanced their own strength at the expense of the Social Democrats, eventually overwhelming and, by June 1948, eliminating the Social Democratic Party. The Communists thereby acquired unrivalled political control, and virtually all Western influence in Hungary came to an end.

The main focus of the study has been to compare and contrast British and American policy toward the sovietization issue. My reading of the evidence indicated that there were significant disagreements over policy. Although both Western governments were opposed to the growth of Soviet control in Hungary, the United States resisted the sovietization process much more aggressively than did Britain. Washington tried to counter most Soviet and Communist moves in Hungary through diplomatic démarche or public confrontation. London, on the other hand, generally chose not to challenge such moves. The divergence between British and American policy, as I have tried to show, resulted from the unequal strength and the dissimilar geographical susceptibility of the two Western powers, and the consequent difference in their ability to withstand Soviet advances.

* * * * *

The principal sources used for the study were the British Foreign Office records in London and the U.S. State Department files in Washington. I am grateful to the staffs of these archives for their assistance in my research. Angela Raspin, archivist of the London School of Economics, placed the Dalton papers at my disposal. Published government material, memoirs, and newspapers have also been drawn upon, as have British Labour Party documents. I. W. Wagner, librarian of the British Labour Party, helped me locate party pamphlets. I particularly appreciate the efforts of Stephen Bird, archivist of the party, for assisting my research in the minutes and correspondence of its International Committee, and for sharing his knowledge of Labour Party politics with me. Of course, any deficiencies in the study are mine alone.

I

HUNGARY AND THE GREAT POWERS, 1918-1945

At various times in their histories the United States and Great Britain have been concerned with Hungarian political affairs. For Britain, the status of East Central and Southeastern Europe has been connected in one way or another with the Eastern Question, a British foreign policy concern since the late eighteenth century. The United States, though it gave little attention to the Eastern Question until the First World War,[1] had considerable sympathy for the Hungarian independence movement of the nineteenth century.

Following the world war, the political situation in Eastern Europe underwent a fundamental transformation, thereby affecting the status of the area in the eyes of Western foreign policy makers. In a state of dissolution for centuries, the Ottoman Empire, which had lost nearly all of its territory in Europe just prior to the war, finally collapsed. In the same period the Austro-Hungarian Empire also disintegrated into smaller units, leaving Eastern Europe with several new or newly enlarged nations. The Russian Empire also fell apart. There, a revolution had placed in power a Communist government, which from the Western viewpoint was so potentially dangerous that it had to be contained, if it could not be overthrown. Containment thus became the strategic value of Eastern

Europe. The area was to serve as a buffer zone, a *cordon sanitaire* as the French put it, to protect Western Europe from Bolshevism. Towards the end of the 1930s, as war clouds began to form, Eastern Europe came under the new threat of Nazi Germany. But this turned out to be only a temporary diversion, for with the defeat of Germany the old Communist menace to Europe again revived, and with the Soviet occupation of Eastern Europe it became more serious than ever.

* * * * *

The centrally located area of the Middle Danube Basin, arched on three sides by the Carpathian Mountains, has historically been a passageway for migrations and invasions between Europe and Asia, and due to geography, has inevitably served as a buffer region between the two continents. Such a migration by the Magyar people was the origin of the Hungarian nation, which upon its adoption of Christianity in the year 1000 became the easternmost bastion of Western culture. Turkish invasion and more than 150 years of occupation in the sixteenth and seventeenth centuries destroyed Hungary's fair degree of prosperity and ended its independence, when Austria's Habsburg rulers claimed the Hungarian throne as their own. As part of the European-wide upsurge of nationalism in the eighteenth century, the Magyars intensified their demands for independence from Vienna. Though the Hungarian Republic of 1849, led by Lajos Kossuth, was short-lived, the weakening of Habsburg rule in the 1860s resulted in the establishment of the Dual Monarchy. This compromise solution returned the throne to Hungary, and entrusted matters of foreign policy and finance to joint Austrian and Hungarian control. Nonetheless, the Austro-Hungarian Empire was socially and politically an archaic structure and did not fully satisfy Magyar national aspirations for total independence. At the same time non-Magyar nationalities inside Hungary, notably Rumanians and Slavs, nurtured their own grievances against Hungarian rule. The strains of the First World War overwhelmed the fragile empire, and some one thousand years after its establishment Historic Hungary came crashing down.[2]

The founding of modern Hungary was a turbulent affair. In 1918 Count Mihály Károlyi rose to power, formed a left-wing government, and, proclaiming independence from Austria, announced a republic. At the same time Serb, Czech, and Rumanian troops saw their chance and occupied two-thirds of Hungarian territory. As all order disintegrated, the

Communist Béla Kun took power, but landlord and peasant counter-revolution, Social Democratic opposition, and invading Rumanian forces overthrew his government in less than five months. A conservative government was set up, but because of widespread disagreement on the question of the monarchy, a regency was established to hold the matter in abeyance. Admiral Miklós Horthy, a counter-revolutionary leader, was elected Regent, a position he maintained until 1944.[3]

Though the Austro-Hungarian collapse gave Hungary full independence from Vienna, the postwar settlement was a grave disappointment to Hungarian nationalists. As a result of the 1920 Treaty of Trianon, Hungary lost more than two-thirds of its historical territory, most of it to Rumania, Czechoslovakia, and Yugoslavia, and nearly two-thirds of its population of all nationalities and about one-third of its Magyar population. The loss of so much territory, on which more than three million Hungarian-speaking persons lived, remained an important irredenta for Magyar nationalists, who were firmly committed to the revision of Trianon.[4]

The United States and Great Britain had a certain degree of sympathy for Hungary's claims at the Peace Conference. President Wilson would have liked to see the notion of national self-determination applied for Hungarians as for other East European nationalities, but it is unlikely, given the intermingled condition of the nationalities, that this could have been achieved. In any case, Wilson thought that Hungary should have kept some of Transylvania instead of surrendering it all to Rumania, even though this would have left Rumanians under Hungarian control. At the Peace Conference Lloyd George also gave consideration, though not support, to Hungary's territorial claims, and there was also some pro-Hungarian sentiment in the British Parliament. Neither the United States nor Great Britain subsequently supported Hungary's desire for treaty revision. In fact France, which supported the Treaty of Trianon at the Conference,[5] played a more active role in Danubian affairs than did either Britain or America, and France was decidedly anti-Hungarian in its foreign policy. This was because France in its attempt to build an anti-German security alliance supported the so-called Little Entente, composed of Czechoslovakia, Rumania, and Yugoslavia. The Little Entente—and thus France—was vitally concerned to oppose any attempt by Hungary to revise the Treaty of Trianon.

Once stability returned to Central Europe following the tumultuous social upheavals of the postwar period, Britain and America were little concerned with Hungary politically for the remainder of the interwar years.[6] Their principal interest was in matters of trade and especially, finance.[7] This in turn corresponded with the needs of Hungary, which to recover from its disastrous postwar condition, not only had to stabilize its own internal political situation, but was also forced to borrow heavily. It did both under the government of Count István Bethlen, Prime Minister from 1921 to 1931. Bethlen managed to persuade peasant leaders to drop their demands for more than very modest land reform and to fuse their party with that of the large landowners. This they did out of a fear of a Habsburg restoration, which had been twice attempted in 1921, and of a revival of Communist agitation. The Social Democrats agreed to support the government and its foreign policy in exchange for their right of existence and an end to persecution.[8] To bolster its troubled economy, Hungary joined the League of Nations in 1922 and applied for a League loan. In 1924 it obtained the loan, which in effect was a British and especially American loan (the principal financial backers) funneled through the international organization. From time to time after that, Hungary drew additional loans directly from private lenders.[9] The loans had the desired effect, and throughout the 1920s, Hungary's economic situation improved dramatically. But after the onset of the depression in 1929 and the eventual freezing of financial assistance from Western bankers, agricultural impoverishment and industrial unemployment soon brought Hungary's recovery to an end.

In 1931, under the impact of the depression, Bethlen resigned. From that point on, Hungary began moving sharply to the right. In part because of the rightward drift, and in part because of its geographical isolation from the Western powers, which in any case refused to sanction Hungary's revisionist policy, Budapest moved ever closer to the Axis camp. But with which wing of the Axis Hungary would align itself— Berlin or Rome—was an issue not finally determined until the very end of the turbulent decade.

Hungary's dilemma was that it needed the help of a powerful state to regain its lost territories. But the growing power of the Third Reich represented more of a threat to Hungary's national independence than a possible basis of support for its territorial aspirations. This was especially the case because Germany's own territorial goals collided with those of Hungary in such key areas of Eastern Europe as Czechoslovakia and the Balkans.

Nearly all political and social groups in Hungary were agreed, more or less, on the German threat. The Jews' hostility toward Nazi Germany was obvious. The Social Democrats and most segments of liberal democratic opinion had no use for a policy of close alignment with the Reich. A pro-German policy also met the opposition of the Legitimists, those, politically conservative, often large landowners, who were particularly perturbed over Hitler's annexation of Austria. Even Hungarian pro-Nazi, anti-Semitic forces—the so-called Arrow Cross Party[10]—had differences with their German mentors. Notably, Ferenc Szálasi, the leader of the otherwise overwhelmingly pro-German Arrow Cross Party, resented Hitler's slighting of Hungary's national ambitions. In fact, the only segment of Hungarian society consistently pro-German was the German ethnic minority, the Swabians. To a significant extent the Swabians constituted a fifth column for Germany inside Hungary—a fact which occasionally produced friction between them and the Magyar population.

On the international front, Hungary could protect its freedom of action from Germany by allying with Italy, thereby playing the two lighter weights of the Axis against the heavier one. Key to a productive Rome-Budapest alliance was the participation of Austria, without which Italy was too weak to challenge Germany, and which in Hitler's hands would create a powerful German threat throughout Europe. Austria, crucial to the fate of Europe, remained a bone of contention between Hitler and Mussolini throughout much of the 1930s.

As long as the Austrian question was undecided, Hungarian statesmen made constant and strenuous efforts to solidify the relationship with Italy. Soon after he came to power in 1932, Prime Minister Gyula Gömbös, a reactionary and anti-Semite, concluded the Rome Protocols, which provided for considerable political and economic cooperation between Rome, Budapest, and Vienna. Thus, Hungary drew itself into the so-called Rome Triangle, which was directed primarily against Germany. Following Gömbös' premature death in 1936, his successor, Kálmán Darányi, a conservative more than a Right Radical, maintained Hungary's pro-Italian orientation.

When Hitler with the Anschluss finally won the showdown with Mussolini in 1938, foreign and domestic pressure on Hungary intensified enorm-
ously. Internally, the Anschluss emboldened the Hungarian Nazis, who
grew increasingly ambitious to seize power for themselves. Externally,
Hitler's annexation of Austria brought German military and economic
power to the very border of Hungary. Italy now lay in the shadow of
Germany, and could no longer stand as an ally with Hungary against
the Reich.

Under such circumstances, and with the threat of war looming dis-
tinctly on the horizon, Hungarians wondered whether they could prevent
an alignment with Germany. It was the only power from which Hungary
could expect help to satisfy at least some of its wide-ranging irredentist
ambitions. Moreover, Hungarians speculated, if war did come and if
Germany won, it would be particularly dangerous to have affronted
Berlin, which could easily place Hungary at its mercy. On the other hand,
a contrasting current of opinion held by Regent Horthy for one, was
that if war came—which Horthy expected—Germany would lose. In any
case, only the most determined Right Radicals were willing to undergo
the ravages of all-out war for the benefit of Hitler. These were the pain-
ful problems with which Hungary had to cope, as Germany's growing
strength drastically limited Hungary's freedom of action.

Despite foreign and domestic pressure, Hungary sought to keep a
safe distance from the Germans and the Hungarian Nazis. Béla Imrédy,
who followed Darányi in the wake of the Anschluss, continued to compete rather than cooperate with the Arrow Cross Party, until charges of
Jewish ancestry drove him from office. His successor, Pál Teleki, sought
to suppress the Arrow Cross early in 1939, though it continued to gain
ground. In foreign affairs, conducted by Count István Csáky, foreign
minister who came into office in the Imrédy government and who was
more accommodating to the Axis than was his predecessor, Kálmán
Kánya, Hungary made certain concessions to the Germans. For example,
Budapest joined the Anti-Comintern Pact in early 1939, and later in the
year withdrew from the League of Nations. But such actions were due to
German pressure rather than pro-German sentiments.

Although Hungary wanted to avoid too close an association with Germany, Budapest never abandoned the ambition to recover its lost territory, and as a last resort it was willing to receive Germany's assistance

toward that end. Germany gave this in the case of Czechoslovakia, when after the Munich crisis Hitler's First Vienna Award sanctioned Hungary's occupation of the Magyar-inhabited region of Southern Slovakia; and in 1939 Germany authorized Hungary to occupy Carpatho-Ruthenia. These events placed Hungary in Germany's debt, as did the Second Vienna Award of 1940, by which Hungary annexed the northern portion of Transylvania. Even so, Hungary offered aid to Germany only sparingly and reluctantly, and did not join the Tripartite Pact until late 1940.[11]

Czechoslovakia, of course, was the stepping-stone into World War Two. Throughout the conflict, Hungarian leaders sought to maintain their freedom of action concerning Germany, though the effort became increasingly unsuccessful. In 1941 Germany invaded Yugoslavia after an anti-Axis coup in that country. Hitler called for Hungarian assistance in the offensive against Yugoslavia, which Hungary refused, though it did permit German transit across its territory. Only after the Germans had launched their attack did Hungary occupy Yugoslav land which Budapest had historically held. After the Germans opened their offensive against the Soviet Union, László Bárdossy, newly appointed prime minister following Teleki's suicide—a suicide prompted by Hungary's having been drawn into the war against Yugoslavia—sent some Hungarian forces in support of the Germans. Bárdossy was himself not a Right Radical, but he wanted to please the Germans, whom he expected to win. The war against the Soviet Union turned out to be costly and difficult, however, and Regent Horthy, who as a lifelong conservative had no desire to see a Soviet victory, nevertheless expected the Germans to lose. Consequently in March 1942 Horthy replaced Bárdossy with Miklós Kállay. Like the regent, Kállay believed that the wisest course was to continue to fight against the Soviet Union, while simultaneously making secret peace overtures to Great Britain and the United States, with which Hungary had exchanged declarations of war.

The strategy of Horthy and Kállay was predicted on the false assumption that the two Western Allies were willing to accept a Hungarian surrender without Soviet participation, and that they were prepared to send an occupation force to East Central Europe. In fact, the United States and Great Britain were not about to make a separate peace with the East European satellites, and in late 1943, at the Moscow and Teheran Conferences, the British and Americans had definitively committed themselves to an invasion of France, and not the Balkans.[12] In the meantime the war against the Soviet Union went horribly, as the titanic Stalingrad campaign in the winter of 1942-43 proved to be the great turning point. In January 1943, Hungary, after a decisive and overwhelming defeat at Voronezh, gave up all offensive operations against the Russians and withdrew most of its forces behind the Carpathians for defense.

Still, the war was far from over, and the Kállay government, unaware of Allied intentions, extended numerous peace feelers towards the West. But by early 1944, Soviet troops were getting close to Hungary, and in this critical situation Hitler, aware of the Hungarian government's disloyalty, demanded from Horthy the appointment of a new government willing to collaborate with the Germans and agree to a German occupation of Hungary. Thus, in March 1944 ended a situation in which Hungary had been able to maintain a certain degree of independence from Germany. Yet Hungarian fortunes changed again in August 1944, when Rumania defected from the Axis and agreed to an armistice with the Allies, a development which temporarily relived German pressure on Hungary. Horthy appointed a new government which proceeded to renew the peace feelers, though he now realized that he had no chocie but to negotiate with the Russians, who forces were already penetrating the Carpathian Mountains. After Soviet-Hungarian discussions had taken place, a preliminary armistice was about to be put into effect when, in October 1944, the Germans abducted Horthy and installed as prime minister Ferenc Szálasi, leader of the Arrow Cross Party. But by this time the Red Army was already on Hungarian territory. As that country became the site of some of the most savage fighting of the Second World War, a new epoch in Hungarian history was about to begin.[13]

* * * * *

As the Red Army drove the Germans westward across Hungary, political life sprang up anew in the cities, towns, and villages over which the battling armies had passed. In order to take provisional charge of local affairs, members of anti-Nazi political parties established municipal and rural councils, which at first worked independently of each other owing to the breakdown in communications. The establishment of the local councils was a basically spontaneous process, though one conducted under the watchful eye of the Soviet authorities. The latter soon intervened actively to control and direct the process, and in December they ordered a temporary administrative center to be set up in Debrecen, the largest city in eastern Hungary and one of the first liberated by the Red Army.

Four Hungarian political parties took part in the establishment and functioning of the new administration. One was the Hungarian Communist Party, most of whose leaders had been living and trained in the Soviet Union and had accompanied the Red Army when it first arrived. During the interwar years, the number of Communists operating in Hungary was no more than a few hundred, and their political influence was minuscule. In the early 1930s, they did, however, make some slight gains in organizing the growing ranks of the unemployed. Closely allied with the Communists, and another element in the new administration, was the National Peasant Party. The Communists had established this party in 1944 to serve as their rural wing, and it purpose was to lead and represent the agricultural proletariat.[14]

Preeminent among Hungarian Communists was Mátyás Rákosi. Born in 1892 to a Jewish family of the merchant class, Rákosi received a respectable education at Budapest's Oriental Institute, where he learned English, Russian, Turkish, and other foreign languages. When World War I broke out, Rákosi joined the Austro-Hungarian army and served as an officer, and was captured by the Russians in 1915. His contact with that revolutionary country converted him to the Communist cause, which he henceforth supported zealously. In 1917 Rákosi participated in the Russian Revolution, and when revolution broke out in his native Hungary months later, Rákosi returned to play a prominent role in that event, serving as a minister in Hungary's red republic. Its collapse forced the now hunted Communist to flee, and he soon arrived back in Soviet Russia. There he worked for the Comintern, in which capacity the Communist agitator returned secretly to Hungary in 1925. But the Horthy regime soon detected and imprisoned him under severely harsh conditions. He spent some fifteen years as a political prisoner until, thanks to the Nazi-Soviet pact of 1939, he was deported back to the Soviet Union. From that vantage point Rákosi observed the war, towards the end of which the hardened revolutionary returned again to his native land, this time accompanied by the Red Army.[15]

Rákosi, known as Hungary's Stalin and unabashedly his protégé, wanted above all total Communist power. But the counter-revolutionary defeat of the Hungarian Communist republic taught bitter lessons to Rákosi, who now understood that in the face of conservative resistance a policy of pragmatic caution and subtlety could be more useful than one of revolutionary bravado and bluster. Rákosi clearly saw how faulty was Béla Kun's refusal to sanction peasant demands for land redistribution, so as to promote immediate collectivization. This time, Rákosi was determined, the Communists would advance gradually through piecemeal consolidation of political power rather than a sudden thrust for it. In the wartorn conditions in which Hungarians found themselves, Rákosi saw the overall situation as favorable for Communist victory, all the more so with the added presence of the Red Army, with therefore little need to advance events hurriedly. At least until 1946 the Hungarian Communist Party pursued a policy based upon coalitionary, popular fronts with non-Communist forces.[16] This gradualist approach was characteristic of other East European Communist parties in the same period.[17]

A third group in the Debrecen administration was the Social Democratic Party, who organizational base was in the industrial areas of Hungary, especially among the skilled workers. The Horthy regime and the Social Democratic leaders had concluded a pact in 1921 guaranteeing the party a legal existence free from persecution. The Social Democrats could maintain a free press, seek parliamentary representation, and carry on trade-union activity. In exchange, the Social Democrats agreed to operate as a loyal opposition, to abstain from activity for the establishment of a republic, not to denounce at home or abroad the regime, and to support the government in all foreign policy issues. As a result of this agreement, by which the Social Democrats commited themselves to a policy of reform rather than revolution, their relations with the Communists, who under Comintern directives denounced the Social Democrats as "social fascists," became strained. In the mid-1930s, when the Comintern changed direction and called for anti-fascist popular fronts, the Communists sought to ally themselves with the Social Democrats, but the latter remained suspicious of Communist intentions, and did not want to jeopardize their legal existence by associating too closely with them.[18]

Participating in the Debrecen administration was finally the Smallholders Party, founded in the early twentieth century by István Nagyatádi-Szabo. A party of the middle peasants, which also managed to attract provincial support from certain professional strata, the Smallholders sought to widen the restrictive franchise existing in Historic and post-World

War I Hungary and gain a measure of land reform. A marked failure to accomplish either objective was the party's hallmark. Following World War II, the Smallholders Party expanded its mainly peasant base significantly to become the gathering place of all right-wing elements.[19]

In the postwar period Ferenc Nagy, the bright, ambitious child of a peasant family in southwestern Hungary, whose talents as a political editorialist led to his rise in the party hierarchy, typified the Smallholder leadership. Cautious and profoundly conservative regarding established society, the young Nagy was appalled by the rural poverty about him, and he sought an easing of peasant burdens. To him this meant modest land redistributions, a lowering of taxation, and a rising of agricultural prices. But he detested the notion of collectivism and the Communists who "intruded" into the villages to promote it.[20] Nagy had the distinction of serving as the last prime minister of the Hungarian old regime, which effectively ended in May 1947.

These four parties, along with the trade unions (which were under Communist and Social Democratic control), formed National Committees throughout liberated areas of the country. Under the nominal supervision of these National Committees—the Soviet High Command had ultimate authority—representatives were chosen for a Provisional National Assembly. In December, this provisional parliament convened in Debrecen and accepted by acclamation a Provisional National Government. The composition of the provisional government had already been decided upon on the basis of discussions, conducted in Moscow without the knowledge of the British and Americans, among representatives of the Hungarian political parties and the Soviet government. The seat of the provisional government remained in Debrecen until April 1945, by which time all German troops had been pushed out of Hungary and the capital was transferred to Budapest. Due to the original site of the Provisional National Government, it is often referred to as the Debrecen government.

In the Debrecen government, the Communists, Social Democrats, and Smallholders held two portfolios each, and the National Peasants one. Moreover, the government included three non-party individuals, two of them generals who had served under Regent Horthy. One of these generals, Béla Dálnoki Miklós, former commander-in-chief of the First Hungarian Army, became premier. Another, János Vörös, former chief of the General

Staff, became minister of national defense. A Smallholder, János Gyöngyösy, became minister for foreign affairs, and another Smallholder,
István Vásáry, took over the finance ministry. The Communists augment their minority strength by acquiring two positions of great importance in war-ravaged Hungary, which was about to embark upon a program
of national reconstruction. Imre Nagy and Jószef Gábor, both Communists, became minister of agriculture and minister of trade and transportation. Communists also infiltrated other departments as deputy ministers.
In an act of political intrigue, Erik Molnár, minister of social welfare,
who had presented himself to the Provisional National Assembly as a
Social Democrat, announced at the first session of the cabinet that he was
a Communist. Of particular significance was the fact that the interior
ministry, a highly important department since it controlled the police
and security forces, was put in the hands of Ferenc Erdei, a member of
the pro-Communist National Peasant Party. Despite these gains, the Communists initially made a genuine effort to cooperate with all government
groupings, which agreed on the need to break Hungary's alliance with
Germany.[21]

The United States and Great Britain approved of this new Soviet-
sponsored regime, although without enthusiasm. H. Freeman Matthews,
director of the State Department's Office of European Affairs, saw the
Debrecen government as a "group of responsible personalities, and not
another 'Lublin Committee' to be imposed on the Hungarians." Although
it was clearly "in all respects 'acceptable' to the Soviets," Matthews added, it seemed nevertheless to be a "well-balanced group representing the
significant pro-Allied political forces in Hungary."[22] The British, in the
words of foreign service officer Michael S. Williams, also characterized
the Debrecen government as a "pretty respectable and representative
gathering."[23]

One of the first and most important acts of the Debrecen government
was to sign an armistice with Russia, Britain, and America. Armistice
discussions had already been taking place with the Horthy government
since September 1944. The pro-German coup in October and heavy
fighting on Hungarian territory thereafter interrrupted formal armistice
negotiations, which were not resumed until the formation of the Debrecen
government late in December. Throughout the latter part of the year,

however, the British and American (and presumably Soviet) governments gave active consideration to possible armistice terms.

Of the various issues to be resolved, two caused serious contention between the Westerners and the Russians. One of these concerned the functioning of the Allied Control Commission in Hungary, a tripartite body which the armistice would set up. Such commissions had already been established in Italy, after that country surrendered in August 1943, and in Finland and Rumania in September 1944 and Bulgaria in October 1944, following the surrender of those nations. The purpose of the control commissions was to enable the Allied victors to direct, theoretically on a tripartite basis, political affairs in the various countries and in general to supervise the implementation of armistice terms, including the demobilization of the former enemies' forces. In fact, however, a division of influence between the Western Allies and the Russians was already becoming evident. In Italy the British and Americans immediately took charge of Italian affairs, while the Soviet representatives on the Allied Control Commission, supposedly an equal partner, was for all practical purposes excluded from meaningful participation.

This situation, which came to be known as the "Italian formula," was exactly reversed in Rumania and Bulgaria, where the Soviet representation on the control commissions assumed control, virtually excluding his British and American counterparts. For example, in both of these Balkan nations the Soviet representative often issued a policy directive in the name of the Allied Control Commission, even though its British and American representatives had not concurred with or had not even been informed of the Soviet decision until after the event. Moreover, the Soviets routinely denied the British and Americans access to local leaders, and also restricted their ability to travel throughout the countries to which they were assigned, even in areas not militarily sensitive. The same type of situation existed in Finland, except that the Finnish Control Commission contained no American representatives (since the United States had not been at war with Finland), and the British representative, though having very little influence, did have access to political leaders and could travel freely throughout the country.

The United States and Great Britain, now wary of applying the "Italian formula" to Hungary, sought in the armistice negotiations to define clearly and improve the status of their representatives on the Hungarian Allied Control Commission. In the period between the armistice signing and the German surrender, known as the "first period," the British and Americans were willing to let the Soviet Union take the lead in Hungarian affairs and were content simply to be consulted before the Russians promulgated policy directives. If they did not agree with a Russian pronouncement and wanted to dissociate themselves from it, they asked that it be issued solely in the name of the Soviet government and not of the Allied Control Commission. But for the "second period," that between the German surrender and the implementation of a Hungarian peace treaty, the British and Americans wanted completely equal and tripartite participation in all functions and aspects of the control commission, and in the armistice negotiations they called for the insertion of a provision guaranteeing this.[24] For its part the Soviet government adamantly opposed any such provision, while the Westerners refused to back down from their demands. The British and Americans finally agreed to sign the armistice without the desired provision, but they simultaneously presented letters to the Soviet Union stating that they regard the matter as open and might later renew discussions as to the functioning of the Allied Control Commission. The Russians did not yield, however, and in response to these letters Foreign Commissar Vyacheslav Molotov indicated that, as far as his government was concerned, the issue was settled and no further negotiations were necessary.[25]

The second difficult issue which arose in the armistice negotiations involved the question of reparations. Originally the Soviet Union demanded that Hungary pay in reparation the equivalent of U.S. $400 million over a period of five years. Of this $80 million would be paid to Czechoslovakia and Yugoslavia, and the rest to Russia. After British and American protests that this figure was excessive, the Soviets reduced their claim to $300 million including $100 million for the Czechoslovaks and Yugoslavs, to be paid over six years.

Actually this concession did not fully satisfy the Westerners, who had additional objections to the Soviet reparations plan. One problem had to do with the price levels to be used as payments. The Russians insisted upon using the 1938 price schedule plus 10 to 15 percent, while the British believed that current (1945) price levels, which had lower value, should be used.[26] Another objection, this one raised by the Americans, concerned reparations taking the form of a fixed monetary payment whatever its value. The State Department preferred instead that "payments should consist in goods to be used directly in reconstruction."[27] To achieve greater influence on reparations matters, the United States also proposed the establishment of a reparations section connection to the Hungarian Allied Control Commission, which would consider the question of reparations on a tripartite basis.[28] The British were of mixed opinion on this suggestion. John G. Ward, acting first secretary in the Foreign Office, thought that his colleagues should "clearly support the American initiative."[29] But John Chaplin, a second secretary, doubted the effectiveness of a reparations section and also feared that it would set an undesirable precedent for a future German Control Commission.[30] In short, the British and Americans, even though they had their own differences on certain technicalities, made a joint effort to reduce Hungary's reparation liability. In the end, the Russians did not accept any major Anglo-American reparation proposals, except for a reduction in the total amount of the reparations bill. But before the issue was settled, the Anglo-Americans and the Russians had fought a contentious debate.

On 20 January 1945, the three Allies and the provisional government of Hungary signed the Hungarian armistice.[31] In addition to the two issues discussed above, the armistice provided for the free movement of Soviet forces throughout Hungary, the return of property removed from the Soviet Union and other Allied countries occupied by Hungary during the war, and the confiscation by the Russians of all German war material as booty (the last two conditions were over and above reparations). Clearly the armistice left the Soviet Union in a quite advantageous position in Hungary. But whether the advantage would turn into unrivalled Soviet dominance was as yet an unanswered question.

* * * * *

The armistice negotiations were the first test of how closely the three wartime allies would be able to collaborate in Hungarian affairs during the postwar period. It must be said that the results of this test augured poorly for future cooperation, for on the two issues of the control commission and of reparations—vitally important issues affecting the political and economic development of Hungary—the Western Allies and the Russians exhibited serious differences. Though the disagreement did not lead to a rupture, there were already visible strains in the Grand Alliance.

In the discussions over armistice terms both the British and the Americans played an active role, making a determined intervention to strengthen, as much as diplomatic means made possible, their position in Hungary vis-à-vis the Soviet Union. This was far from an easy task, as the less than successful Western effort in the armistice negotiations demonstrated. And it became even more difficult once all of Hungary, from which the invading Red Army was driving German forces, fell under Soviet military occupation. The question that faced the British and the Americans was how to respond to this new reality in Hungary, where Soviet force had become paramount.

II

THE POLITICS OF IMPOTENCE:
ANGLO-AMERICAN RECOGNITION OF
THE HUNGARIAN GOVERNMENT

As the year 1945 opened, Hungary was the scene of fierce combat between German troops, who still occupied about one-half of the country, including its capital city, and the Red Army, steadily advancing from the east. Although it required several months of major conflict before the Russians completed the expulsion of all German forces from Hungary, the trend of battle was clear. Gradually, step by step, the Red Army spread throughout the Danubian nation, and occupied it completely by April.

The political situation was far less predictable than the military one. At the turn of the year the Soviet-sponsored Debrecen government had been in existence for less than two weeks. As a coalition comprising all political groupings to the left of nazism, the political orientation of this provisional government was an unknown factor, and so was the degree of influence that the Soviet Union might exercise over it. Having come into existence without a formal, nationwide vote—an impossibility given the state of active warfare—it was clear that the government, to legitimize itself, would have to hold an election at some future time. But when such an election might be held, and in what circumstances remained uncertain. To enhance its position, the new government sought foreign

17

recognition, especially from Britain and the United States. But London and Washington were reluctant to enter into diplomatic relations with the Debrecen regime, preferring to withhold judgement until the direction of Hungarian politics could be clarified.

Hungary's situation reflected the political uncertainty facing much of Europe in January 1945. That Germany was headed toward a decisive military defeat was obvious; the only question was when it would occur. But what was then to be the fate of the collapsing Third Reich was an unsettled problem, and one which became all the more pressing the tighter the Allies drew their noose around it. Also undetermined was the status of Eastern Europe, throughout much of which communist influence, Soviet and non-Soviet, seemed to be on the ascendant. The British and American reaction to this development remained to be seen. In the meantime Western Europe, in a phenomenon characteristic of a society shaken by serious warfare, was in a state of social and political turmoil. In the Far East, an eventual Allied triumph could not be doubted, but appeared to lie on a yet distant horizon.

The scope of the political problems facing the wartime Grand Alliance in 1945 was so enormous that the Big Three governments in the course of that year deemed it necessary to hold two summit meetings and several conferences on the foreign ministerial level in their continuing effort to regulate the delicate transition from war to peace. Yet the magnitude of the difficulty and the extent of Inter-Allied disagreement were such that most issues remained unresolved, or even were further complicated by year's end. The return to stability was a long and tortuous process, as the involved attempt to reach a solution in Southeastern Europe demonstrated.

* * * * *

The issue of Eastern Europe forced itself on the attention of the British and Americans, when the Russians, in mid-1944, resumed their westward offensive and moved into position to strike out beyond their own frontiers. The future of Eastern Europe, including Hungary, now became a pressing problem.

There was considerable divergence of opinion between the United States and Great Britain on how to handle that problem, a divergence which reflected the two countries' differing outlook on the broad issue of spheres of influence. American political leaders, like President Roosevelt and his Wilsonian secretary of state Cordell Hull, rejected in principle the notions of balance of power and local political arrangements imposed from outside, especially when they openly smacked of colonialism. Whether of course fact met theory, as witness U.S. treatment of the Phillipines or adherence to the Monroe Doctrine, is another question altogether. But the myth persisted among Americans, who were themselves tucked safely between two oceans, that the United States should settle for nothing less than self-determination for all nations. H. C. Allen, the historian of Anglo-American relations, explains this phenomenon by noting that the Americans, having "made a continental nation out of a wilderness. . .find it difficult to appreciate the depth of European divisions."[1]

British statesmen, by contrast, who have insured their country's national survival precisely by a clever manipulation of European divisions, harken to no such myths nor do they shrink from seeking just the most effective balance of power to hold any potential aggressor at bay. Winston Churchill easily fit into the British tradition of balance-of-power politics, and his well worn remark in 1942 that he "did not become the king's first minister in order to preside over the liquidation of the British Empire" clearly demonstrates his role as a confirmed imperialist. Similarly, his actions in the latter years of the war showed his concern to maintain a suitable balance of power in Southeastern Europe.

In May and June 1944, Churchill and his foreign secretary, Anthony Eden, began pressing U.S. officials to accept a wartime division of responbility in Southeastern Europe between the Anglo-Americans and the Russians. They proposed that any such division would apply only to wartime military operations and not to the postwar political settlement. The British believed that the Kremlin would insist that governments in the area be at least friendly to the Soviet Union, though not necessarily Communist. That made it important to consolidate British control in Greece and Turkey in order to maintain influence in the Eastern Mediterranean. American leaders rejected such proposals, which they believed despite British assurances, would lead to the postwar establishment of spheres of influence. The Americans called instead for non-exclusion and equality of opportunity for all governments and social systems. In October 1944, when Churchill went to Moscow for talks with Stalin, Roosevelt, at the urging of presidential adviser Harry Hopkins, wrote to the British and Soviet leaders, that "in this global war there is literally no question, either military or political, in which the United States in not interested."

The clear implication was that Roosevelt would not be bound by any decisions reached in his absence. Not to be swayed, Churchill pursued his plans for a division of Southeastern Europe between East and West. In the meeting with Stalin, Churchill presented his so-called "percentages" proposal, according to which the Soviet Union would receive a predominant influence (90 percent) in Rumania, while Britian would get the same percentage in Greece. Churchill also suggested that the Soviet Union get 75 percent influence in Bulgaria, 90 percent in Rumania, and that Yugoslavia and Hungary be divided 50-50.[2]

Historians have given much attention to Churchill's curious percentages proposal, which was certainly impractical if not altogether "childish," as Adam Ulam calls it.[3] Charles Bohlen, Soviet specialist in the State Department, compared trying to divide influence over a country to saying that someone should be partially pregnant.[4] Although it is difficult to see how such an agreement could have been carried out, however, Churchill's proposal and its reception by the American and Soviet governments sheds important light on Big Three diplomacy.

Churchill did not inform U.S. officials of his percentages proposal either before or after he had presented it to Stalin. But America's utter refusal to be drawn into any discussion about even a wartime division of responsibility demonstrates its already uncompromising anti-Soviet attitude. In his letter to Churchill and Stalin, Roosevelt insisted that America had global military and political interests. While Albert Resis perhaps forces greater chronological precision than is warranted when he argues that the Cold War began the day that Roosevelt sent that letter,[5] his outright rejection of a sphere of influence for the Soviet Union even in an area so crucial to it as the Balkans surely contributed significantly to the onset of the Cold War.

As for Stalin, it is questionable how seriously he could have regarded Churchill's proposals, in view of Roosevelt's refusal to extend his *carte blanche* to Britain. Nevertheless, Stalin's interest in the area, if not already apparent from the Red Army's advances into it, was clearly evident by his willingness to deal. The British demand for so little in Rumania and Bulgaria must surely have pleased him.[6]

For Churchill's part, his desire to bargain indicated on the one hand his interest in a spheres-of-influence agreement, above all to protect Greece. On the other hand his proposal of 50-50 for Hungary proves that he did not desire simply to hand that country, historically tied to the West, over to the Soviet Union if he could prevent it.[7] According to Vojtech Mastny, Churchill "abhorred a rigid partition of Europe and hoped to preserve Western influence in its eastern part."[8] In this regard it is worthwhile to recall the serious British effort to win concessions from the Russians during the Hungarian armistice negotiations of January 1945. The Americans, who also intervened during these negotiations, certainly had no intention of handing over any nation to a Soviet sphere of influence.

While these developments proceed on the diplomatic front, the military situation moved quickly towards the inevitable Allied victory. With the end of the European war in sight, the three governments in February convened a summit meeting at Yalta to discuss the problems of peace. As far as Eastern Europe was concerned, the Yalta Conference devoted most attention to Polish affairs and very little to questions relating to Hungary, Bulgaria, and Rumania, the former German satellites now under Soviet occupation. What the Yalta Conference did produce, inspired by the American delegation, was the "Declaration on Liberated Europe," which affirmed the right of liberated peoples to "solve by democratic means their pressing political and economic problems" and "create democratic institutions of their own choice." The declaration also stated that the three Allies would jointly consult when they deemed it necessary to fulfill the declaration's terms.[9]

But the Yalta declaration proved no mechanism to achieve its stated objectives. Even more serious was its open-ended nature. The Westerners and the Russians obviously had entirely different conceptions of democracy. It was impossible for any of the three governments to conduct itself any way it pleased in liberated nations and still argue that its actions fell within the terms of the declaration. In coming months and years conservative critics attacked the Yalta declaration as a "sell out" to the Soviet Union.[10] The document's one achievement, as Charles Bohlen, a member of the American delegation, stated several years later in defense of the declaration, was that it "formed the foundation of almost every diplomatic protest" made by the United States in connection with the East European events.[11] Certainly Secretary of State Edward R. Stettinius exaggerated highly when he labelled the Yalta agreements a "diplomatic triumph" for the British and Americans, who he claimed won greater concessions from Russia than they gave in return. "The real difficulties with the Soviet Union," so he argued, "came *after* Yalta when the agreements were not respected."[12] But even if adequate enforcement machinery could have been established, the declaration was far too ambiguous to be effective.

Yalta was a brief diplomatic interlude that had virtually no influence on the course of events in Eastern Europe. Soviet control over the region increased steadily. In March 1945, within a month of the Yalta Conference, a Soviet-directed coup in Rumania put the left wing firmly in charge there. In Poland, the Russians made no more than cosmetic changes in the Moscow-oriented Lublin government, though Yalta had called for the reorganization of that regime "on a broader democratic basis." The Yalta accords soon proved to be very hollow indeed.

Under such circumstances, the British and Americans still had to come to grips with, what was for them, a rapidly deteriorating situation in Eastern Europe. By this time, in the post-Yalta period, Western policy makers had examined the alternatives and formulated their positions, but the differences between them continued to be sharp.

In March 1945, Sir Orme Sargent, then deputy under-secretary and soon to become permanent under-secretary at the British Foreign Office, and thus an extremely important official, produced a noteworthy memoandum which sheds considerable light on British thinking towards the East European situation. In this pessimistice appraisal, Sargent argued that there was a "fundamental disagreement" between the Anglo-Americans and the Russians "as to the meaning of 'democracy'," and that the Western form of democracy had "never flourished" in Eastern Europe except for Czechoslovakia. One should not expect "the exhausted and impoverished, in fact 'proletarianised'" populations of those countries "to put up any fight for parliamentary institutions which in any case they have never learnt to rely on or respect." In the meantime, Sargent continued, Rumania and Bulgaria were already either "definitely Communist or at any rate totalitarian in character and policy" and "very much the same development" would probably occur in Hungary, Yugoslavia, and Poland. In Greece and Italy, the situation was "more promising" only because of the presence of British rather than Soviet troops. Sargent contended that the time was "fast approaching" when the Foreign Office would have to consider seriously "how far and how long it would

the fore late in May, when Stalin proposed to Truman and Churchill
t they recognize the governments of Rumania, Bulgaria, and Finland
mediately, and the Hungarian government as well in the near future.[19]
Except for Finland, which was not under Soviet occupation, the
mericans opposed recognition. According to a State Department brief-
paper, not only would recognition imply "approval of the present
representative governments" and thus help to "entrench them in
wer" in the Balkan states, but it would also mean the "abandonment"
the attempt to put into practice" the Yalta declaration and "discour-
democratic elements in those countries and probably pave the way
their elimination from the political scene." This, in turn, "might well
courage the repetition of the same process" in other Soviet-occupied
untries, a high price to pay for a momentary easing of relations with
Soviet Union. The United States therefore advised the Soviet Union
t it could not recognize the Balkan governments, which were "neither
resentative of [n]or responsive to the will of the people," particularly
he cases of Bulgaria and Rumania.[20]

The British government had a totally different approach to the prob-
. While the British completely agreed with the American view that
Balkan governments, especially in Rumania and Bulgaria, were un-
resentative, they believed that further Western efforts to obtain genu-
ly democratic governments in the area were useless—the Russians
uld be counted on to block it in the future as they had in the past. As
British saw it, they and the Americans should instead conclude peace
aties with the Soviet statellite governments as soon as possible and
ablish diplomatic relations with them. Once peace treaties had been
ned and ratified, British thinking went, the Russians would be obliged
withdraw their occupation forces—or at least they would have to
eal their intention of maintaining permanent garrisons in the three
untries. Moreover, the normalization of relations between the Anglo-
mericans and the Balkan states would perhaps allow the West to improve
position in those nations.

The British were unable, however, to convince the Americans to cease
ssing for broader governments, leaving one frustrated Foreign Service
ficer, Duggald L. L. Stewart, to question the State Department's ability
"recognize a brick wall."[21] The dispute between London and Wash-
gton lasted well into July, by which point the wartime allies has arranged

continue to fight "the losing battle of enforcing" the Yalta principles.
Though he held out hopes of success in Italy and Greece, and of miti-
gating "the purely totalitarian character" of the Yugoslav and Polish
governments, he saw no chance at all of forestalling completely Communist governments in Hungary, Rumania, and Bulgaria. He suggested
frankly that the Foreign Office abandon an "untenable" position and
"without further protest or argument" simply "accept tacitly" the existing
Balkan governments, "no matter what their political colour" may be.

Sargent recommended this "unheroic course," as he termed it, so as
not to endanger the "fundamental" British policy of postwar cooperation
with the Soviet Union for the sake of an issue "not vital" to British
interests in Europe. At the same time he suggested that Eastern Europe
was absolutely vital to the Russians—"an essential part of their security
system"—for they were creating out of this area "a *cordon sanitaire*
against Germany," which they would "not lightly abandon." Moreover,
he argued that the Soviet Union would require the governments in the
cordon sanitaire "to be modelled on totalitarian lines" so that their
foreign and military policies would "continue to be in accordance with"
the Soviet Union itself. Sargent noted in conclusion that acceptance of
the establishment of left-wing governments, which he recommended,
would entail and "explanation" to the United States government, which
was actively pursuing implementation of the Yalta declaration.[13]

Sargent's formulation represented a classic portrayal of the spheres-
of-influence policy. The idea was to divide Europe between Soviet and
Anglo-American regions, neither encroaching upon the other, and thereby
to enable East and West to coexist with a minimum of friction. Britain
had pursued such a policy since 1944, at which time it had, however,
still sought a measure of influence in Hungary, as indicated by Churchill's
50-50 proposal to Stalin and Britian's determined effort in the Hungarian
armistice negotiations. By March 1945, on the other hand, having achieved
almost no success in the armistice discussions and with nearly all of Hungary occupied by Soviet forces, Britian had written off Hungary as lost
to the Soviet sphere. But in the meantime American policy makers continued to oppose a spheres-of-influence strategy on any terms, and they
did not cease to invoke the Yalta declaration against the left-leaning
East European governments. Possible Soviet repercussions did not deter
the Americans, for whom Soviet collaboration was less important than it

was for the British. Typical was the attitude of Averell Harriman, the American ambassador in Moscow, who argued that "our relations with the Soviet Government will be on firmer ground as soon as we have adopted a policy which includes on the one hand at all times a place for full cooperation with the Soviet Union but on the other a readiness to go along without them if we can't obtain their cooperation." He added that "although we should continue to approach all matters with an attitude of friendliness we should be firm and as far as practicable indicate our displeasure . . . in each case they fail to take our legitimate interests into consideration."[14]

An even more notable view was that expounded by George F. Kennan, chargé d'affaires in Moscow and director of the State Department Policy Planning Staff from 1946 to 1949. On the question of spheres of influence Kennan's views were not representative of other American policy makers, though this is not astonishing for the intellectual and historian who had a reputation among his colleagues for his often eccentric opinions. Many years later H. Freeman Matthews, director of the Office of European Affairs in the postwar period, acknowledged Kennan's central role in developing the containment policy. At the same time Matthews described Kennan as a "very sensitive, very touchy" individual, one who became "frustrated" very easily, a "loner" with a "brilliant mind."[15] Kennan himself described his own position in Dean Acheson's State Department, from which he resigned in 1950, as occasionally that of "a court jester, expected to enliven discussion, privileged to say the shocking things, valued as an intellectual gadfly on hides of slower colleagues, but not to be taken fully seriously when it came to the final, responsible decisions of policy."[16]

Shortly before the Yalta conference, in a personal letter to Charles Bohlen, Kennan lambasted the Soviet Union, whose "political aims in Europe are not, in the main, consistent with the happiness, prosperity or stability of international life on the rest of the continent." Kennan argued against virtually any collaboration with the Soviet Union, and even denounced the prospective World Security Organization, which had "no basis in reality." He also proposed that the American political representatives in Eastern Europe should be withdrawn, for their presence undermined "the respect we enjoy abroad." Somewhat surprisingly, and for U.S. policy makers atypically, Kennan advocated that the Russians and

the Americans "divide Europe frankly into spheres of ourselves out of the Russian sphere and keep the Russia Unlike the British, however, Kennan did not suggest a par so that the United States could better cooperate with th but rather because America seemed indisposed to argu sians. "Lacking the will" to oppose them "with all tl diplomatic resources at our disposal," he told Bohlen, " [Eastern Europe] off." He added: "Where the Russia there our world stops; beyond that line we should no voices unless we mean business."[17] But he would hav the United States did "mean business," which he clearl have had successful results. As he wrote several months la States were to "muster up the political manliness to deny moral or material support" for its consolidation of p Europe, the Russians could probably be driven back at

In short, the British, who sought an accomodation w were willing to partition Europe and thereby placate tl Americans either refused to acknowledge the loss of and continued to attempt to influence events there desp the Russians, or, as in the somewhat exceptional case wanted to challenge the Soviet hold in Eastern Europe. should admit defeat and partition of Europe, though stil cooperation. As of mid-1945, therefore, the American ar for Eastern Europe were clearly disparate.

* * * * *

Once fighting on Hungarian territory creased, the Debr set about the task of resuming normal political life. This a general election and restoring diplomatic relations world, especially the three major Allies.

The more immediate of these issues was that of diplon In March 1945 both Western governments sent politic with the rank of minister to Hungary, but on the expli that their presence was unofficial and did not constitute The British minister was Alvary D. F. Gascoigne, and the F. Arthur Schoenfeld. Meanwhile there was no Hungaria official or unofficial, in either London or Washington. formal relations with Hungary and other ex-German sa another summit. In view of American intransigence, the British decided to let the United States take the matter up with the Russians once again. Should the effort fail—as the British expected it would—the Americans might then be willing to join with Great Britain, either at or after the Potsdam Conference, in negotiating peace treaties.[22]

By the time the Potsdam Conference opened, the recognition question had not been resolved, and it was not long before serious and substantial disagreements emerged between the Russians and their Western Allies over this and other Balkan issues. The American delegation initiated the debate when, in the first days of the conference, it introduced a proposal calling for "the immediate reorganization of the present government in Rumania and Bulgaria, in conformity with" the Yalta declaration. Following the reorganization of those governments to include "all significant democratic elements," the three Allies should accord diplomatic recognition to, and conclude peace treaties with, these new governments. Finally, the proposal appealed to the Allies to assist "in the holding of free and unfettered elections."[23]

Several days later, the Russians countered the American proposal with one of their own. Arguing that "due order" existed in Rumania and Bulgaria, as well as Finland and Hungary, and that the "legal power" had "authority" and was "trusted" by the population of those states," the Russians saw "no reasons for interfering in the domestic affairs of Rumania or Bulgaria." The Soviet proposal went on to recommend the speedy recognition of all four governments by Britain and America. Then, presumably to deflect attention from the Soviet-occupied Balkans, and perhaps to split the British and Americans,[24] the Russians proposed that the three Allies "take immediate measures towards the establishment of a democratic government" in Greece, a country in which "no due order still [existed], where law [was] not respected, where terrorism [raged] directed against democratic elements."[25]

The total divergence of the two proposals immediately led to a sharp dispute. The Soviet proposal particularly enraged the British, who at that moment were intervening militarily in the Greek civil war. Foreign Secretary Eden opened a meeting of the foreign ministers by denouncing the Soviet description of the situation in Greece as "a complete travesty of fact." The present Greek government, Eden pointed out, had proposed elections in which "all parties would participate." In Bulgaria, by contrast,

where an election was schedulted to take place, "the vote would be only
for or against a set list." That, said Eden, "did not meet the British idea
of democracy." He also raised the issue of press censorship, asserting that
representatives of the press were free to go to Greece and report on conditions there, a situation "unfortunately" not possible in either Rumania
or Bulgaria. Replying to these arguments, Molotov, on the question of
elections, assured his Western colleagues that "there was no reason to fear
delay or that elections would not be free." Concerning freedom of the
press, he claimed that there were more British than Soviet representatives
in Rumania and Bulgaria. Admitting that "censorship had been hard
during the war," he promised that it "would be better now." Secretary
of State James Byrnes supported Eden's contention of press censorship
in Rumania and Bulgaria, and unfavorably contrasted the situation there
to that in Greece. Throughout the meeting, Byrnes also continued to
urge implementation of the Yalta declaration through supervised elections. Molotov, however, still "saw no reason" for supervised elections in
Bulgaria and Rumania, and rejected the idea absolutely.[26]

Unable to agree on a course of action in the Soviet-occupied Balkans,
the conferees were deadlocked. Continued discussion over the next several
days, both among the foreign ministers alone and together with the heads
of government, failed to resolve the disagreement, and a breakdown of
the conference seemed possible. It was avoided when Byrnes decided to
offer compromise solutions on certain key problems. On one of the most
important of these, the recognition question, he dropped the demand for
Allied-supervised elections and announced his willingness to accept a
Soviet proposal, according to which the three governments would "consider each separately in the immediate future the establishment of diplomatic relations" with Finland and the Balkan states.[27] This proposal
would have left the difficult question of recognition to each individual
government, thus avoiding the necessity for unanimous agreement.

Churchill demurred, arguing that the compromise proposed by Byrnes
"did not reflect what they had been saying, and would be covering with
words. . .a difficulty which had not been removed around the conference table."[28] No other way could be found to break the deadlock, however, and ultimately the conferees—who by this time, following the defeat
of the Conservatives in the British general election, included a Labour

Party premier and foreign minister—accepted the Byrnes compromise formula, which stated, as written in the Potsdam communique:

> The three governments agree to examine each separately in the near future, in the light of the conditions then prevailing, the establishment of diplomatic relations with Finland, Rumania, Bulgaria, and Hungary to the extent possible prior to the conclusion of peace treaties with those countries.[29]

Byrnes' compromise enabled the three governments to end the conference without a public display of Allied disunity. Nevertheless, the agreement scarcely resolved the problem of recognition, now left to each separate government, which could establish full, partial, or no relations as it saw fit. In the meantime, the Soviet Union still wanted Western recognition of the Balkan states, and the United States still refused to extend it. The effect of the Potsdam agreement was to defer, but not resolve, the conflict.[30] On the other hand, their success in keeping the issue alive underscored the continuing interest of the Americans in the Balkans and manifested, to the British as well as the Russians, the refusal of the United States to accept Soviet domination of the area.

The Potsdam Conference, the last of the wartime summits, settled only a few of the political problems that had emerged during the war; many more were left to be dealt with later. Before passing on to that, a word should be said about the new British foreign secretary, Ernest Bevin, whose first official duty was to replace Eden at the Potsdam Conference. It was not long before Bevin and the new prime minister, Clement Attlee (who, as leader of the Labour Party, had sat at the conference table with Churchill) demonstrated that Labour's ascendance as the ruling party would not significantly alter British foreign policy. The British Labour delegation, to all appearances at least, approached Conference-related problems in exactly the same way as had the Conservatives. A few years later, Secretary Byrnes wrote that the replacement of Churchill and Eden by Attlee and Bevin did not alter Britain's stand on conference issues "in the slightest, so far as we could discern." This he deemed an impressive "continuity in foreign policy."[31]

Also noteworthy was Bevin's maiden parliamentary speech as foreign secretary, in which he dispelled any question there may have been that he, a socialist, would be more favorably disposed to the left-wing Balkan governments than the Conservatives. The new governments set up in Bulgaria, Rumania, and Hungary, he told the House of Commons, "do not, in our view, represent the majority of the people, and the impression we get from recent developments is that one kind of totalitarianism is being replaced by another."[32] Clearly, whatever Bevin's socialism may have meant, it did not mean approval of Soviet Communism as exercised in Southeastern Europe. At the same time, as events were to show, he was also not inclined to come to blows with the Soviet Union over the fate of the Balkan countries.

* * * * *

The surrender of Japan one month after the conclusion of the Potsdam Conference made formal peace with the defeated Axis powers and their satellites an urgent political priority as attention turned to the work of postwar international reconstruction. Of course, there were serious and substantive disagreements between the Western powers and the Soviet Union as to the basis of that reconstruction, and thus of the peace. And there were tactical disagreements with the British and Americans as to whether peace with the Balkan states should be an immediate goal or await the establishment of more acceptable governments. Nevertheless, the achievement of a formal peace settlement, whenever and on whatever terms, was one of the burning issues to which the Allies now turned their attention.

The U.S. State Department had given thought to the process of treaty drafting since before Potsdam, and had concluded that the experience of the 1919 Paris Peace Conference—"a full, formal peace conference without preliminary preparation," and one "conducted in a heated atmosphere of claims and counterclaims"—was something to be avoided. Consequently, the United States recommended that the Potsdam Conference establish a Council of Foreign Ministers, to consist of the Big Three plus France and China (that is, the Big Five). The immediate task of the proposed Council would be to draw up treaty drafts with the former German satellites and, once a German government was established, with that country as well. The Council would also be empowered to take up any other issue it chose to consider. The Potsdam Conference adopted the American proposal in its basic form,[33] and the Council of Foreign Ministers served, though with only limited success, as a medium of multilateral discussions until late 1947, when it broke down completely.

The first session of the Council convened in London in early September, a month after the Potsdam Conference ended. Soon after the session opened, the Soviet delegation introduced peace treaty proposals for the Balkan ex-German satellites, which were brief documents calling for the treaties to be based upon the respective armistice agreements.[34] The British and Americans objected, noting, as an American delegate pointed out in an internal memorandum, that the proposals would permanently give the Soviet Union "all the advantages" of the armistice agreements and remove even the "small measure of joint Allied participation" presently existing.[35] They submitted counterproposals designed to guarantee such concepts as freedom of speech, religion, political belief, and public meeting, and for the withdrawal of Allied troops. The latter meant in reality only Soviet troops, who alone occupied the Balkans north of Greece. The American draft also provided for multipartite rather than unilateral Soviet control over reparations and equal Allied access to the trade, raw materials, and industry of the former enemey nations.[36] As these proposals would have reduced, if not eliminated, Soviet preponderance in the Balkans, they were certainly unacceptable to Moscow. The Council session thus began on a rather inauspicious note.

Yet even before a discussion of treaty terms could get underway, other issues quickly sidetracked the negotiations. One was the continual problem of recognition. As Byrnes told Molotov, the United States would not sign treaties with governments it did not recognize, and it would not recognize the Bulgarian or Rumanian governments in their present form. The British, repeating their performance at Potsdam, preferred not to make yet another attempt to reorganize the Balkan governments. But once the United States had initiated such an effort by introducing a proposal to implement the Yalta declaration, the British joined in the American denunciation of the Bulgarian and Rumanian governments.[37]

The result was a heated and almost hostile debate, as the Westerners accused the Rumanian and Bulgarian governments of being unrepresentative and called for their reorganization. The Russians rejoined that the governments were not unrepresentative and that the people supported them. In addition Molotov directly charged that the British and Americans opposed these governments for being friendly to the Soviet Union, pointedly noting that the Western powers had supported Balkan governments in the past hostile to the Soviet Union. He insisted that the Soviet Union could not tolerate a hostile government in this area. At the same time he countered Anglo-American claims of the unrepresentative character of these Balkans governments by arguing that the Italian and Greek governments, supported by the West, were themselves unrepresentative. Byrnes and Bevin disputed the latter point and assured Molotov that they did not oppose the Balkan governments because they were friendly to the Soviet Union, but because they were undemocratic. In this manner the discussion went on until an impasse was reached.[38]

In a surprise move, the United States in September, when the Council was holding its session, announced its intention of recognizing the Hungarian government. According to Leslie Albion Squires, a secretary of the United States Mission in Hungary, Byrnes and his advisers decided to restore relations "not so much in connection with the effect in Hungary as in Bulgaria and Rumania. It was felt . . . that the restoration of normal diplomatic procedures between Hungary and the United States would emphasize and give added validity to our refusal to do business with the present governments in Rumania and Bulgaria."[39] It is possible that Byrnes timed the move to coincide with the Council session, presumably hoping to appease Molotov and win concessions from him. If so, he failed. The ill-will generated by the Soviet-Western dispute over Bulgaria and Rumania overshadowed any concillatory effect of the American recognition of Hungary.

Another dispute arose over a matter of procedure. The Soviet delegation interpreted the Potsdam protocol to mean that the Council of Foreign Ministers, when working on peace treaties, should be composed only of states signatory to the armistices. The Western position was to permit the entire Big Five to participate in all treaty discussions, though only signatory states would have the right to veto.[40] This procedural dispute quickly led to a breakdown of the London talks. Of course, the substantive disagreements on treaty issues and the recognition question were so fundamental that success at London was highly improbable in any case.

The collapse of the September discussions was a setback for Byrnes in his effort to reach an acceptable settlement in the Balkans through the Council of Foreign Ministers.[41] The setback was only temporary, for Byrnes successfully began mending fences and brought about a resumption of talks before the year ended. But before we turn to these talks, it is necessary to examine political developments in Hungary.

* * * * *

The most important of those developments during the second half of 1945 was the holding of local and general elections, for which Hungarian political parties had been preparing since August. Washington and London favored elections as a step towards the restoration of stability, but were concered about the conditions under which they would be held. There was ample evidence that the Communist Party was receiving considerable financial and material assistance from the Soviet occupation authorities in the form of automobiles, trucks, gasoline, newsprint, and money, while the moderate Smallholders Party, favored by the British and Americans, was hardpressed for funds. Added to this concern was the fear that the Communists would press for an electoral law similar to one recently passed in Bulgaria, which required the prior certification for "non-fascist attitude" of each voter and a single national slate of candidates which the electorate had either to accept or reject. In Bulgaria this electoral law led to a left-wing victory.

The Hungarian parties eventually agreed to schedule municipal elections for the Budapest area early in October and national parliamentary elections a month later. One Western fear was removed when the Hungarian Communists, certainly in accordance with Soviet officials, did not demand a common electoral list for the October municipal election. Every party was allowed to run its own candidates and present its own party program, although the Social Democrats and the Communists, who had already agreed upon a policy of cooperation, decided to submit a common slate of candidates, thereby forming a left bloc. The government did disenfranchise a number of potential voters with records of rightist behavior, but exclusions were not on a scale wide enough to affect the elections significantly. On the whole it was in fact conducted quite fairly. Surprisingly, this election gave the Smallholders just over 50 percent of the vote, while the Communist-Social Democratic bloc polled not quite 43 percent. The Smallholder victory was striking, because the electorate contained the largely working-class neighborhoods of Budapest. The November general elections, in which many rural, typically conservative regions would participate, promised an even larger Smallholder showing. The British and Americans were encouraged.

Soon after the Budapest election, the Hungarian Communists—no doubt embarrassed by their lackluster performance—began pressing once again for a common electoral list in the November general elections. To the Smallholders such a move was certainly reprehensible since it would probably deny them their anticipated victory. After intensive interparty discussions, it was finally decided to permit separate party lists, but the four-party coalition was to remain in power irrespective of the election results. As it turned out, the Smallholders won with 57 percent of the popular vote, the Communist-Social Democratic slate received 34 percent, while the pro-Communist National Peasant Party got nine percent. In the wake of this election, by all accounts conducted fairly, the British government recognized Hungary,[42] as the United States had done two months earlier.

A new political crisis erupted when the Communists in post-election interparty consultations demanded the important Interior Ministry, which controlled the police. Though the Smallholders initially resisted, the threat of a Communist resignation from the government—which could have sparked labor agitation and Soviet economic reprisals—caused the Smallholders to back down, leaving a Communist, Imre Nagy, as Interior minister. A Smallholder, Zoltán Tildy, became prime minister, while a Communist, Mátyás Rákosi, and a Social Democrat, Árpád Szakasits, the leaders of their parties, each became a deputy prime minister. János Gyöngyösy, Smallholder foreign minister in the Debrecen government, retained his post. The Cabinet portfolios as a whole were divided among nine Smallholders, four Communists, four Social Democrats, and one National Peasant. In sum, the new government contained a sizable left-wing representation, bolstered by Communist control over the Interior Ministry and the continuing Red Army presence on Hungarian territory. Balanced against these factors was the influence that the Smallholders wielded in holding the remaining half of the Cabinet seats, including the premiership. Though facing powerful left-wing forces, those of the center and center-right, embodied in the Smallholders Party, were stronger in Hungary than anywhere else in Soviet-liberated Europe, with the possible exception of Czechoslovakia.[43]

The election episode was a critical test of the Anglo-American response to Soviet advances in Hungary, for it demonstrated the extent to which Washington and London were willing to assist the anti-Communist moderates—particularly the Smallholders—at a crucial point.

Prevailing opinion in the British Foreign Office at the time was that the West had very little hope of successfully opposing Soviet influence in Hungary, which the London government frankly expected to become and remain a Soviet satellite for years to come.[44] This pessimistic outlook was consistent with Foreign Office opinion throughout 1945. Guided by such an assessment, Britain avoided direct intervention in the Hungarian situation and gave no special encouragement or support to the Smallholders. Even during moments of acute crisis, when the Communists were pressing for an obviously manipulated election, the attitude of the Foreign Office was that the anti-Communist forces themselves should resist attempted Communist encroachment and not rely upon or expect outside assistance.

An indication of British policy toward Hungary during the election crisis was the reaction by one Foreign Service officer to a report by Minister Gascoigne in Budapest on a conversation he had had with Béla Zsedenyi, a leading Smallholder politician. According to Gasciogne, Zsedenyi requested that the British and Americans take action through the Allied Control Commission to ensure that free elections would be held. He even suggested that the two Western nations send troops to Hungary. Back at the Foreign Office, Second Secretary John M. Addis took Zsedenyi's request as "an attempt to justify before the event Hungary's submission to the Russian-Communist programme and to lay the blame in advance on" the British and American governments, and he labelled Zsedenyi's request for British troops "a farcically impracticable suggestion." Addis concluded pointedly: "If these Hungarian politicians explained frankly that they were going to give into Russian-Communist pressure without an attempt at a struggle, one would have more sympathy for them. For there is not much else they can do."[45] This reflected the general Foreign Office opinion, which tended to place responsibility for resistance to the Communists—such as could be mounted—on the Hungarian moderates themselves.[46]

Washington was no more prepared to intervene directly in Hungarian affairs during the election crisis than was London, and it certainly had no intention of engaging military force in the region. In Budapest, Minister Schoenfeld peformed much as had his British colleague. Though he warned the State Department that the Smallholders might not be able to withstand Communist pressure, unless assisted from outside, he was not free, in the absence of instruction, to do any more than to speak "in general terms" of the American commitment to the Yalta declaration.[47] To a prominent anti-Communist banker, Baron Ullman, who requested American funding for the Smallholders Party, Schoenfeld replied that democracy could be won only "by necessary personal sacrifice" from local forces and not by external intervention. He added that this had been the case since the time of the Magna Carta.[48] Without tangible assistance, such assurances had little value, of course, for the besieged Smallholder and other anti-Communist forces.

Yet American policy during the Hungarian election crisis was in certain subtle respects more aggressive than that of the British. In the first place, the United States did inform the Hungarian government and Smallholder leaders that it would consult with the Soviet and British governments on the Hungarian situation if the Hungarian government requested such action.[49] Though this offer placed much of the burden on the Smallholders themselves—who declined to request such consideration, presumably for fear of Communist reprisals—it reflected a more active approach than the British. It should also be recalled that the United States continued to raise issues pertaining to Rumania and Bulgaria—but closely assocated with the situation in Hungary itself—during the Potsdam Conference and the September session of the Council of Foreign Ministers. In short, the United States was willing to intervene diplomatically to resist Hungarian Communism, but in terms of material or military assistance it did, like Great Britain, virtually nothing on the local level.

* * * * *

While these events were proceeding in Hungary, Byrnes in late November began making efforts to reconvene the Council of Foreign Ministers, whose first session had broken down in discord two months earlier. Byrnes strongly desired to resume talks, not only because he wanted to reach a settlement on issues facing Europe, but also because he felt a personal commitment to the success of the Council of Foreign Ministers, whose establishment had largely been his work at the Potsdam Conference.

Despite the failure of the London meeting in September, Byrnes was hopeful that a new conference would produce positive results. It was not that the Balkan issues blocking agreement at London had been resolved. True, the United States had agreed to recognize the Hungarian government, but the much thornier problems of Rumania and Bulgaria remained.

Byrnes believed, however, that if only the Big Three foreign ministers attended, without France and China, whose participation in the peace-making process the Soviet Union found objectionable, then the Russians would be more amenable to a settlement.

Byrnes succeeded in persuading the Russians to renew the discussions, and arrangements were made to convene another conference in Moscow. Byrnes approached the Russians without first consulting the British, who were quite displeased over his unilateral action. Bevin furthermore was wary at the prospect of undertaking without adequate preparation a new foreign ministers' conference, in which difficult problems remained to be resolved. Bevin feared that the conference would lead only to another failure, which would leave matters even more deadlocked than they were after the collapse of the London meeting. He regarded a failure as all the more likely, because the foreign ministers, expected to attend the opening session of the United Nations General Assembly in early January, would be working under a time limit. Nevertheless, there seemed no alternative but to participate in the scheduled conference, which Bevin therefore agreed to do. The Moscow Conference of Foreign Ministers began in mid-December.[50]

One issue to be resolved was the procedure for drafting the peace treaties. Though the conferees devoted considerable time to it, suffice it for now to note that they resolved it satisfactorily.[51]

Of greater immediate importance was the difficult recognition question. Although London and Washington had recently recognized Hungary, they had yet to establish relations with Bulgaria and Rumania, and both Western allies still held widely divergent views as to whether they should do so. The Americans continued to press for reorganized governments in those two nations according to the Yalta declaration before extending recognition. The British maintained, and periodically sought to convince the Americans, that the only practical course was to recognize the existing governments and conclude peace treaties with them.[52] But the Americans refused to discontinue the attempt to win more satisfactory governments, and the Foreign Office, once again, agreed to give the effort "general support," though it had little faith that it would succeed.[53]

In Moscow, Molotov and the Soviet delegation refused as always to agree to a radical reorganization of the Rumanian and Bulgarian governments. But the Russians did propose certain compromises similar to the

Yalta agreement concerning Poland, which promised cosmetic thought not necessarily genuine efforts toward more representative governments. To break the yearlong deadlock, Byrnes agreed to a compromise formula. Though it required considerable Soviet-American argumentation on the precise wording, the Moscow conferees agreed on two protocols concerning the Rumanian and Bulgarian situation.[54] On Rumania, it was agreed that two representatives of opposition (non-Communist) parties would be placed in the government, and that this reorganized government should hold "free and unfettered elections" in which "all democratic and anti-Fascist parties" would have the right of participation. A subministerial, tripartite commission would proceed to Rumania to oversee these tasks, which, once accomplished, the British and Americans would follow by recognition. As for Bulgaria, it was agreed that the Soviet Union would give "friendly advise" to that government "with regard to the desirability" of including in it two opposition politicians. On the condition that Bulgaria accepted the advice, the British and Americans agreed to extend recognition.[55]

In the wake of the Moscow decisions the British and Americans extended recognition to the Rumanian government early in 1946; however, they withheld recognition from Bulgaria for almost two years. Even so, the Moscow protocols did not lead to any fundamental overhaul of the Rumanian and Bulgarian governments. The Westerners, who never came to view those regimes as democratic, remained at loggerheads with the Soviet Union for years over the status of the Balkan nations. The importance of the Moscow Conference, as well as of the London session of the Council of Foreign Ministers and of the Potsdam Conference, was not in achieving a reorganization of the Balkan governments—which they failed to do—but in demonstrating that the United States, seriously concerned over East European developments, was willing to intervene on the level of diplomacy to counter Soviet influence in the area. The various conferences also demonstrated that Great Britain, which saw the ascendance of Soviet Communism throughout much of the region as inevitable, was nonetheless willing to support the American denunciation of pro-Soviet regimes.

The Moscow Conference of Foreign Ministers also marked the end of a decisive year in East European history. From the Western perspective, the situation in Eastern Europe had deterioated gravely in the period between the Yalta and Moscow conferences. One by one the nations in the region fell firmly into the Soviet grip, and by the end of 1945 only Hungary and Czechoslovakia maintained even a semblance of independence from Moscow. In the case of Hungary, the Russians and their clients in the Communist-led Hungarian left bloc had steadily increased their influence to powerful, though not yet decisive, proportions. The November elections, while placing in power a government with a nominal Smallholder majority, did not lessen this influence.

* * * * *

Mounting Communist political power was one aspect of the revolution sweeping Hungary and other East European nations in the postwar period. The other important facet to the process of sovietization occurred on the economic plane, and it presented the British and American governments with yet another serious challenge. The political foundations of the Western powers conditioned their response to East European developments.

III

THE POLITICAL FOUNDATIONS OF BRITISH
AND AMERICAN POLICY TOWARD EASTERN EUROPE

Ever since 1945, when the British Labour Party assumed office in its first majority government, the question has arisen as to whether it has pursued a socialist policy. The question is logical and flows from the nature of the organization. The Labour Party—the British branch of European social democracy—was an amalgam of socialists and trade unionists, who coalesced at the turn of the century to form a political party. The declared goal of the Labour Party (the name it finally adopted in 1906) was to foster the interests and aspirations of labor. Unlike radical socialists on the continent, however, Labour Party adherents did not insist upon the need for class struggle and violent revolution to achieve their objectives, which could be gained, according to Labourites, through parliamentary activity and gradual reform. At the end of World War II, the Labour Party finally won the opportunity to put its program into effect.[1]

But did the Labour Party implement a socialist policy in foreign and domestic affairs?[2] Did socialist principles motivate its actions? Or did the Labourites abandon these principles and, like their non-socialist predecessors, serve the interests of the British state—which, despite Labour's accession to power, had not undergone any fundamental socio-economic transformation? An examination of Labour Party pamphlets, along with other material, suggests an answer to these questions.

40

Broad agreement exists among historians and other scholarly observers of postwar Britain that Labour's foreign policy amounted to a continuation of, and not a deviation from, the foreign policy of the wartime, Conservative-led coalition. If this was in fact the case, then the Labour Party could rightly be accused of having abandoned the principles of a socialist foreign policy, which it had once espoused before coming into power.

A political scientist, Michael R. Gordon, who makes this claim, defines a socialist foreign policy as constituting four principal elements: internationalism; international working-class solidarity; anti-capitalism; and anti-militarism and antipathy to power politics. Gordon argues that the postwar Labour government rejected these principles as "utopian and therefore a poor and dangerous guide" in the conduct of foreign affairs. Instead, Labour carried on a traditional foreign policy, which meant "self-regarding promotion of national interests, defense of a far-flung imperial and commercial network, and management of a European balance as a condition of British security—all backed, whenever necessary, by the application of force."[3]

One historian who believes that the Labour Party abandoned socialist principles in foreign affairs is M. A. Fitzsimons. Writing in 1953, Fitzzimons states:

> The question of a socialist foreign policy arose only to become absurd. The continuity of British foreign policy prevailed because British interests remained the same and the suspicion of state for state survived.

In all important matters of foreign policy, whether support for West European defense, opposition to Soviet expansionism, or withdrawal from the empire (a withdrawal which, Fitzsimons argues, the Conservatives also could not have avoided, had they been in power), Labour policy was virtually identical to Conservative policy. "The foreign policy of the Labour government was Churchillian in its major lines," concludes Fitzsimons.[4] Another historian, F. S. Northedge, writing in 1962, maintains a similar viewpoint, succinctly demonstrated by his statement: "Labour's accession to office made scarcely any difference on the main lines of foreign policy which the [war-time] coalition government had already decided."[5]

There is not universal agreement that Labour abandoned its socialist principles upon acceding to power in 1945. Nevertheless, adherents of the opposing view, that postwar Labour policy was based upon socialist principles, appear to be limited to partisans of the Labour Party. An example is Elaine Windrich, who argues in her obviously sympathetic *British Labour's Foreign Policy* (1952) that the party's conduct of foreign affairs has conformed with a socialist program. According to Windrich:

> Labour has consistently opposed the balance of power, secret diplomacy, alliances and ententes, militarism, and imperialism. It has upheld the doctrines of international co-operation, open diplomacy, self-determination of nations, arbitration, collective security, and the rule of law in international relations. While in the opposition, the Labour Party has advocated these propositions; while in office, it has, whenever possible, applied them in practice.

Windrich's qualification with the words "whenever possible" is quite significant, for she admits that there were certain issues—she refers to the Labour government's maintenance of diplomatic relations with Franco's Spain—in which Labour Britain did not carry out a socialist foreign policy. But she attributes deviations from a socialist foreign policy to "the inheritance of previous commitments and the necessity of concurrence from other foreign powers," in other words, to factors over which the Labour government presumably had no control. She concludes by arguing that "only if the long-range goal of a world 'co-operative socialist commonwealth' were achieved, would it be possible for the British Labour Party to apply, in all instances, a truly socialist foreign policy."[6] Thus, even Labour partisans are obliged to modify the judgement that the postwar Labour government carried out a socialist foreign policy, and note that the party faced external constraints, which rendered its foreign policy less than completely socialist.

Another proponent of the notion that the postwar Labour government practised continuity in its foreign policy—though he did not put the matter in those terms—was the wartime Conservative foreign secretary Anthony Eden. Writing in 1960, Eden said that he and Bevin "had been good colleagues during our years in the war cabinet"—in which Bevin had been minister of labour and national service—"and often discussed foreign affairs together." Concerning Bevin's tenure as foreign secretary, Eden commented that "Bevin was shrewd and he soon saw that the problem of his term of office would be how to withstand the growing Soviet appetite." Bevin's "enduring memorial," Eden remarked complimentarily, calling Bevin a "man of stature and sincere conviction," was to lead the country—which "at the close of the war . . . was in no mood to be alerted" to the Soviet danger—to share his judgement about Soviet expansionism. As for Bevin's performance at the foreign office, Eden observed,

> Though my handling of some events would have been different from his, I was in agreement with the aims of his foreign policy and with most that he did, and we met quite frequently . . . . In Parliament I usually followed him in debate, and I would publicly have agreed with him more if I had not been anxious to embarrass him less.[7]

If any doubt remains that the Labour government's foreign policy was a continuation of the Conservative's, it is useful to refer to the left-wing challenge that almost immediately confronted the newly installed, supposedly socialist government. As the wartime Grand Alliance broke down acrimoniously, which happened very soon after the end of the war—and, in fact, had already begun to happen in the closing months of the war—dissident Labourites began to accuse the government of having betrayed the principles of socialist foreign policy, principles which the government, now in power, should be seeking to implement. Instead, the dissidents clamoured, the government had embarked upon a Tory, pro-capitalist foreign policy. The significance of the left-wing revolt was in further demonstrating that the accession to power of the Labour government did not alter the nature of British foreign policy. If it had done so, and if Britain had begun practising a socialist foreign policy, then there would have been no basis for the rebellion. It was the fact of continuity in foreign policy that gave cause to the accusation of socialist betrayal.

There is no need to recount the story of the left-wing Labour rebellion, the main aspects of which have already been treated in considerable detail.[8] It is sufficient to note that leftist dissent began to emerge soon after Ernest Bevin's maiden parliamentary speech as foreign secretary on

20 August 1945. In this address, Bevin expressly refused to alter the war-time coalition's policies of maintaining diplomatic relations with Franco Spain and of supporting the royalist Greek government—foreign policies that the British left had attacked as reactionary—and at the same time he denounced the Soviet-sponsored Balkan governments as totalitarian. This speech represented a clear intention on Bevin's part to continue the foreign policy line of his Conservative predecessor.

After this address, and as Soviet-Western relations went from bad to worse and Great Britain seemed to move ever closer to the American side of the widening East-West schism, dissent in Labour ranks grew, both among the rank-and-file constituency and within the Parliamentary Labour Party. A high-point in the left-wing dissident movement was reached in November 1946, marking the onset of the parliamentary revolt. At that time 57 Labour "rebels," in defiance of Party discipline, attached a critical foreign policy amendment to the Debate on the Throne Address. This amendment called on the government to "so review and recast its conduct of international affairs as to . . . provide a democratic and con-structive socialist alternative to the otherwise inevitable conflict between American capitalism and Soviet communism." In the debate that followed, left-wingers took occasion to attack many aspects of the government's foreign policy. In the end, no one, including the rebels, voted for the amendment, but some 70 Labourites abstained. The Conservatives voted with non-rebel Labourites to defeat the amendment by over 350 to zero. Nevertheless, the parliamentary revolt brought the breach in Labour ranks, which had been brewing for over a year, sharply to the surface.

After the November revolt, a number of the left-wing parliamentarians began to meet regularly during the winter of 1946-1947, and in May 1947 they drew up a pamphlet entitled *Keep Left*. Fifteen members of Parliament, advocating a "more drastic socialist policy," appended their names to this tract, while three of them, R. H. S. Crossman, Michael Foot, and Ian Mikardo, took credit for writing it in its final form. *Keep Left* is one of the most important documents of the left-wing rebellion—perhaps the single most important. It serves, as its inspires intended it to do, as a statement of principles of the Labour rebels. After the publication of this pamphlet, the left-wing Labour parliamentarians were often referred to collectively as the "Keep Left" group.

It should be stressed at the outset that the rebel parliamentarians were not pro-Soviet. Though they admired Russia's planned economy, they also believed that its political structure was undemocratic and totalitarian. *Keep Left* labelled Soviet communism and American capitalism as "bleak alternatives." The pamphlet condemned the establishment of what it called satellite governments in Eastern Europe, and even referred to them as police states. *Keep Left* also denounced Soviet actions in Iran, and furthermore asserted that Moscow's attitude during the 1946 peace conference and in the United Nations Organization was uncooperative. It is worthwhile to remark that the left-wingers' antipathy to Soviet Communism rendered their critique of the Labour government all the more striking. The fact that the government's foreign policy aroused the indignation not only of Communists—which it certainly did, though that is scarcely surprising—but even of non-extremist, relatively moderate socialists, indicates just how traditional the government's policy was.

In any event *Keep Left*'s main villain was the British, not the Soviet government. In fact, the Soviet Union's aggressive actions, according to *Keep Left,* were mainly a product of the accumulated—and justified— suspicions that the Soviet leadership had built up over the years toward the Western powers. Britain's own lack of cooperation with Moscow, under Foreign Secretary Bevin's foreign policy, had further contributed to Soviet mistrust. *Keep Left* declared that Britain must avoid too close association with the United States, which sought to lead a worldwide alliance against the Soviet Union. To promote international cooperation and understanding, Labour Britain should serve as a "third force" between the twin extremes of American capitalism and Soviet Communism. It was Labour's responsibility to "heal the breach" between the two contending powers, and "to save the smaller nations from this futile ideological warfare." Labour should "set an example in British foreign policy of genuine social democracy," and give a lead to similar progressive forces elsewhere. Along such lines, Britain should take steps to form an alliance with Socialist Europe, especially France, to prevent the division of the continent into two opposing blocs. But, *Keep Left* admonished, Britain could not fulfill these goals if it had become "the junior partner and the advance outpost of an Amercian dominated system of 'collective security against communism.'"[9]

Soon after the publication of *Keep Left,* the Labour Party leadership published an official rejoinder, called *Cards on the Table.* Written by Hugh Dalton, chancellor of the exchequer and head of the International Subcommittee of the party's National Executive Committee, and Denis Healey, secretary of the party's International Department, *Cards on the Table* sought to justify the Labour government's foreign policy on the basis of soicalist principles. In fact, the pamphlet was a ringing affirmation that the government, and along with it the Labour Party leadership, had completely adopted a traditional foreign policy, based upon power politics and quite devoid of anti-capitalism or international working-class solidarity.

"As socialists," *Cards on the Table* declared, "we of the Labour Party want in all spheres a policy which will promote the spread of democracy and social progress." Claiming that this goal was the premise behind Labour's foreign policy, the tract went on to explain that, given the existing international situation, the postwar Labour government was not in a position to "choose among infinite possibilities the precise policy best calculated to achieve a world socialist millenium." The Labour government could achieve its foreign policy objectives only if Britain, led of course by the Labour Party, survived as a world power. Consequently, to insure this survival was to be a fundamental tenet of Labour's foreign policy. However, *Cards on the Table* continued, postwar Britain, weakened and overextended as it was, could not defend itself alone against other powers that might seek to expand at Britain's expense. The tract left no doubt that such an expansionist power was the Soviet Union, which had launched a "sustained and violent offensive against Britain" and sought to fill Britain's place in Europe and the Middle East. Under these circumstances the United States, which with the recent promulgation of the Truman Doctrine had indicated its intention of bolstering Great Britain against Soviet expansionism, played a progressive role. For "if, as it appears," *Cards on the Table* explained, "the U.S.A. is about to take the weight of Russian expansion off British shoulders, Britain will be freer to pursue a constructive initiative for improving Big Three relations."

Now this flirtation with the United States—a capitalist big power and thus a principal scoundrel in the eyes of the left-wing rebels—required considerable justification on the part of the Labour Party leadership. *Cards on the Table* defended the Anglo-American "understanding" on the basis that, not only was America bolstering Labour Britain's position as a world power, but that American society itself had certain progressive aspects. For example, the American working-class was not totally power-less, for despite the absence of an American labor party "the 15 million organised workers [had] decided the result of every American election since 1932." And if the merger, then under consideration, between the A.F.L and C.I.O. should take place, American working-class power would be further enhanced. Moreover, argued *Cards on the Table,* Anglo-American cooperation was in the best interests of the Soviet Union as well as of Britain, for it served to restrain any anti-Soviet impulses that might arise in the United States. According to the tract,

> the existence of Labour Britain as a stable world power is a protec-tion to Russian security and a guarantee against anti-Soviet aggression. For so long as Britain plays a decisive part in the defense of American security, it is impossible for America to adopt a policy of world-aggression without British agreement. The nature of the military co-operation between America and Britain makes it impossible for either to fight if the other remains neutral.[10]

Cards on the Table amounted to a thorough repudiation of the prin-ciples of a socialist foreign policy. Yet, neither the Labour government nor the party leadership could ignore the vocal, left-wing minority. Its criticisms touched a raw nerve among the supposedly socialist Labour-ites, and forced the government and the Party leadership to defend Labour's foreign policy on the grounds that it was a sound—if pragmatic—application of socialism. *Cards on the Table* and its non-leftist adherents started from the premise that Britain had become a socialist country, once the Labour Party had acceded to power—a premise which only a Labourite is obliged to accept. Then they proceeded to justify every governmental foreign policy action on the basis of the need to maintain Britain as a world power. From its position as a world power, Britain would be able to defend and spread its socialist principles.

Of course, the philosophical justification for a policy is less important than the policy itself. In the case of *Cards on the Table* the object was power politics, to preserve Britain's role as a world power. Would a Con-servative government have adopted a different program? The Labour

government was willing to withdraw from important imperial commitments, admittedly a major innovation in British foreign policy. Besides
this exception, however—and it is a moot point whether the Conservatives could have avoided doing the same even if they had been in power—
it seems unlikely that they would have behaved very differently from
Labour. The only difference would have been that the need to justify
policy as socialist would not have encumbered the Conservatives. And
therein lies the sole contrast—Labour carried on a traditional foreign
policy, and labelled it, rather ludicrously, but out of necessity, socialist.

The left-wing rebellion, it may be noted, continued to be a thorn in
the side of the Labour Party leadership and of the Labour government.
The intensity of the rebellion waned somewhat beginning in the latter
half of 1947 and lasting until 1950. The reason for this had to do with
the string of seemingly quite aggressive Soviet thrusts during these years
of heightening Cold War. The establishment of the Cominform and later
Tito's expulsion from that body, the rejection of the Marshall Plan, the
Czechoslovakian coup, and the Berlin blockade—all had the effect of
hardening even left-wing opinion against the Soviet Union. Only a comparatively small, hard core of Labour leftists continued to try to lay the
blame for the international discord on Bevin's head rather than Molotov's
or Stalin's. Nevertheless, the establishment of a certain degree of concensus in Labour foreign policy was short-lived, for the rearmament question and the outbreak of the Korean War in 1950 gave renewed life to
the leftists and reopened the breach, which has been an enduring factor
in Labour Party politics ever since the first postwar Labour government.[11]

However, it is important to note that, at least during the tenure of the
government, the left-wing rebels never actually jeopardized the Labour
Party's leadership, or forced it or the government to revamp its foreign
policy. On no foreign policy issue, whether on Greece or Spain or any
other matter, did the Labour government modify its program as the left-
wing urged. Nor did the Labour Party. Thus, for example, reference to
the reports of the Labour Party annual conferences demonstrates numerous leftist-inspired resolutions on foreign policy repeatedly defeated—
with never a single victory.[12] A policy statement like *Cards on the Table*
is perhaps the most significant evidence of all. It shows that the left was
not totally inconsequential—it was strong enough to force the party leadership to conceptualize government foreign policy in a socialist framework.

But it was not strong enough to force the government to alter its foreign policy. Beyond terminology, nothing changed, and the postwar Labour government and the Labour Party leadership did not shift at all from their traditional foreign policy.

In fact, however, a shift toward a socialist foreign policy was not a real option, for now that the Labourites were in a position of power, and were responsible for the interests of the British state, they had no alternative but to carry out a traditional foreign policy, a policy designed to protect the great-power status of the United Kingdom. And it should now be clear, it was precisely such a foreign policy that the Labour government and the Party leadership pursued. Any attachment that the Labour leaders may once have had to the principles of a socialist foreign policy, they completely abandoned in the postwar period. It may confidently be asserted, in short, that what motivated the Labour government was not a socialist foreign policy, of which it had not a trace.

* * * * *

In the eyes of American officials, the Soviet Union was the cause of the revolutionary upheavals occurring in Eastern Europe. The United States possibly could contain or even reverse the effects of those upheavals, American policy makers believed, depending upon the influence it could exert on the Kremlin. Secretary of War Henry L. Stimson summed up the importance American leaders placed on Soviet-American dealings when he wrote in 1945 that "the great basic problem of the future is the stability of the relations of the Western democracies with Russia."[13]

But whether the United States could best exercise such influence thorough a policy of cooperation or confrontation with the Soviet Union was the great question facing U.S. foreign policy makers in the first critical months of the postwar period, when the course of Soviet-Western relations was in the crucible. On each side of the question stood two competing factions in American ruling circles. Henry Wallace, the leading light of the cooperationists, blamed the United States for posing a greater threat to the Soviet Union than it presented to America. An Anglophobe to begin with, Wallace believed that Britain represented a nearly equal danger to international peace and stability as did Russia. Wallace was a universalist during the war, but for the postwar period he saw a spheres-of-influence settlement as inevitable, with the Soviet Union receiving its own sphere in Eastern Europe.[14]

The confrontationists saw little hope of working out a *modus vivendi* with the Soviet Union, which they perceived to be an inherently aggressive and seditious power. Soviet power had to be contained, politically by a ring of anticommunist countries stretching from Europe to the Middle East to East Asia, and militarily by bases in those countries whose abundant armaments should be trained on Russia. Confrontationists, barring the special breed of isolationists, were universalists in the war and remained so afterwards. For them, abandoning Eastern Europe to the Russians would be both treacherous and foolish, for it only would encourage the Soviets to seek yet more territory in the future. Although not one of the more knowledgeable or educated of the confrontationists, Harry Truman became one of the most influential.

Truman represented the ideal of the smalltown American youngster who grows up to become president, for this is precisely what happened to the intelligent and energetic farmer's son from Independence, Missouri. Truman, who failed as a businessman and lacked formal education, managed via local Democratic Party politics to rise from obscurity and occupy the offices of U.S. senator, vice-president, and quite fortuitously president. The idea that there could be compromise with the immoral Soviet Union and its leaders was a foreign concept to the Baptist-raised Truman, who had been trained to see the world largely in good-and-evil terms. For Truman the Soviet Union was a bully to its neighbors, a tyrant to its own people, and an evil force that had to be met head on.[15]

From the outset Truman demonstrated a propensity to confront the Russians. Less than two weeks after assuming the presidency, Truman challenged what he believed were Soviet violations of Yalta. On April 23, in his first important discussion with a Soviet official, Truman caustically and undiplomatically rebuked Foreign Commissar Molotov for his government's policies in Poland. Nevertheless, throughout 1945 Truman wavered in his approach to the Soviet Union between one of cooperation and confrontation. A week after his sharp exchange with Molotov, for example, the president informed adviser Joseph Davies of the incident and sheepishly asked him, "Did I do right?" Suspicious of Soviet intentions since taking office if not long before, Truman still continued the preparatory negotiations already underway on the United Nations. And although he was convinced that the Kremlin was imposing a Communist government on Poland, Truman did not object to the seating of that government in the U.N. In May, Truman sent the ultraliberal Harry Hop-kins as his personal envoy to Stalin, and the more conservative Davies as his representative to Churchill. In July the president went to Potsdam to try to iron out differences with the Russians, and in the coming months he permitted his secretary of state James F. Byrnes to try to do the same. But a frustrated Truman came home from 17 days of hard bargaining at Potsdam convinced, "Force is the only thing the Russians understand."[16]

Throughout the year, therefore, Truman engaged in discussions with Russia. But he combined them with an underlying anti-Soviet posture that brooded of an unwillingness to engage in any substantive compro-mises. Beginning in 1946 the Truman administration even abandoned all but the most perfunctory efforts at dialog.

James Byrnes, the new secretary of state, soon presented himself as an obstacle to Truman's impulse toward a confrontationist policy. In large part the differences that emerged between Truman and Byrnes were personal. There was serious rivalry between these two independent-minded politicians. In the 1930s Byrnes was mentor to Truman, the junior senator from Missouri. When the presidency suddenly fell on his shoulders in 1945, the confused Truman, who had had little experience in foreign affairs, naturally called upon his former teacher. Actually, Byrnes, a South Caro-lina lawyer and former Supreme Court justice, had about as little foreign-policy expertise. But during the war years he had been very close to President Roosevelt and active in the White House, so much so that he was informally known as the "assistant president." Truman by contrast had been the classic example of the unused and isolated vice-president. Without international background in this particularly trying period in world affairs, and lacking his own ready-made political base upon which to begin his new administration, Truman could well rely upon the power, connections, and inside knowledge of the politically sophisticated Byrnes.[17]

Byrnes envied Truman, a political junior who rose by chance to become president—a post which Byrnes believed should have been his. Further-more, as secretary of state Byrnes acted condescendingly toward Truman, and he managed foreign affairs quite independently, a style of work which significantly contributed to tension between the two. "Byrnes's personal style was to operate as a loner, keeping matters restricted to a small circle of advisers," wrote Charles Bohlen in his memoirs. "Byrnes was his own man," Bohlen continued, "and demanded the freedom to operate that

way. This method of operating inevitably ran into conflict with Truman's
strong views on the prerogatives of the President."[18] The historian Charles
Mee places similar stress on Truman's and Byrnes' clash of personality
rather than on any political differences:

> The difficulty between the two men was not that Byrnes was in-
> sufficiently combative—he was certainly combative—but that Byrnes
> kept tooting off on his own without informing Truman of what he
> had planned. Truman was intent upon having close control of for-
> eign policy.[19]

Without question the area of political agreement between Truman and
Byrnes was substantial, and certainly overrode any disagreement. Both of
these politicians, who had been raised and had prospered in the West and
who as patriotic Americans had never entertained a single subversive idea,
had fundamental hostility toward communism in general and the Soviet
version in particular. Truman, Byrnes, and for that matter nearly all American officials assumed the essential malevolence of the Soviet system. The
Kolkos thus argue that "the only real division between Truman and
Byrnes was one of ego and tone."[20]

Although the differences between the two men were small, in the extraordinarily difficult period of 1945, even nuances could become magnified
to such an extent that disagreement over means would obscure agreement
over ends. On the tactical question of how to deal with the ceaseless
Soviet problem, Truman and Byrnes came to disagree strongly and ir-
reconeiliably.

Byrnes had nothing in common with Henry Wallace's approach to the
Soviet Union, for the latter viewed Russia's situation sympathetically
and believed that it deserved to be given an equal standing in the world
community. By contrast, Byrnes was very conservative in both international and domestic affairs. Viewed simply from an ideological standpoint, Byrnes' inclination would have been as confrontationist as Truman,
and had a policy of confrontationism been successful he probably would
have followed it. But at the London Council of Foreign Ministers, which
was Brynes' first attempt to show down the Russians, such a policy did
not halt Soviet gains in Eastern Europe, and the necessity for a different
approach to the problem therefore presented itself. Already possessed of

a sharp personal antipathy toward Truman, Byrnes was more than willing to try another tack. This was especially so because Byrnes came from a different background and mindset. A shrewd, calculating lawyer and a most able administrator, Byrnes came to value above all the art of compromise and adjustment. Throughout his long and successful career, he had become skilled in the technique of backroom political deals. He became the "fixer" for President Roosevelt, and now that Truman called upon his services Byrnes would use his negotiating talents to make a deal with the Russians.[21]

But far from easily arranging a great peace to settle the problems of the postwar world and still leave the United States with preeminent global power, Byrnes found the Soviet Union to be a novel type of opponent, whose tendency seemed to be not to seek compromise but to strive obstinately for its objectives. Byrnes described Molotov as a man who "will win your reluctant admiration by the resourcefulness he exhibits in his delaying tactics."[22] Clearly, what the Soviet Union sought in the postwar period was to achieve international recognition of its great-power status and retain its own sphere of influence in Eastern Europe. Byrnes' failure to reverse Soviet gains in Eastern Europe brought him into disfavor with Truman.

Byrnes originally had placed great hopes on using the American monopoly of the atomic bomb to force an acceptable Soviet policy in Eastern Europe.[23] The critical test of the bomb as the arbiter of international affairs was the London Council of Foreign Ministers held in September 1945. Instead of achieving his coveted breakthrough at London, however, Byrnes encountered unmovable Soviet resistance to altering its policies in the Balkans. In response the United States refused to grant recognition to the Bulgarian and Rumanian governments, and the conference broke up ignominiously. Byrnes' great hope for the bomb proved illusive.

Despite his serious failure at London, Byrnes' own political position did not yet suffer. The press and public widely blamed the breakdown on Molotov, and to the secretary of state's own surprise Byrnes was applauded—rather than denounced as he expected to be—upon his return from London. Still the old horsetrader Byrnes, who was determined to play the great peacemaker and cap his diplomatic career with the conclusion of peace treaties, continued to seek progress on the difficult Balkan issue. Nevertheless, at the Moscow Conference of Foreign Ministers in December 1945, Byrnes found again that the only kind of agreement he could make with the Russians was a bad one. But this time he took it, for the frustrated and disillusioned secretary was impatient to get on with the peace-making process, even if its results turned out to be less than those for which he had once hoped. Soviet stonewalling tactics had succeeded.

Truman learned of the Moscow conference agreements through the radio, for Byrnes had not even consulted the president before reporting the results to the nation. Byrnes' lack of consultation surely annoyed Truman, although no more so than the agreements themselves. He and influential advisers around him, notably Admiral William D. Leahy, were very displeased. By the end of 1945, the Truman administration was more than six months old, but its foreign policy continued to fare poorly. It had not succeeded in stemming the tide of sovietization in Eastern Europe; on the contrary the floodwaters were rising. Problems were mounting in Iranian Azerbaijan, where Soviet troops had ensconced themselves to support a native rebellion. And the situation was far from satisfactory in Korea and China, where Communist forces had secured huge tracts of territory. In reaction to his wave of negative news conservative voices in the press and politics were beginning to cry appeasement, as indeed were members of the president's own entourage. The Moscow agreements, which won the West nothing more than cosmetic changes in the Bulgarian and Rumanian governments, were a dismal dissapointment to anyone, like Truman, who wanted an undiluted victory to stop the Soviet advance.[24]

The Moscow conference proved to be the turning point in the Truman-Byrnes partnership. According to the historian Robert L. Messer, that personal change simultaneously marked the increasing political divergence and incompatibility between Byrnes' continuing efforts at compromise and Truman's increasingly resolute commitment to Cold War confrontationism. In a memorandum Truman wrote soon after the Moscow conference which the president claimed to have read to Byrnes, Truman strongly condemned policy up to that time as too conciliatory and harshly summarized his overview with the remark, "I am tired of babying the Soviets." Precisely what Truman may have said to Byrnes in the one or two meetings they had after the secretary's return from Moscow, and to what extent Truman gave Byrnes a verbal dressing down, remains unsettled

sed the loan, although ineffectually, arguing that it
pport Britain's experiments in collectivism.[37]
ericans, Byrnes and especially the Midwesterner Tru-
ncerns about the British. So did officials in the State
submitted a briefing book to Truman, shortly after
marizing possible points of Anglo-American friction
Nevertheless, the overwhelming preponderance of
sentiment toward Great Britain was favorable. In the
hostility from the Soviet Union, whose traditions
ged markedly from those of the United States, the
was a refreshing source of strength in a difficult world.
ences between the two Atlantic nations, they were
pared to their points in common.

n the change from the Tory to the Labour Party soon
nor one unaccompanied by any radical revision in
asteful to conservatives, the victory of Labour was
n liberals and labor circles. The domestic consequ-
government, despite a wave of nationalizations in
ld scarcely be called communistic. Most important,
ent retained the policies and personnel of its Tory
gn affairs, at least as far as Europe and the Soviet
d.[39]

States had little difficulty working with Great Brit-
the Conservative or the Labour Party. The funda-
ook of the two countries coincided, and they both
munism and its extension beyond Eastern Europe.
e itself, however, the United States lacked a clear
ritain demonstrated no interest in trying to preserve
that region, the United States stubbornly refused
a to the Soviet Union. Yet at the same time the
l to take military action on behalf of Eastern Europe
tantial economic aid to the region, although at least
ry to prevent its sovietization. The historian Geir
hat American officials were caught between their
ersalism," according to which "the United States
role everywhere," and the practical difficulties and
hs that compelled the United States to modify its

questions. Whatever the case, it had become clear to Truman as a result of
the conference that he and his secretary of state, and the two different
approaches to the Soviet Union that they represented, could no longer
work together. Byrnes resignation was now a matter of time.[25]

As it was, Byrnes remained in office throughout 1946, so that he had
the opportunity to complete his coveted peace treaties. After January
1946, however, Byrnes was no longer an independent man but the com-
pliant executor of Truman's foreign policy. He never again agreed to
make major concessions for the purpose of concluding a spectacular if
unequal agreement with the Soviet Union, as he had done at the Moscow
Conference of Foreign Ministers. When he bargained, he did so quietly
and to achieve businesslike accords.[26] The peace treaties are the best
example. A major disappointment to the West in general, and to no individual more than Byrnes himself, his long-sought treaties scarcely achieved
the *pax americana* he wanted. Far from preventing the sovietization of
Eastern Europe, they confirmed it. On the other hand neither Byrnes
nor any Westerner could have accomplished more, and the treaties did
have the simultaneous result of strengthening American influence in
Western Europe.[27]

By 1946 administration foreign policy had become an undilutedly
confrontationist one. Truman no longer sought to compromise, and the
stalemate in the Council of Foreign Ministers discussions over Germany
—the refusal of either East or West to attempt German unification—
indicated the breakdown of communication and the hardening of the
division of Europe. Soviet power could go no further west, but the United
States could not roll it back eastward. On the international stage the
Cold War had begun.

The politics of anti-Sovietism also permeated the American domestic
scene. An anticommunist witchhunt did not develop for several years,
for that required the Berlin crisis of 1948, the Communist victory in
China and the Soviet explosion of an atomic bomb in 1949, and the outbreak of the Korean War in 1950. But from the start of the postwar era
and the breakdown of the Grand Alliance, Americans unlike the British
pursued little or no substantive debate over the need to contain or reverse
the advance of Soviet power. No one could doubt the fact that the Soviet
Union had significantly pressed its political influence far westward. But

few questioned whether that possibly could have had its beneficial aspects to the populations involved. Could a forcible levelling and proletarian re-molding of society have had any progressive consequences? Was not at least the resolution of the endless national conflicts between Magyar and Rumanian, Pole and Czech, Serb and Bulgarian, and of course German and Russian, one positive result of the *pax sovietica*?[28] Few of the established political institutions debated these questions. Business corporations and organized labor were firmly tied to the Cold War consensus,[29] as was the press.[30] And the Republican "opposition" prided itself on carrying out a "bipartisan" foreign policy—in other words, one without a debate.

The driving force behind bipartisanship, its "symbol"[31] and "chief Congressional architect,"[32] as he has been universally described, was Senator Arthur H. Vandenberg, Republic from Michigan. In the 1930s he was an acknowledged isolationist, or "insulationist" as he preferred it. After Pearl Harbor he gradually reversed his position and came to support an interventionist approach to foreign affairs. During the war Vandenberg became his party's principal spokesperson on foreign affairs and in 1946 he was promoted to the chairmanship of the powerful Senate Foreign Relations Committee. In support of Roosevelt's United Nations plan, Vandenberg made a widely acclaimed Senate speech in January 1945,[33] in which he publicly announced his conversion from isolationism. Vandenberg was instrumental in lining up often substantial congressional majorities for the Truman administration's foreign policies, even after the 1946 Republican landslide. George Marshall praised the senator for the "decisive influence" he exercised on behalf of White House foreign-affairs initiatives.[34] Such efforts included Vandenberg's work in the peace-treaty negotiations of 1946, during which Vandenberg worked closely with James Byrnes and played an important role, as well as active and successful legistlative support on behalf of the Greek-Turkish aid bill of 1947, the European Recovery Program of 1948, and congressional endorsement of West European unification (the Vandenberg Resolution of 1948).

There was a left and right wing flanking the mainstream of American politics. The conservative isolationists, who refused to follow Vandenberg in 1945, did not challenge the anti-Soviet basis of American policy, but they did refuse to sanction American involvement in political and financial burdens abroad to oppose communism—no doubt a contradictory position and one which hardly affected administration policy.[35] One element in

the American political es
Party, was willing to over
brace it, and treat the So
interests and security co
out of the cabinet in Sep
dismal performance in th
its influence in the Ar
foreign-policy issues, wi
was fortunate in workir
census.

In a troubled and r
support and instinctive
Union. The close simi
and political tradition
a long-lasting Anglo-A
ing from the closest w
between two sovereig
inate its efforts with
at all levels worked ve
widely recognized ho
agreed with each othe
natural, the two cou
in the face of the co

Americans did hav
can public about th
long traditions of i
many Americans ass
were fearful of get
East for the sake of
The differing politi
England was yet ar
solidity of Anglo-
Labour Party in
isolationists, believ
slide to socialism
anti-British, anti-
Truman administr

conservatives oppo
would be used to su

Like many Am
man shared such c
Department, which
he took office, su
in foreign affairs.
public and official
face of increasing
and objectives dive
presence of Britain
Whatever the differ
at most nuances com

Furthermore, eve
proved to be a mi
policy. Though dist
welcome to Americ
ences of the Labou
the late 1940s, cou
the Labour governm
predecessors in fore
Union were concerne

Clearly the United
ain, whether led by
mental political outl
opposed Soviet Com
As for Eastern Euro
policy. While Great B
Western influence in
to relinquish any are
United States decline
or even to infuse subs
the latter was necess
Lundestad theorizes
commitment to "uni
should play an active
lack of realistic optio

universalism. America's vacillation and "nonpolicy" continually provoked the Kremlin but never succeeded in preventing or reversing the sovietization of Eastern Europe. By contrast Great Britain was committed to withdrawing from what it considered to be a "non-crucial" region.[40] In the end the divergence between these two viewpoints proved to be the major problem in Anglo-American relations, as the two allies faced the sovietization of Eastern Europe.

IV

CONFLICT OVER THE HUNGARIAN ECONOMY, 1945-1946

The Soviet Union sought to gain predominant influence not only over the political life of Hungary, but also over its economic structure. These were complementary goals, for the stronger the control of the Hungarian government by pro-Soviet elements, the easier could such elements institute those sweeping changes in the Hungarian economic system which characterized its transformation from a mainly privately-owned to a state-owned economy. At the same time, the consolidation of those radical economic measures reinforced and accelerated the left-wing movement of Hungarian politics.

The British and American governments opposed the economic process at work in Hungary, a process which aided the political advance of Soviet-style Communism westward. It also brought into play an important and immediate financial consideration, for the increasingly severe restraints which left-wing forces were placing on private ownership threatened British and American as well as other Western investments in Hungary. The capitalist-oriented governments in London and Washington made serious efforts to protect the imperiled foreign property of Anglo-American private investors. But the leftist elements in Hungary and other East European nations—and their Soviet patrons—had no intention of retreating from their economic drive, and thus emerged a serious diplomatic clash between East and West.

* * * * *

A consistent trend of Soviet action in those countries of Eastern Europe which the Red Aarmy occupied at the close of the war was to support and direct state interference in their economic structure. This process occurred in successive stages and at a basically uniform rate, though somewhat more or less rapidly in various countries depending upon local conditions. At the end of this process, which in all cases had been completed by 1948, the economic system in Eastern Europe had come to parallel that of the Soviet Union itself. Most nationalization occurred in major industries and finance, resulting in nearly total state ownership in those sectors, ranging to least nationalization in agriculture, where a pre-war, peasant-based economic structure lingered on for a number of years.[1]

The similarity of Soviet economic activity through much of Eastern Europe clearly suggests that it was a conscious policy of the Kremlin leaders to remold the region's economy in the Soviet image. At what point the Soviet government decided to adopt such a course—whether prior to or concomitant with the military occupation of the area—is, however, a moot point, and for present purposes an unimportant one. What is relevant to note is that the Soviet drive to communize the economy of Eastern Europe faced different problems in the liberated Allied nations of Poland and Czechoslovakia than in the defeated enemy states of Hungary, Rumania, and Bulgaria. In the latter, communization of the economy was an easier undertaking in that the Soviet Union had won by conquest the right to station troops, extract reparations, and confiscate German war material. By contrast, the Allied nations of Eastern Europe were supposedly sovereign, independent countries over which the Soviet Union had no political or economic jurisdiction.

Soviet inroads into the economies of the former German satellites of Southeastern Europe began with the signing of the armistice agreements.[2] The Hungarian armistice of January 1945 stipulated that the Hungarian provisional (Debrecen) government would provide for the occupational needs of the Soviet armed forces. Specifically, Hungary would place at the disposal of the Soviet High Command, as it required, industrial and transport enterprises, means of communication, power stations, public utilities, and fuel storage facilities. These occupational supplies, or requisitions, ensured that the Soviet Union would be able to maintain a military force on Hungarian soil ready to back up any future policy ordered by the Kremlin. The military occupation, being the financial responsibility of the Hungarians alone, cost the Russians nothing. The armistice also awarded to the Soviet Union as booty all German war material in Hungary, a further economic gain for Russia, though at the expense of the Germans, not the Hungarians.[3]

The armistice opened another, major avenue for Soviet economic encroachment in the form of reparations. All Allies agreed that Hungary, as an enemy state that had launched an attack on the Soviet Union, should be held liable for war reparations payments to the Russians. A dispute arose only over the amount of reparations Hungary should pay. In the tripartite armistice discussions held in Moscow early in 1945, the Anglo-American negotiators, it will be recalled, sought a lower reparations figure than did the Russians, and the Soviet demand was indeed reduced from $320 million to $200 million. But even the lesser amount was a substantial liability and reparation payments were a severe drain on the Hungarian economy for the next several years.

In part because of the reparations burden, and in part because of wartime destruction and dislocation, an inflation of astronomical proportions gripped the nation in the latter part of 1945 and throughout most of 1946.[4] In circumstances of such economic hardship, Soviet ability to extract reparations represented a powerful lever of control over the Hungarian leadership. Whenever the Russians wanted to reduce pressure on the government, they could, and did, lessen the reparations burden by such means as postponing demands for payment or not insisting on penalties for late payments. In June 1948, by which time a fully pro-Soviet government had been installed in Budapest, the Russians cut the remaining $130 million reparation debt by one-half in a single stroke—a clear example of a Kremlin reward for political loyalty. But, until the Hungarian government was firmly under Moscow's control, the Soviet Union had the legal right and the military means to hold over Hungary's head the threat of intensifying reparation demands as a reprisal for any anti-Soviet action.[5]

Another crucial factor affecting the future status of the Hungarian economy concerned German assets in that country. Under the terms of the armistice agreement, the Soviet Union was entitled to expropriate, as war booty, all German-owned property and other assets found in Hungary. In their implementation of this provision, the Russians tended, however, to ignore the fact that much of the property "owned" by Germany in Hungary during the war had been owned by British and American interests until the Germans took it over. Also, certain bona fide German enterprises contained significant Anglo-American investments. Soviet failure to make these distinctions therefore quickly led to conflict with Britain and the United States.

The most important of these disputes arose in the case of the Hungarian oil industry, in which American investments amounted to some $59 million, almost all of it owned by the Standard Oil Company of New Jersey. British investments were slight, but the British—who had substantial investments in the Rumanian oil industry, as did the Americans —were nevertheless concerned because of the principle involved.

During the war, the Germans had seized control of the oil industries and petroleum installations in both Hungary and Rumania. As the Red Army cleared the Germans out of these countries, Soviet technicians and engineers quickly took charge of the oil fields and refineries, removed equipment, quartered troops in company housing, used company workshops to repair military vehicles, examined company records, and curtailed the movement of company staff.[6]

As early as January 1945, the British and American governments protested to Moscow about this Soviet intrusion in Rumanian oil companies owned by British and American interests. Following these complaints, such Soviet activity ended for a time, but in April the Russians again began removing equipment from British, though not American, installations. Then, in May, Soviet technicians took control of Hungarian-based petroleum plants owned by the American subsidiary MAORT (the Hungarian-language acronym for Hungarian American Oil Corporation). After receiving reports on the situation from MAORT representatives and American officials, the State Department ordered its Mission in Budapest to bring the matter up in the Allied Control Commission. This did not, however, cause the Russians to cease their activities on MAORT property, and two months later the State Department ordered yet another protest to be lodged, this time with the Allied Control Commission for Austria, which had jurisdiction over certain Hungarian-related issues.[7] By the time the Potsdam Conference convened in mid-July, the status of the Hungarian petroleum industry was, however, still unresolved and remained a serious point of contention.

The issue was in fact discussed at Potsdam, albeit only with specific reference to the Rumanian situation, which of course implicitly affected the status of Hungarian oil as well. Debate focused on the Soviet contention that the petroleum enterprises which they had seized, and from which they had removed equipment, were German-owned. The British and Americans did not object in principle to Soviet seizures of German property as war booty or for reparations, but they argued that the property in question belonged to their nationals, and not to Germans. The Russians, arguing that the Germans during their occupation of Hungary and Rumania had confiscated the petroleum plants, added German equipment, and used the enterprises in the anti-Soviet war effort, claimed that they had become German owned.[8] To a certain extent the Soviet argument was reasonable, and the Russians were doubtlessly entitled to some oil equipment or products. On the other hand, the dubious claim to virtually all British and American petroleum property was a transparent effort to seize the bulk of the foreign-owned petroleum industry in the Balkans for Soviet use. Short of a military intervention, however, there was little the British and Americans could do, and despite their efforts at Potsdam they failed to win any promise that the Soviet measures would be halted.

The British and American representatives did, however, win certain minor Soviet concessions. The Big Three agreed to an American proposal, attached as an annex to the Potsdam Conference Protocol, according to which "the burden of reparation and 'war trophies' should not fall on allied nationals." Moreover, the annex continued, the United States looked "to the other occupying powers" for the return of property "wholly or substantially owned by allied nationals," for the removal of such property to cease, and for the "adequate, effective and prompt compensation" for such property if it could not be returned. Although it might seem that the implementation of this proposal would have been given complete satisfaction to the British and Americans, it actually lacked all force because it spoke about the removal of "allied" property. The Soviet position, of course, was that the removed property was Axis-owned. The Russians refused to consent to a British proposal that a committee of three Allied nationals of non-interested states be formed to adjudicate this dispute, but the Big Three eventually agreed to form bi-lateral Anglo-Soviet and American-Soviet commissions to study the problem.[9] As it turned out, these commissions had no effect on the status of the Balkan petroleum industry, which continued to fall under increasing Soviet control.[10]

Beyond the question of oil property, the Potsdam negotiators also gave attention to the broader issue of the disposition of German external assets as a whole. The conferees came to easy agreement that the Soviet Union was entitled to confiscate all German investments in Hungary, Rumania, Bulgaria, and Finland; at the same time the Soviet Union renounced all claims to German property in any other country.[11] While there was quick agreement on how to apportion German external assets, the Potsdam decisions did not, however, specifically define what was meant by "German" or by "assets." As a consequence of this ambiguity, the Russians were able to extract considerably more property from the Balkan nations than the Western leaders at Potsdam had intended. Thus, as in the instance just described, the Russians were able to advance the dubious claim that the Balkan oil properties were German-owned. The British and Americans disputed this, but, in the absence of a precise definition of the word "German," the issue remained unresolved. The Russians, nevertheless, maintained possession of the oil properties.

Similarly, taking advantage of the failure of Potsdam to define specifically what constituted an asset, the Russians introduced a myriad of claims which rebounded against the interest of Hungarian and foreign-owned investments in Hungary. For example, did assets mean gross or net assets? When a dispute over this later arose, the United States interpreted assets to be net, meaning that assets had to be balanced against liabilities. The Russians, however, said that assets meant gross assets and that they did not have to take into account liabilities. The discrepancy between such competing claims amounted to tens of millions of dollars in Soviet demands on Hungarian-based property.[12]

Although the Soviet interpretation of what constituted German external assets was excessive and served to increase the Kremlin's demands on Hungarian-based property to a considerable extent, it should be understood that German assets invested in Hungary were in fact substantial, even if one applied the most rigid of interpretations. And as a result of the Potsdam decision all of these assets, invested in such actually or potentially productive enterprises as mining, manufacturing, transportation, and finance, now became Soviet assets. Moscow was able to use these substantial resources not only as a basis for economic demands on Hungary beyond the $200 million in reparations awared by the armistice, but more importantly as a device to penetrate and control the Hungarian economy.

The Soviet method of economic penetration soon became clear. At various times in 1945, the Soviet Union concluded trade agreements with East European nations, including Hungary, which ensured that the bulk of their foreign trade would be directed towards Russia, whereas before the war most Eastern European trade was with Central and Western Europe, particularly Germany. Of even greater significance were the so-called economic collaboration agreements, which the Soviet Union concluded with Rumania in mid-1945 and with Hungary a few months later. These agreements provided for the establishment of joint (or joint stock) Soviet-Rumanian and Soviet-Hungarian companies, which were the principal device by which the Soviet Union was able to gain control over those nations' economies. In the case of Hungary, joint companies were first set up in the fields of aviation, river navigation, petroleum production, and bauxite-aluminum production.

The ownership of the Soviet-Hungarian joint companies (the principle was the same in Rumania) was to be equally divided between the two nations. The principle of equal ownership was no more than theoretical, however, for the operating procedures governing the joint companies guaranteed that real control would rest with the Soviet Union. Moreover, the burden of furnishing the initial capital investment was placed mostly on Hungary. This was because the Hungarian capital contribution was to consist of its presently existing assets, while nearly all of the Soviet contribution was to come either from Hungarian assets acquired by the Russians through reparations or requisitions, or from German assets invested in Hungary and inherited by the Russians as a result of the armistice and confirmed as theirs at Potsdam. Thus, the Soviet Union was able to obtain half ownership and full control of various enterprises in crucial sectors of the Hungarian economy and operating on Hungarian soil, through which it acquired extraordinary influence over the nation's economy. And Moscow achieved this result with virtually no obligation to export any capital whatsoever.[13]

* * * * *

It was quite apparent to the British and American governments that the Soviet Union had everything to gain from the economic collaboration agreement, which promised to legitimize and regularize Soviet economic control over Hungary. At the same time, the agreement threatened to eliminate any chance for the two Western nations, or for any nation except the Soviet Union, to retain an economic foothold in Hungary. This was especially disconcerting for the Anglo-Americans who twenty years earlier had concluded commercial treaties with Hungary granting them most-favored-nation treatment. The collaboration agrement would effectively put an end to such privileges.

Along with the election crisis, the question of the economic collaboration agreement was one of the most pressing issues to develop on the Hungarian political scene in the final months of 1945, and, like the elections, it became an issue important in Soviet-Western relations. The question of the collaboration agreement arose after the Soviet government and two left-bloc members (a Communist and a Social Democrat) of the Hungarian government signed it in August. Final ratification (which required the approval of the cabinet as a while as well as the National Assembly) would normally have been a mere formality, but it was delayed as a result of opposition by the right wing of the Smallholders Party.[14] In the ensuing period, as the State Department learned from Minister Schoenfeld in Budapest (who himself was kept informed through contacts with high-ranking Smallholder politicians), Soviet authorities applied "increasing pressure" on the Hungarian government to ratify the agreement. Schoenfeld, in effect, urged Washington to resist Soviet coercion by suggesting that "American failure to express disapproval" of the agreement had "discouraged" non-Marxist circles and "given support" to pro-Soviet elements.[15]

Against the background of such reports, the State Department sent a letter to Moscow in October objecting to the proposed agreement on the grounds that the "long-term arrangements" for which it provided were of "common concern" to other signatories of the Hungarian armistice and should await the conclusion of a peace treaty. The American note also expressed concern that some of the proposed arrangements "might work out to prejudice United States interests in Hungary and to deny to countries other than the Soviet Union equal access to Hungarian raw materials and markets and equality of opportunity to trade with Hungary." Finally, the State Department affirmed its desire that the three wartime Allies concert their efforts and take joint action to rehabilitate the Hungarian economy.[16] Shortly after the presentation of the note to Moscow, Schoenfeld informed Hungarian Prime Minister Béla Miklós of the Smallholders Party about the letter. Miklós, Schoenfeld reported, "expressed great satisfaction at this action."[17]

The American note had no effect on the Soviet government. Two weeks later, Deputy Foreign Commissar Vyshinski replied that there was "no foundation for the uneasiness shown" by the United States regarding the economic agreement. He assured the American government that it contained "no element of discrimination" and created "no difficulties in economic relations" between Hungary and third countries. The American request that the Soviet-Hungarian economic agreement be delayed until the conclusion of a formal peace treaty was rejected. One reason to proceed immediately with the economic agreement was, Vyshinski stated, that the distressed Hungarian economy required assistance. In addition to this, he added pointedly, the United States had concluded economic agreements with Italy even though no peace treaty had been signed.[18]

Moscow's insistence that the Hungarian government ratify the economic collaboration agreement continued unabated,[19] and there was very little the United States could do to resist such pressure. Hungary ultimately ratified the agreement on 20 December 1945. Yet, despite the failure of the attempt to prevent ratification, the United States continued diplomatic efforts to curtail the growing Soviet involvement in the Hungarian economy. In March, July, and September 1946, the State Department in letters to Moscow protested the state of economic affairs in Hungary and called for tripartite collaboration in its economic rehabilitation. These notes also referred to the Yalta Declaration's stated aim of Allied cooperation in assisting liberated nations "to solve by democratic means their pressing political and economic problems." These representations also failed to have any impact, either on the Hungarian economic situation or on Soviet-Western collaboration. The Soviet Union rebuffed them as sharply as it had the one of October 1945.[20]

For both political and economic reasons the British were as concerned as the Americans about the Soviet-Hungarian—and the Soviet-Rumanian—

economic collaboration agreements. Duggald Stewart, referring to Rumania, minuted that the agreements "militate[d] against direct British interests" in that country, particularly in the oil and Danube shipping industries.[21] Southeastern Europe was certainly important to Britain and other European countries as a source of agricultural products, such as grain and timber.[22] John Coulson, apparently fearing a spillover affect toward the west, argued that, if the Balkans fell into the Soviet sphere, the loss of this supply would "seriously damage" British interests in Central Europe.[23]

On top of the short-term economic threat, whose seriousness some Foreign Office personnel doubted, the long-term political threat to the region was indisputable. Orme Sargent's main concern about "Russian economic penetration" was the danger it posed to Southeastern Europe's "political independence."[24] Michael Williams did not see an economic threat, because neither country had been or was likely to be an important market for British goods. "From the political point of view," however, the agreements were "much more objectionable since they provide[d] for a very large measure of Russian infiltration into both countries."[25] Similarly, William Hayter believed the economic collaboration agreements were not doing "any actual damage to our commercial interests," since there was then very little British trade with those two countries. His "real objection" to the agreements was "the fact that they tie[d] the economy of [Hungary and Rumania] to the Soviet economy and thus render[ed] them subject to excessive Soviet influence."[26]

In view of their appraisal, the British, like the Americans, sought to forestall ratification of the Hungarian agreement. To a large extent the two Western governments were able to work in conjunction with each other, though they had certain tactical differences. One of these was that London preferred to direct its protests to the Soviet Union at a relatively low level, specifically through the Hungarian Allied Control Commission. The United States, by contrast, immediately brought the issue up at the highest level, presenting it, as we have noted, in a formal letter directly to Moscow in October. Nevertheless, once the United States had thus taken the lead—afterwards informing the British Foreign Office of the text of the letter—London decided to support the American action by sending a similar letter to Moscow.[27]

Another difference in approach concerned the nature of the representations that Washington and London made to the Soviet Union. After the failure of the Anglo-American effort in October, the British Foreign Office revised its policy from one of protesting the substance of the collaboration agreement itself to one of demanding that the Russians make available the precise text of the agreement. The British had come to believe that, until they had received the official terms of the economic agreements, they would be unable to force a discussion on the subject with the Russians, who would simply go on "stalling" (as Duggald Stewart put it) and denying that the agreements were prejudicial to Western interests.[28] Such a policy change represented a significant retreat, and one with which the Americans refused to go along. Rather than make the demands for copies of the texts the centerpiece of their tactics, the Americans persisted in protesting the Soviet-Hungarian collaboration agreement and the resulting Soviet economic dominance in Hungary on substantive grounds. Thus, all three protest letters of 1946 appealed for tripartite collaboration in dealing with the Hungarian economy, the same demand that the United States had made in 1946. By themselves these tactical divergences were minor, but they did represent a discernible difference in emphasis: the united States pursued its point far more aggressively than did the British.

Although the British and Americans were able to work together on Balkan economic problems with a minimum of friction for a time, the greater American combativeness eventually limited the possibility of coordinated action. By January 1946, shortly after Hungary had ratified the collaboration agreement, the Foreign Office was clearly beginning to lose hope of even acquiring the texts of the Balkan collaboration agreements.[29] When the State Department in March, following its protest to Moscow on the Hungarian economic situation, formally requested that the British Foreign Office make a similar protest,[30] the British were in a quandary. John Coulson minuted how he disliked making such a representation, noting that it was "unlikely to have any effect." On the other hand he argued to his colleagues, "we could not possibly refuse to support such a strong lead by the U.S."[31] Ultimately the British went along with the United States, but their lack of enthusiasm was unmistakable.[32]

* * * * *

Another way for the West to try to counteract Soviet domination of the Hungarian economy was to offer material assistance. Theoretically at least, such assistance could serve to reestablish political and economic ties between the West and the Danubian nation. Both the British and American governments pondered such a policy, and in the latter part of 1945 and in 1946 they had periodic discussions on the subject with pro-Western Hungarian officials (pro-Soviet Hungarians were not interested in obtaining Western aid). During these talks, the Hungarians expressed their desire for loans and credits, reconstruction supplies, assistance from the United Nations Relief and Rehabilitation Administration (UNRRA)—in which the British and Americans, as the two largest contributors, had decisive influence—and restitution of Hungarian-owned property looted by Germany in the closing months of the war and currently located mainly in the American zones of occupation in Germany and Austria. Among the looted property were Danube River barges and more than 30 million dollars worth of gold.[33]

Within the British government, there was some sympathy for assisting Hungary economically. The feeling was, however, that Britain, then in the throes of its own economic crisis, could not afford to provide any type of direct assistance such as loans, credits, or supplies to Hungary. For example, an under-secretary at the Board of Trade, A. E. Welch, speaking during an interagency review of the Hungarian economic situation held in November 1945, explained that the United Kingdom's "present limited capacity [was] strained to the utmost to meet even the immediate requirements of more deserving claimants such as the Empire and the Allies."[34] On another occasion, in December, Edmund L. Hall-Patch, assistant under-secretary of state in the Foreign Office, similarly argued against contributing to Hungary's economic recovery: "To the U.S.A.," noted Hall-Patch "this might be unpalatable but not impossible. To us, in our present financial straits, it would be quite out of the question."[35] Michael Williams expressed support for directing a small amount of UNRRA assistance to Hungary, but Hall-Patch's opinion against doing even that prevailed, in part because the UNRRA funds were already earmarked for other recipients. In fact, the only economic commitment that Britain was willing to make towards the rehabilitation of Hungary was to resume trade relations with it.[36] Even so, Welch of the Board of Trade, who advocated such a policy, stressed the restraints that Britain would have to place on this trade. If Hungary were to buy British goods, Welch stated, it in turn would be required to sell its produce back to Britain or to other nations in the sterling area.[37] As a matter of fact, because of Hungary's trade obligations to the Soviet Union, this requirement effectively eliminated any chance for Anglo-Hungarian commerce, which for some time remained non-existent. Ultimately, therefore, Britain took no action to assist Hungary economically.

The United States played a more active role in assisting Hungary's rehabilitation. A policy of economic intervention began shortly after the November 1945 election, which led to the installation of a nominally Smallholder-led government. Explaining that the United States might be able to sell reconstruction equipment to Hungary on a credit basis, Byrnes informed Schoenfeld of the State Department's desire "to encourage the newly formed" government "by giving full consideration to such means as may be available to contribute to the economic recovery of Hungary." This would support the Hungarian government's desire "to maintain and increase economic and commercial ties with the United States."[38]

Schoenfeld expressed his strong approval of such a policy and urged that it "be accelerated and encouraged." By February 1946, however, he perceived that the Hungarian economy was sliding further under Soviet domination, and he suggested that in a "relatively short time" Hungary "may be expected" to "become an economic colony" of the Soviet Union "from which western trade will be excluded and in which western investments will be totally lost." Still, he did not regard the situation as hopeless, and he continued to stress Hungary's pressing need for American assistance, which he clearly implied had been inadequate. But by May, Schoenfeld concluded that the situation had deteriorated beyond salvage, and he described "present day Hungary" as "virtually" a "Soviet economic colony." He now advised against any economic assistance to Hungary—with the "possible exception of limited help given on humanitarian grounds"—since Soviet economic demands would neutralize its effects. If the United States were to give aid to Hungary, Schoenfeld argued, it should do so only in the context of Soviet-American relations as a whole and without any expectation of improving the Hungarian economic situation.[39]

At various points in 1946, even beyond the time that Schoenfeld recommended, the United States did provide certain forms of aid to Hungary. In January, after strong support by the United States government, UNRRA approved a four million dollar relief program for Hungary. At about the same time the United States granted Hungary a long-term, low-interest credit for the purchase of up to ten million dollars worth of American-owned surplus property. In June, following a state visit by the Hungarian prime minister and other government members to Washington, the credit was raised to 15 million dollars, and the United States announced that it would return Hungarian gold and some of the other Hungarian-owned property it held in Germany and Austria. This type of sporadic aid continued into 1947. In February of that year, the United States gave yet another 15 million dollar credit to Hungary.[40]

On the whole, American aid was spotty and by no means sufficient to have any appreciable effect on the Hungarian economy. It could neither loosen its connection with the Soviet Union, nor satisfy the Hungarian Smallholders, who repeatedly requested that American aid be increased. But this the United States was unwilling to do, partly because it did not have unlimited funds at its disposal, and partly because it was reluctant to supply large quantities of aid to a nation which was under obligation to pay reparations to the Soviet Union.[41]

In short, while it is true that the United States intervened much more actively in Hungary with economic aid than did Britain, it did not dispense financial aid extravagantly, or even generously. That it played a more ambitious economic role can probably be attributed to the fact that it was better equipped to do so. Unlike Britain, which emerged from the war in a weakened economic condition, the United States had grown more powerful, both economically and militarily, and was obviously capable of providing more assistance to foreign nations than its British ally.

* * * * *

Soviet inroads into the Hungarian economy adversely affected Anglo-American interests both in the long and the short terms. The short-term threat was of an economic nature, and imperiled whatever investments the two Western nations had in Hungary; the long-term threat was political, portending an expansion of the Soviet system westward. In the case of the immediate, economic threat—which the rapid Soviet intrusion and seizure of Western-owned oil property strikingly exemplified—British and American reactions were virtually identical. The two Western Powers strongly protested Moscow's actions, notably at the Potsdam Conference, where the Balkan oil question was an important topic of discussion. At Potsdam there was no discernible difference in approach between the British and the American delegations, both of which pressed vigorously (albeit unsuccessfully) to protect their interests in the petroleum industry. On the other hand, the long-term, political threat, embodied in the Soviet-Hungarian economic collaboration agreement, produced sharply contrasting Anglo-American reactions. Although both Western governments engaged in diplomatic efforts to forestall ratification of the agreement and, once ratified, Soviet domination of the Hungarian economy, the Americans fought more assertively and persistently.

But aggressive diplomacy by itself costs nothing—with the possible exception of tranquil international relations, whose value is intangible and subject to interpretation. On the other hand, what possesses real and objective value is material wealth, and with this the United States parted only sparingly, a fact which the issue of financial assistance brought bubbling to the surface. Though the United States believed, up to a certain point at least, that financial aid might induce the Hungarian government to maintain a pro-Western course, it doled out such aid as though with an eyedropper. It is true that American officials in time came to believe that continued financial support would not produce the desired effect, but it is noteworthy that they came to no such belief regarding diplomatic protests, which to all appearances had no more effect on the course of events. In short, as long as the contest over Hungary was a diplomatic one, Washington acted far more aggressively than London. But when it came to risking something tangible, the United States backed away sharply from its aggressive stance and demonstrated that it was no more willing than its British ally to bet on the outcome.

The Soviet Union, meanwhile, was making steady inroads into the Hungarian economy. The creation of joint Soviet-Hungarian companies was but one step in this process, as was the early confiscation of a number of industries—notably the oil industry—on the pretext that they were German-owned and therefore war booty. But it would take wholesale nationalization of all important industrial enterprises, Hungarian as well as foreign-owned, and under a Communist government, to establish the sort of control over the Hungarian economy to which the Russians obviously aspired. And this could not be accomplished as long as the Smallholders Party retained its majority and continued to exercise its moderating and restraining influence. More radical political changes than those already wrought had to be effected before the Soviet Union could harness the Hungarian economy to its own.

V

1946: A YEAR OF UNEASY TRANQUILLITY

As early as March 1946, the Soviet Union had acquired enough power in Eastern Europe for Winston Churchill to speak of the descent of an iron curtain from the Baltic to the Adriatic. By the end of the year, Poland, Rumania, and Bulgaria had been brought almost totally within the Soviet orbit. Of the East European countries occupied by the Red Army at the end of the war, only Hungary and Czechoslovakia remained relatively independent of Soviet domination, their independence a result of the countervailing strength of anti-Soviet, pro-Western political parties.

In Hungary, the Smallholders Party emerged from the November 1945 general election as the rallying point for anti-Soviet opinion, while the Communist-led left bloc embodied the Smallholders' chief political opposition. There was continuous tension between these two antagonistic forces throughout 1946, but occasional conflicts were kept on a relatively restrained level. While the left bloc strengthened its position during this period, the Smallholders remained an important though embattled element in Hungarian politics.

While this political maneuvering proceeded in Hungary, the Paris Peace Conference of 1946 became a forum for international competition between the Soviet Union and its Anglo-American and other adversaries. These discussions, which concerned the former satellites of Germany, including Hungary, led to the conclusion of peace agreements in February

76

1947. The deliberations were long and contentious, a fact resulting from—
and in turn contributing to—the international East-West division which
was already beginning to crystallize.

Like the internal events of 1946 in Hungary, the peace discussions and
the ensuing peace treaty were transitional developments in the resolution
of the Hungarian situation—not in themselves decisive, but steps toward
a final settlement. And, also like internal Hungarian events, the peace
negotiations kept alive often latent but ever-present strains between pro-
Soviet and pro-Western political forces. Hungarian affairs did not burst
into a full-scale crisis until 1947, but the antagonistic atmosphere of
1946 laid the foundation for the coming showdown.

* * * * *

According to the procedure worked out by the Moscow Conference
of Foreign Ministers in December 1945, the peace-making process was
to consist of three basic stages. In the first stage, the Council of Foreign
Ministers would convene early in 1946 to draw up treaty drafts. In the
second stage, these drafts would be submitted to a peace conference,
which was to meet in Paris no later than 1 May 1946. In addition to the
Big Five, the peace conference would also include "all members of the
United Nations which actively waged war with substantial military force
against European enemy states," a total of twenty-one. It was also agreed
to permit each enemy state to present its views at the conference. In the
third stage, the Council of Foreign Ministers would reconvene to consider the recommendations of the conference and draw up final texts of the
peace treaties, which would then come into force upon ratification by the
Big Five.[1]

The actual course of events proceeded roughly along the lines envision-
ed, but at a slower pace and with considerable bickering. The Council of
Foreign Ministers session, convened in January 1946, was beset by serious
disputes over a number of issues and lasted far longer than expected. Even
with the delay, many problems were so persistent that they prevented the
foreign ministers from completing the treaty drafts, and the council eventually decided to present unfinished drafts to the peace conference.

Amid fanfare the conference, to be held in Paris, finally convened in
late July, nearly three months beyond the projected deadline. James
Byrnes, who had already devoted countless hours to his long-sought
goal of concluding peace treaties, led the U.S. delegation to the conference.

To win senatorial support, necessary for the ratification of treaties, and continue efforts at bipartianship, Byrnes invited Arthur H. Vandenberg and Tom Connally, the ranking Republican and Democratic members of the Senate Foreign Relations Committee to accompany him.[2] On the British side the stormy tempered Bevin, after only a year in office and already a veteran of several encounters with Molotov, was unable to attend the first half of the conference due to illness. In his place stood the prime minister himself, the mild-mannered but politically astute Clement Attlee, who did not normally involve himself closely in foreign affairs, a subject he was content to defer to his foreign secretary.[3] Hector McNeill, parliamentary under-secretary in the Foreign Office, and Gladwyn Jebb, Bevin's deputy in the Council of Foreign Ministers, were other key members of the British delegation.[4] Vyacheslav Molotov, now with the more Western-sounding designation minister (rather than people's commissar) for foreign affairs, led the Soviet delegation, while Foreign Minister János Gyöngyösy headed the Hungarian.

Whatever high hopes surrounding its opening, the conference proved unable to resolve a number of disputes, concluded its proceedings in mid-October, and turned the unfinished business back to the Council of Foreign Ministers. Meeting in New York in November and December, the council made such slow progress that Secretary Byrnes threatened to abandon the effort to conclude the peace treaties. When Molotov realized that Byrnes' threat was not idle and that the Soviet Union would win no further American concessions (at least this is how Byrnes explained Molotov's behavior), the Russians quickly agreed to many points which they had resisted throughout the year. On certain matters the Russians yielded outright, on others they called for minor, apparently face-saving changes in terminology, while a few questions on which no agreement was forthcoming were dropped from consideration.[5] In their final form, the five peace treaties were signed in Paris on 10 February 1947. Following ratification by all the governments concerned, the treaties came into force in September.[6]

To a large extent, the peace treaties were based upon the armistice agreements that all German satellites had previously signed, and those agreements were patterned after the first one, signed by Italy in 1943. There was thus a considerable similarity among the treaties, except for provisions relating to problems peculiar to only one country. The Hungarian treaty, like the others, provided for the repeal of racial, religious, and othe discriminatory legislation, the release of prisoners confined because of sympathy for the United Nations, the dissolution of fascist-type organizations on its territory, and the arrest and surrender for trial of war criminals. The treaty also provided that the Hungarian armed forces would be "closely restricted" to the task of providing internal order and border defense. Although all Allied forces were to be withdrawn within ninety days of the coming into force of the treaty, the Soviet Union could "keep on Hungarian territory such armed forces as it may need" to protect the lines of communication with its troops in Austria.[7]

Another and particularly important provision common to all five treaties governed the status of the ex-enemies' commercial relations with other nations. In the case of the Hungarian treaty, Article 33 provided that, for a period of eighteen months after the coming into force of the treaty, Hungary would "make no arbitrary discrimination" against the goods of any one of the United Nations in favor of another, and also stipulated that all United Nations nationals would receive most-favored-nation treatment "in all matters pertaining to commerce, industry, shipping and other forms of business activity within Hungary."

Both the United States and Great Britain strongly desired this provision in order to halt the increasing Soviet monopolization of the Hungarian economy, a trend which deeply concerned them. At the same time, the Soviet Union obviously wanted to maintain its own free hand in Hungary and keep out Western competition. No doubt the Russians would have wanted to omit any equality-of-treatment provisions whatsoever, but the Western nations would certainly have objected. To get around it, the Russians proposed that most-favored-nation treatment not apply to those branches of industry or commerce where "private enterprise does not take place." This would have excluded a great deal, since a portion of Hungarian enterprise was already nationalized, and much of the rest was under state control or in the process of being nationalized. To counter the Soviet proposal, the British and Americans agreed to specify that the United Nations would not have the right to engage in business activity which is "a monopoly of the Hungarian State."[8] While such a provision would have excluded the West, it would also have excluded the Russians by preventing them from operating their joint Soviet-Hungarian companies. In any case all of this became academic, for the parties decided not to pursue either proposed addition, which accordingly did not appear in the treaty.

However, the Russians were able to insert in the treaty an important exception to the equality-of-treatment principle. They proposed that business activities "customarily" excluded from most-favored-nation treatment in prewar Hungarian treaties, as well as business activities "which relate to relations with neighboring countries," would not have to conform with most-favored-nation treatment. Since prewar Hungarian treaties often contained exceptions to the most-favored-nation principle—as commercial treaties often do[9]—and since Hungary was a "neighboring" country of the Soviet Union, the Soviet proposals would have eliminated virtually all force behind the equal treatment provision.

The British and Americans agreed to the exception for business activities "customarily" excluded in prewar treaties, but they strongly objected to the proposed exception for neighboring states. The American delegation argued at the Peace Conference that an exception for neighboring states would lead to "the establishment of a closed regional system of preferential arrangements" and "permit the establishment of a new and rigid economic regionalism in Eastern Europe which would have no historical validity." The British delegation simply noted its concern "that equality of terms should be given to all the United Nations without discrimination."[10] At the New York session of the Council of Foreign Ministers, the Russians agreed to drop the exception for neighboring countries but not the customary exceptions from most-favored-nation treatment, and the clause guaranteeing the latter exceptions was retained in the treaty. As a result the Soviet Union was able to strengthen its control over the Hungarian economy and to continue its exclusion of Western competition with at least a veneer of legality.

In addition to political and economic questions, the peace treaty discussions also dealt with certain border and national minority issues which were of great importance to Hungary and its neighbors. As a holdover from the pre-1919 era, there were some two million ethnic Magyars in what had once been Historic Hungary, but which became Czechoslovak and Rumanian territory as a result of the Treaty of Trianon. Motivated by a powerful irredentism, Hungarian nationalists (but not the Communists, who followed Moscow's lead in territorial and nationality questions, as in others) greatly desired a rectification of what they perceived as an injustice both to Hungary and to the Hungarian minority in bordering countries. At the 1946 Paris Peace Conference, these proponents of

Hungarian nationalism argued their case in the hopes of effecting a territorial adjustment in Hungary's favor.[11]

Although the United States and Great Britain gave some attention to the question of Hungaro-Czechoslovak relations, they had little reason to become deeply involved in the issue and sought instead to persuade the two affected governments to settle their differences through bilateral negotiations.[12] The Hungaro-Rumanian dispute, on the other hand, became an object of more serious Anglo-American interest. The dispute concerned the status of Transylvania, the northern part of which Hungary seized from Rumania in 1940. Rumania now demanded that the whole province be returned, while Hungary wanted to retain a portion of it. Neither the United States nor Great Britain had a direct interest in the Transylvanian problem, but there were distinct political implications involved. Ever since the Soviet-directed installation of the Petru Groza regime in March 1945, Rumania had been closely tied to Moscow. Hungary, on the other hand, where the Smallholders Party continued to be a serious opposition force and nominally led the coalition government, resisted Soviet domination. Logically enough from its standpoint, the Soviet Union consistently supported the territorial aspirations of Rumania at the expense of Hungary, a fact made clear by the Soviet performance at the peace conference.[13] Reversely, Anglo-American support for Hungary's territorial claims as against Rumania's would have served to strengthen the pro-Western elements in the Hungarian coalition and counter Soviet influence in that country.

It is quite clear that such reasoning motivated the United States. For example, Schoenfeld in Budapest, urging State Department support for Hungary's territorial goals, argued that it was more important for the United States "to consider the effect of a frontier revision on Hungarian internal politics than on Rumanian internal politics inasmuch as Hungary is still a twilight zone in respect to Soviet expansion whereas the shadows falling on Rumania are already of deeper hue."[14] Similarly, John C. Campbell, an adviser to the American delegation, acknowledged that a border rectification proposed by Hungary would both create economic "complications" and fail to solve the ethnic minority problem. Nonetheless he supported it because of its "important political effect in Hungary." As he argued:

It would probably improve the position of the present coalition regime in Hungary and avoid a situation whereby the Smallholders Party could be charged with complete failure to obtain in the peace settlement even the granting of Hungary's most reasonable claims.[15]

On the basis of such thinking, the United States gave some support at the peace conference for the Hungarian position. In the face of Soviet resistance, however, it did not press the point, which was after all not so crucial for Washington as to warrant a major East-West split. The American delegation stated that it was not "a strong supporter" of returning all of Transylvania to Rumania, but, "in view of the desirability of reaching unanimous agreement," it would not insist upon continued consideration of the problem. It expressed the hope that progress might be made through bilateral negotiations between the two disputants "toward a mutually satisfactory settlement of the outstanding questions."[16]

British thinking on the Transylvanian question was identical to the American, but London was not willing to press for such a border adjustment. According to a Foreign Office briefing paper, "it would be useless to raise the matter" of Hungary's claim to Transylvanian territory "in view of the intransigent attitude" already demonstrated by the Russians on this point.[17] However, the British did consider at one point proposing a clause in the Rumanian treaty guaranteeing the rights of the Magyar minority in Rumania.[18] Although the British decided against pressing for even this limited proposal, the political impulse behind it is clear. The Foreign Office hoped that such a clause "would go far to give the Hungarian Smallholders the necessary strength to enable them to rally behind them the bulk of the Hungarian people and to withstand pressure from the extreme left."[19]

In short, the British and Americans failed to win any territorial gains for Hungary at the peace conference. Whether success along these lines would have had any effect on the internal political situation in Hungary is, of course, problematical. In any case, it remains noteworthy that both the British and the Americans saw an opportunity to make use of Hungarian irredentism as a device to support and encourage the anti-Communist Smallholders. That they could not have their will prevail reflected the declining ability of the West to influence East European affairs. There can be no doubt that the peace treaties were a positive achievement for the Soviet Union, for they helped consolidate its control over Southeastern Europe. For example, the Allied Control Commissions in Hungary, Rumania, and Bulgaria were to be terminated. While these had never been effective instruments for Western interests, they gave the British and Americans at least the legal right to intervene in the affairs of these Balkan nations.

With the coming of peace came *de jure* sovereignty. Theoretically, this meant that neither East nor West could interfere in Hungarian affairs. In fact it meant that the West was totally excluded, while the Soviet Union, through its patron relationship with the Hungarian Communist Party, could maintain and enhance its already significant political influence. Also, although they treaty called for equality of treatment in trade and commerce, it was loosely enough constructed to allow the Soviet Union to continue its monopoly position in the Hungarian economy.

It should finally be recalled that the peace treaties permitted the Soviet Union to retain some troops in Hungary and Rumania to protect its lines of communication with Austria. This continued presence of the Red Army in the two Balkan nations clearly enabled the Soviet Union to impose its will if necessary. In sum, the peace treaties helped to confirm and stabilize the status quo, which in the case of Southeastern Europe meant confirming what was increasingly becoming a pax sovietica.[20]

This was not, however, a one-way process. The advantages that the peace treaties gave the Soviet Union in the Balkan region, they also gave the West in Italy. In that country the Allied Commission,[21] which included a Soviet representative, was terminated when the Italian peace treaty came into force, and with the restoration of Italian sovereignty the Soviet Union lost any legal right to intervene in Italian affairs. It is true that the Russians could try to influence the affairs of Italy through the Italian Communist Party, but they lacked the leverage provided by a military presence. Thus, the peace treaties strengthened the hand of the Soviet Union in Southeastern Europe and of the Western Powers in Italy. In so doing the peace treaties advanced a trend in progress since late 1944: the division of Europe into two spheres of influence, one Western and the other Soviet.

* * * * *

The November 1945 general election demonstrated that a clear though not overwhelming majority (57 percent) of the Hungarian populace favored the pro-Western Smallholders Party over the three leftist parties. The magnitude of the Smallholders' victory appears more substantial when measured against the vote cast for each individual leftist party. The Communists won 17 percent of the vote, as did the Social Democrats, while the National Peasant Party, closely allied with the Communists as their rural wing (but soon to dwindle to insignificance in Hungarian politics), took 9 percent. The Smallholders could legitimately claim the status of Hungary's majority party.

However, the leftist parties were able to array a number of important factors against the Smallholders' majority mandate and thereby to enhance their own political power. One such factor was the very nature of the Communist Party, whose well organized and highly disciplined structure led by Moscow-trained agitators such as General Secretary Mátyás Rákosi, made it a decisive force and the dominant one on the left. Despite the Smallholders' majority showing in the 1945 election, the Communists subsequently demanded that a coalition government be established—lest they foment social disorders against a purely Smallholder government— and they won for themselves and the other two parties of the left half of the cabinet seats. Moreover, inside the coalition the Communists were able to obtain strength beyond numbers by acquiring particularly important ministries, such as those which controlled economic affairs and the police. Beyond the realm of government, the Communists and the Social Democrats had virtually total control over the trade unions and could utilize working-class power, intrinsically a highly centralized and easily organizable force, for leftist political purposes. What capped the Communists' ability to augment strength was the formation in March 1946, on Communist initiative, of a left bloc. All three leftist parties, which collectively gathered a substantial minority vote of 43 percent, agreed to act as a coalition and adopt a common political program, and this forged the three lesser parties into a powerful political opposition.[22] Thus, as the year 1946 got under way, a number of potentially serious challenges from the left confronted the Smallholders Party.

Probably the last non-controversial political event in Hungary in the immediate postwar years occurred in January 1946, when the newly-elected National Assembly formally abolished the monarchy and established the Third Hungarian Republic (the short-lived republics of 1848-49 and 1918-19 were the other two). In February, Zoltán Tildy, a Smallholder who had been prime minister since November, assumed the office of president, a largely ceremonial post, while Ferenc Nagy, also a Small-holder, became premier. Nagy, who soon revealed himself to be a moderate among the Smallholders—neither so far to the right that he refused to work with the Communists, nor so far to the left that he was willing to serve as a tool in Communist hands—became the final bulwark against left-wing advance: the leftists could not seize complete political control in Hungary until Nagy was removed from the political scene; but once he was removed, they had an unimpeded path to power. It is noteworthy that in his memoirs, written shortly after he was deposed in mid-1947, Nagy compared his rule in Hungarian politics to that of other Eastern European anti-Communist leaders such as Stanislaw Mikolajczyk of Poland, Rumania's Iuliu Maniu, the Bulgarian Nikola Petkov, and Eduard Beneš of Czechoslovakia, all of whom the local Communists, with Soviet backing, overthrew one by one.[23]

For the first few weeks of 1946 the Hungarian political situation remained outwardly calm. Towards the end of February, however, conflicting political currents began to emerge and threatened to undermine the existing stability. The cause of the mounting tension was leftist demands in the National Assembly for passage of the so-called Defense of the Republic bill, which would have created new categories of criminal offences with obvious political applications and strengthened the powers of the police, already largely under Communist control. In the face of left-wing pressure for the enactment of this bill, and because of lingering resentment over the Communist-inspired economic collaboration agreement which the Hungarian government had ratified two months previously, some members of the Smallholders Party, who soon emerged as its most virulently anti-Communist, right-wing faction, began to make open denunciations inside parliament of the Communists and the Red Army occupation.

Apparently in response to this defiance of the Kremlin and its Hungarian supporters—the first public challenge the Russians had faced since they entered Hungary more than a year before—the Communists launched a political offensive. On 3 March, they made a widely publicized verbal attack against the right-wing Smallholders. A few days later, the leftist parties demanded from Prime Minister Nagy certain political and economic concessions, one of the most important of which was that he purge the Smallholders Party of twenty-two members of its right wing. Then, in what turned out to be the climax of the crisis, a massive street demonstration of over 100,000 people, organized by the left bloc, was staged in Budapest on 7 March. The crisis was resolved when the Smallholder leadership on 12 March formally acceded to all of the leftist demands, which besides the purge of the right-wing Smallholders also included the establishment of a program to purge the civil service, the nationalization of certain industries, and the placing of others under state supervision.[24]

Closely observing these events, Western foreign policy officials were quite perturbed over the developing situation in Hungary, and no less so over Nagy's handling of it. His policy, so he explained to the British and American representatives, was to maintain the existing coalition government, even if that meant yielding to left-wing demands to some extent. Nagy believed that if he refused to make concessions, the leftist parties would have resigned from the coalition and then, through the use of strikes and disorders, proceeded to incapacitate the Smallholder government.[25] Although the British and Americans sympathized with the embattled premier's difficult position, they also thought he conceded to left-wing pressure much too readily and could offer greater resistance to it. "Although one can appreciate their difficulties," noted A. Russell of the Foreign Office, "the Smallholders . . . are displaying a peculiarly spineless attitude in the face of the Communists."[26]

In view of what the British and Americans saw as irresolute leadership on the part of Nagy and the Smallholders Party, they considered whether they should encourage the Nagy government to take a stronger line against further demands from the left. Opinion within both the State Department and the Foreign Office was somewhat divided on this question. Among the Americans Ben Cohen, State Department counsellor, and in the Foreign Office William Hayter, did not want to encourage Smallholder resistance. They believed that an overly defiant posture might provoke Soviet retaliation, such as a left-wing coup d'état, and that in the event of such a Soviet reprisal the British and Americans could do nothing to assist the Smallholders.[27] But H. Freeman Matthews' view, about which he did not "feel strongly," was that the two Western powers should offer "mild encouragement" to the Smallholders Party.[28] Christopher Warner favored more strongly a policy of encouraging "the anti-Communist parties to stand up to the Communists and to be true to their principles, so far as they can." He argued that to a large extent the Communists were "bluffing" and that in the face of Smallholder resistance they would back down, at least for the present. He suggested that, if the Communists were in fact prepared to stage a coup d'état, forcing them to take such illegal action openly was better than yielding to their demands without obliging them to stage a coup.[29]

Despite this ambivalence, prevailing opinion within the two Western governments favored making an approach to encourage Nagy, and their representatives in Budapest were instructed to speak with him along these lines. However, the limited encouragement offered rendered this approach almost ineffectual. According to their instructions, Gascoigne and Schoenfeld separately advised Nagy that "continual concessions" to the left bloc could in the end lead only to the "negation of the people's mandate" given the Smallholders Party in November 1945. They also emphasized—and this was the key—that the problem was "one for solution by the Hungarians themselves."[30] The meaning of this advise was inescapable: the British and Americans wanted the Smallholders to stand up to leftist pressure, but they would not come to their assistance if needed. Such counsel could scarcely have given much encouragement to Nagy and the Smallholder leadership. Strangely, Nagy did not record the incident in his memoirs.

In any case, once the Smallholders had yielded to the leftist demands in mid-March, the political situation settled down and an atmosphere of relative calm prevailed for more than two months. Then a new crisis erupted. On 21 May, Béla Kovács, secretary general of the Smallholders Party and a close associate of Nagy, presented a list of demands to the left bloc on behalf of the Smallholders. These demands called for, among other things, holding provincial elections, handing over fifty percent of the police positions in the Interior Ministry to the Smallholders, and halting "arbitrary action" by the political police. After intensive discussions in late May and early June between Smallholder representatives on the one hand and members of the left bloc and the Soviet political representative in Hungary on the other, the leftists on 5 June agreed to give a number of important police positions to Smallholders, abolish the political police in the provinces, and hold provincial elections in the near future.[31]

Like the March crisis, this new emergency ended quickly. The agreement by the left bloc to meet some of the Smallholder demands ended the crisis atmosphere, and once again political tranquility returned. It soon became apparent, however, that the leftists did not intend to abolish the provincial political police or admit Smallholders into the police, and the question of provincial elections remained open. Although the left's failure to honor its commitment could have produced a Smallholder backlash and upset the recently restored quietude, the Russians one month later struck first and provoked yet another crisis, more serious than the first two. This time, London and Washington would become more deeply involved.

On July 7, Lt. Gen. Vladimir P. Sviridov, Soviet representative and acting chairman of the Hungarian Allied Control Commission, presented Premier Nagy with an extensive list of sweeping demands, including the dissolution of the Boy Scouts and the Catholic Youth Organizations (which the Soviet Union argued were fascist or pro-fascist), "strong measures" to be taken against the Catholic clergy under the leadership of the Prince Primate of Hungary Cardinal Mindszenty (whom the Soviets claimed to be inciting people against the Red Army), the resignation of the Smallholder undersecretary of justice, Zoltán Pfeiffer, and the arrest of several Smallholder parliamentary deputies. The Prime Minister agreed to some of the demands, such as dissolving the youth organizations, but he refused to dismiss Pfeiffer or arrest the deputies. In other cases, he applied evasive techniques. Instead of disciplining of the Catholic clergy, he simply called publicly upon them to refrain from anti-Soviet propaganda and promote cooperation with the occupation forces.[32]

Nagy's refusal to comply with some of the demands no doubt seriously angered the Russians, but their anger was temporarily deflected by a challenge from another direction. The unilateral Soviet presentation of demands to the Hungarian prime minister incensed both the British and the Americans. Such action contradicted the statutes of the Allied Control Commission as revised by the Potsdam Conference to deal with the postwar period. Under the revised procedure, the commission chairman (always a Russian) was to issue directives to the Hungarian government only after "coordinating" them with his Western colleagues.[33] The British and Americans also questioned the necessity of disbanding the youth organizations. London and Washington noted that the commission the previous

April had agreed that the Hungarian government be regarded as having fulfilled that aspect of the Hungarian armistice (article 15) which required the dissolution of fascist organizations. On the basis of these complaints the British and American governments, after consulting with each other on joint action, decided to instruct their commissioners to raise these issues with General Sviridov, with the objectives of having the Soviet demands suspended, forcing the Russians to explain their action, and acquiring the text of the Soviet demands on Premier Nagy (who actually had informed the British and Americans already).[34]

The Allied Control Commission met on 24 July to discuss the Soviet demands, but the session was anti-climatic. The British and American commissioners, Maj. Gen. O. P. Edgcumbe and Brig. Gen. George H. Weems respectively, pressed General Sviridov on the various matters involved, but he was evasive. He also refused to hand over a copy of his letter to Nagy on the grounds that he could not do so without authorization from his superiors.[35]

The stalemate in the Control Commission left the matter unresolved for the time being. The Russians did not press Nagy to comply with those demands he had so far managed to avoid and they even allowed the Catholic Youth Organizations (but not the Boy Scouts) to regroup under different names. The British and Americans, for their part, abandoned their efforts to press the issue seriously.[36] The tense situation of July, like those of March and May-June, any one of which could have escalated into a major crisis, quickly dissolved into a state of political calm.

But the relaxed atmosphere was short-lived, for further rumblings developed in the fall. One of these concerned the formation of an ultra-rightist party, the Freedom Party, by a group of politicians expelled from the Smallholders Party the previous March under Soviet pressure. In July, the Soviet representative on the Allied Control Commission, without consulting his Western counterparts, informed Nagy that the new party could be officially established (the functioning of political parties required the authorization of the control commission). But in September, when the Freedom Party became associated with Cardinal Mindszenty and received his support, the Russians, again without prior consultation, rescinded their authorization and moved to suppress the party.[37] The British and Americans, meanwhile, decided from the outset that it woudl be best not to show support for this party, lest they appear to be intervening improperly in Hungary's internal affairs. The Americans, though not initiating any action on the party's behalf, were, however, prepared to defend its right to exist if the Russians sought to disband it.[38]

The issue lay dormant until the Soviet action in September brought it to the surface. With the authorization of Acting Secretary Dean Acheson, General Weems—but not his British counterpart—quickly challenged the Russians in the Allied Control Commission on the grounds that they could not unilaterally suppress a political party. Apparently as a result of this pressure and that of Prime Minister Nagy, who also defended the Freedom Party's right to function, the Russians let the party remain, though with the proviso that its activities be directed toward "strengthening Hungarian democracy."[39]

During the next several weeks other disquieting events occurred, all of which followed the familiar pattern. In the latter half of October the left bloc presented a new list of demands to Nagy, calling among other things for state control of all banks, reform of public administration, and a state monopoly over the publication of school books. Nagy acceded to these demands, but in November, when the leftists also claimed certain cabinet seats which had become vacant through attrition, he refused, insisting that the positions be given to candidates acceptable to the Smallholders Party. In the face of Nagy's strong opposition, the leftists retreated and accepted his ministerial recommendations.[40]

Nevertheless, Nagy's inclination to resist the left bloc was not unlimited, for he decided not to insist upon holding provincial elections, an issue which had remained unresolved since June. As László Ecker-Racz, a political associate of Nagy, explained to Schoenfeld and Alexander Knox Helm (the new British minister to Hungary as of July 1946), Nagy made this decision because he believed that his party would win an overwhelming victory in fairly conducted provincial elections. This, in turn, would either provoke Soviet retaliation or simply cause them to falsify the election results. Thus, Nagy was willing to postpone provincial elections until after the Red Army withdrew from Hungary.[41]

And there the situation stood in November, as the events of fall resolved themselves inconclusively. The antagonistic forces on each wing of the political spectrum—the Smallholders Party on one side (and even further to the right the Freedom Party, though still a minor factor in Hungarian politics) and the left bloc on the other—continued to face each other in an atmosphere poisoned by unrelenting rivalry and intermittent crisis. Under such circumstances, a renewal of conflict loomed as an ever present threat to political stability.

* * * * *

Mátyás Rákosi, leader of the Hungarian Communist Party, said in 1952, well after his party had seized total power four years earlier, that the Communists had attained victory by slicing off the non-Communist elements in the coalition government "like pieces of salami."[42] If such salami-slicing was actually their tactic, the Communists may be said to have cut their first slice in March 1946, when the Hungarian left bloc demanded and achieved the expulsion of more than twenty right-wing Smallholders from that party. This divided and weakened the bourgeois opposition in general and its main rallying point, the Smallholders Party, in particular. But it did not destroy the Smallholders, who remained an important factor in Hungarian politics. Indeed, soon after the March events they were bold enough to make their own demands on the left bloc, albeit unsuccessfully. And the Communist-led left bloc continued to pressure the Smallholders Party and demand further concessions from it. Some of these it granted; others it resisted. By the end of November 1946, the left bloc had advanced its position but had not eliminated the Smallholders from the scene. Hungarian politics remained perched in a delicate equilibrium.

While the left bloc and the Smallholders were vying for power in what was still a low-key competition, the British and Americans remained largely out of the picture, intervening little in Hungarian affairs, though observing events closely. To the extent that the governments in London and Washington became directly involved, they did so primarily across the conference table during the 1946 peace talks—and in these they were prominent participants—rather than in the day-to-day events in Hungary. The British and Americans did not remain totally aloof, however. At one point they both encouraged the Nagy government to adopt a stronger posture toward left-wing pressure, and on another occasion they made a diplomatic intervention in the Allied Control Commission against the Russians. Perhaps because of their limited role in Hungarian events throughout the year, the two Western governments exhibited little discernible difference in approach. But an indication that such a difference lay hidden below the surface was the fact that the Americans, but not the British, were willing to intervene on behalf of the right-wing Freedom Party when the Russians threatened it with suppression.

Until November 1946, the political conflict was fought on a relatively restrained level. Though periods of serious crisis occurred, they were all brief and resolved themselves with relative ease. But in December a new crisis emerged. Unlike the previous ones, this one intensified. No solution was found until the existing coalition government had been overthrown.

VI

THE COUP D'ETAT OF 31 MAY 1947:
TRIUMPH OF THE LEFT WING

As of December 1946, Hungary was still relatively independent of Soviet control, a situation increasingly anomalous in post-World War II Eastern Europe. Barely six months later, however, Hungary's unique status came to an end after a continuous barrage of Soviet- and Communist-directed assaults—including the forced expulsion and often the arrest of leading Smallholders—undermined the Smallholders Party to the point of annihilation. This process culminated at the end of May with the resignation of Prime Minister Ferenc Nagy exacted under Communist pressure. His outster was the decisive blow which crushed his party and marked the end of its ability to withstand leftist encroachment. A bourgeois opposition remained, but as a result of the May coup it no longer had an organizational focus. Instead it became fragmented into several minor parties, which the Communists easily eliminated one by one.

In the meantime, the British and American governments were deeply concerned about the destruction of the Smallholders Party and the incapacitation of Western-oriented opposition forces. The successive crises of 1947 presented London and Washington with the most precarious situation they had yet faced over Hungary, a country which momentarily became a focal point in already embittered East-West affairs. The gravity of the events and the lightening speed with which they sometimes occurred hindered the two Western allies in agreeing upon a joint policy in this situation. At times, their respective approaches to the Hungarian question began to diverge so widely as to become a source of friction in Anglo-American relations. Nevertheless, their common hostility to the process of sovietization in Hungary was a unifying bond between them. Both Western powers realized that the events unfolding in 1947 greatly advanced Soviet control in Eastern Europe, and they observed the Hungarian situation with much apprehension.

* * * * *

For anti-Communist forces in Hungary, the year 1946 ended under very inauspicious circumstances. In mid-December, the left-bloc parties resumed the political offensive conducted sporadically during 1946. Now the agitation took the form of street demonstrations in Budapest, organized and staged by the leftists on an almost daily basis. In order to see what the Prime Minister had to say about the situation, the British and American ministers, Alexander Knox Helm, who had replaced Alvary Gascoigne in July, and H. F. Arthur Schoenfeld, interviewed Nagy on 11 December. He indicated to them that he intended once again to make concessions, this time in the form of a cabinet reorganization agreeable to the left bloc.[1]

Although political tension had reached a very high level, the existing state of affairs was not extraordinary, and, as a member of Helm's staff commented, there was "nothing in the situation to prove that it [would] not resolve itself as often before."[2] Instead of resolving itself, however, the crisis intensified. In the last week of December, the Communist-controlled Hungarian political police, in what turned out to be the first of a series of bombshells dropped by pro-Kremlin forces, carried out a wave of arrests and took into custody some 250 to 300 individuals. Rapidly following up these arrests, the Communist press announced on New Year's Eve the uncovering of an anti-government conspiracy by an organization they called the Hungarian Unity Society. The charges were not groundless; the conspiracy did exist, as the British and American governments soon recognized and privately admitted. The so-called Hungarian Unity movement comprised elements from various political parties, and above all from the Smallholders Party. Also involved were many individuals—including active and retired army officers—not formally associated with any political party. The political complexion of this underground movement was ultrarightist, and its goal was the restoration of the prewar

Regency, the Hungarian old regime. The conspirators, who had collected stores of arms, also planned to set up a rival government-in-exile in the event a Communist government was established in Hungary.[3]

Although the British and Americans conceded in private that there had been an anti-republican plot, they also believed that the Communists, drawing the other parties of the left bloc behind them, were vigorously exploiting the conspiracy to their own advantage. Indeed, in an intelligence study of the conspiracy, the Americans criticized the conspirators for launching this intrigue, not because of its goals, but because the Soviet occupation made its success impossible and its discovery rendered anti-Communists, especially the Smallholders, vulnerable to attack. As soon as the wave of arrests began in late December, both Western governments as well as anti-Communist Hungarians engaged in widespread speculation that the Communists, in league with the Soviet occupation authorities, were trying to eliminate any centers of bourgeois resistance and consolidate their own position before the Hungarian peace treaty came into effect and most Soviet troops left. Sometime prior to that point, it was suspected, the Communists would bid for power. Such a scenario accorded with the timing of the situation, for the coming into force of the peace treaty— which had been completed in December 1946 and was scheduled to be signed in February 1947—seemed imminent; it eventually came into force in September 1947.

Whatever the intentions of the Communists and Russians may have been, it is clear that the conspiracy provided them with the opportunity to strike hard at pro-Western elements in Hungary. Arrests of accused conspirators continued into the new year. The Communists soon began demanding not only the expulsion of various Smallholders from their party, but also that the parliamentary immunity of certain Smallholder deputies be suspended, making their arrest legally possible. Since many of these Smallholders had in fact been involved in the conspiracy, the party leadership had little alternative but to comply with these demands, though it tried to limit the scope of the purges. Nevertheless, the Communists maintained relentless pressure on the Smallholders and other pro-Westerners and made it plain that they might intensify their demands. This might involve a reconstruction of the cabinet to the left, as Premier Nagy had anticipated in December, and perhaps also new elections, which anti-Communists feared would result in a rigged leftist victory.[4]

Fearful that Hungary's coalition government would be overthrown and replaced with a Communist one, london and Washington observed the unprecedently intense and sustained leftist attack on pro-Western circles with growing apprehension. In order to forestall or delay a possible Communist takeover, the British and Americans sought to bolster the already shaky coalition by various means. One of these was economic. To strengthen Hungary's ties to the West, the United States in mid-February doubled the $15 million surplus property credit it had granted Hungary the year before.[5] Similarly, the British government underwrote ninety percent of a £5 million (a little more than $20 million) wool loan provided through a British bank. This move represented a slightly more aggressive economic policy than that adopted by the British in 1946, when they decided against giving financial aid to Hungary because of Britain's own economic difficulties.[6]

Another method of buttressing the anti-Communist forces was to rely on that minority faction of the Hungarian Social Democratic Party which opposed alliance with the Communists. Although both the British and the Americans nurtured relation with the right-wing Social Democrats, the British in particular looked upon them as a possible brace to hold back further Communist advance. In fact, the Foreign Office tried to use British Labour Party influence to keep the Social Democrats from falling completely under Communist domination. But such attempts at persuasion failed to produce the desired effect, for the pro-Communist left-wing Social Democrats remained dominant and in control of the party.[7]

The British and American ministers in Budapest, with the backing of their superiors, also encouraged Nagy to resist concessions to the leftists. Unlike March 1946, when the question of offering such encouragement caused a minor controversy among foreign policy officials, no opposition to offering such advice emerged this time. But no direct political assistance was offered to Nagy, who had to face left-wing pressure without assurances that the Western powers would aid him if he needed it.[8]

In the meantime, the Communist offensive continued unabated. The political tension rose again in early February, when the Communists accused Secretary General Béla Kovács of the Smallholders Party of being involved—as he indeed was—in the anti-republican conspiracy. In late February, the Communists intensified their attack on Kovács—who thereby became the focal point in the new phase of the political crisis—by demanding that the Smallholders Party act in the National Assembly to suspend his parliamentary immunity, a move which would have meant certain arrest. Though Kovács voluntarily resigned his party post, the Smallholders on 25 February defiantly refused to lift his immunity. The Russians settled the issue by force later that day. Accusing Kovács of having plotted against their occupation forces, the Soviet authorities arrested him.[9] He would never been seen again and is presumed to have died in Soviet captivity.

It was a devastating blow to the viability of the Smallholders Party. The Russians had now unmistakably demonstrated that they were prepared to intervene directly in Hungarian affairs. Reviewing Kovács' arrest, Michael S. Williams of the Foreign Office recalled the events of July 1946, when the Russians unilaterally made a number of political demands on the Smallholders Party in the name of the Allied Control Commission. The British and Americans had then succeeded in neutralizing the Soviet maneuver by protesting against the failure to consult them. This time, however, the Russians had acted in their own name on the grounds that Kovács threatened the occupation forces' security. Such action, Williams concluded, was within the powers of the Soviet High Command under the terms of the armistice, which left the British and Americans "no technical ground for complaint."[10]

Kovács' arrest touched off an immediate crisis in Soviet-Western relations. For the Americans, although they recognized that Kovács had been seriously implicated in the plot, had no inclination to be bound by "technical" considerations. On 1 March, John D. Hickerson, deputy director of the Office of European Affairs, urged upon his State Department superiors that the United States "immediately" take "energetic action" in response to the Soviet Union's abduction of Kovács.[11] His recommendation was accepted, and on 5 March an extremely sharp protest note was presented to the Allied Control Commission with copies to all interested parties. Soon thereafter, it was also released to the press.

The American note condemned the "pattern of recent political events" involving "foreign interference in the domestic affairs of Hungary in support of repeated aggressive attempts by Hungarian minority elements to coerce the popularly elected majority." These "minority elements" were identified specifically as the "Hungarian Communists, together with other members of the Leftist bloc." The Soviet High Command was denounced for its "direct intervention" in Hungarian affairs by arresting Kovács, an action which had "brought the situation to a crisis," and for having taken this step "unilaterally." On the basis of "its present information," the United States government believed the charges against Kovács to be "unwarranted," and it called for a tripartite investigation through the Allied Control Commission of the "facts of the present situation, including the case of Mr. Kovács and the conspiracy."[12]

The American protest put the British on the spot. They objected to the line of argument set forth in the American note, maintaining that the Russians had the legal right to arrest Kovács "if," as Williams said, "they had a watertight case against" him, as the British believed they did. The British also disapproved of the note for associating the Social Democrats with the Communists by reference to "other members of the Leftist bloc." Christopher Warner would have preferred some expression like "pro-Communist groups." Nor did the British believe that the Russians would consent to a three-party investigation as requested by the United States. Even so, the Foreign Office, anxious to maintain a common front with the Americans, hesitated to withhold British support from them.[13] Consequently, the British ambassador in Moscow and the minister in Budapest were instructed to join in the call for an investigation, but not to endorse the arguments employed in the American note.[14]

In Budapest, Helm was as unenthusiastic about the American note as were his colleagues in the Foreign Office. Describing its impact, he contended that, "instead of doing good," it had done "positive harm." Only the rightists were "delighted," Helm reported, while the Social Democrats saw the note as an "encouragement to reaction" and had been drawn even closer to the Communists.[15] To the extent that this process had occurred, it was a setback for the British policy of splitting the anti-Communist Social Democrats away from their party's left wing.

Schoenfeld, for his part, was equally critical of British policy, which he did not believe to be sufficiently assertive. He particularly faulted the British for not offering stronger support for the American note. Their failure to do so, he implied, had rendered the Smallholders more reluctant to resist Communist encroachment.[16]

Clearly, an Anglo-American tactical disagreement had crystallized around the question of where in the Hungarian political spectrum the most effective bulwark against the advancing Communists might be found. The Americans continued to rely upon the Smallholder Party, as they had done since 1945. By contrast, ever since the new Communist offensive got underway in December 1946, the British increasingly saw the Smallholders as no match for the pro-Soviet forces and hoped instead that the right-wing Social Democrats could obstruct the Communists in their apparent grasp for total power. On the whole, British expectations were limited and aimed at slowing down, rather than reversing or halting, the sovietization of Hungary.

Anglo-American friction grew sharper in the weeks ahead. On 8 March, three days after the Americans had delivered their protest note, General Sviridov flatly rejected the call for a tripartite investigation of the Hungarian situation. He noted that the Hungarian authorities were investigating the anti-republican conspiracy, and the inquiry proposed by the Americans would therefore be an "open intervention" into Hungary's internal affairs and a "rude violation of the legal rights" of its judiciary. Sviridov also described the American intervention in the Kovács case as an "attempt" to infringe on the legal rights of the Soviet occupation authorities to defend their armed forces located on Hungarian territory."[17]

The Soviet response left the issue unresolved and the Americans dissatisfied. Schoenfeld urged that the State Department follow up its note by presenting yet another, since the "inconclusive handling of our controversy" with the Russians would "do nothing" to strengthen the resolve of the Smallholders Party to restore its authority. Secretary Marshall and Under Secretary Acheson agreed. On 17 March, the United States delivered to the Hungarian Allied Control Commission a second note along lines similar to the first one and repeating the call for a three-party investigation. The note also criticized the manner in which the Hungarian government was conducting its investigation of the conspiracy, charging in effect that the Communists were dominating the investigation despite their minority parliamentary status. Furthermore, the note implied that the arrest of Kovács had been politically motivated. This second note was also sent to the Soviet, Hungarian, and British governments and released to the press.[18]

The British were dismayed. They would have preferred to leave the Soviet note unanswered and let the matter drop. They were also concerned about what could be done if the Russians rejected the new American note. And they were reluctant to defend Kovács; they were convinced he was guilty and that the Russians could prove it. As G. T. C. Campbell of the Southern Department commented, "we would be on a bad wicket if we intervened on his behalf."[19] In Budapest, Helm and British General Edgcumbe especially objected to American criticism of Soviet and Hungarian Communist behavior in the Kovács case and the conspiracy investigation. They insisted that in these matters Soviet and local Communist conduct was legally defensible and that unlawful or politically motivated action would be very difficult to prove.[20]

In the end, however, the Foreign Office, still wanting to keep "in step" with American policy, repeated its handling of the first United States note. The Russians were informed that the British supported the American call for an investigation of the Hungarian situation, including the Kovács case, but did not endorse the terms of the American note. But in order to prevent further misunderstandings and lack of Anglo-American coordination, the Foreign Office instructed its Washington embassy to discuss the Hungarian question with the State Department and request that the British be consulted before the Americans made any further moves over Hungary.[21]

In a move surprising to no one, the Russians again rejected the call for an investigation of the Hungarian question. The American note, General Sviridov said, failed to touch upon any issues not already answered in his previous note. He defended the procedure used by the Hungarian government in investigating the conspiracy, arguing that it was in complete accord with the laws and constitution of the Hungarian Republic. As for the suggestion that the Russians had political motives for arresting Kovács, Sviridov, "solely in order to forestall [the United States] from making any further mistake," declared that Kovács had "fully acknowledged his guilt in crimes committed against the Soviet Army as well as his participation in the plot."[22]

Once again the question was what response, if any, Britain and the United States could make. Neither the Foreign Office nor Helm was inclined to answer Sviridov's letter, but Schoenfeld was, and he proposed to the State Department that yet another démarche be made. The State Department decided, however, to call a halt to the acrimonious exchange of notes. Schoenfeld was advised that the first two notes had in the main accomplished the American objectives: they had reemphasized the continued American interest in Hungary and "assisted in checking" the deterioration of the Smallholders' position. A third note could only recapitulate points already made and would not add to the "forcefulness" of the previous ones. The Department would, however, "continue to press for [an] expeditious extension [of] additional economic assistance,"[23] presumably to maintain influence with the Hungarian government.

The American decision to discontinue the exchange of notes eased the atmosphere of growing tension in Anglo-American relations. The British, both fearful of exacerbating their relations with the Russians and anxious to promote close ties with Washington, now had less reason to worry about being caught in the middle of a Soviet-American conflict over Hungary. Hoping to reduce Anglo-American friction still further, the British Ambassador in Washington, Lord Invershapel, on 21 March asked Under Secretary of State Acheson that the State Department henceforth consult the Foriegn Office before taking action on Hungary. Acheson agreed to attempt to do so, and he apologized for not consulting with the British on the first two notes. The failure to consult, he explained, was due to the urgency of the situation.[24]

In the meantime, the gradually mounting East-West conflict continued to be reflected in Hungary. The Soviet arrest of Kovács, and the arrest by the Hungarian Communist police of hundreds of other anti-leftists, were severe blows to the pro-Western forces in Hungarian society, and particularly to the Smallholders Party.

In early March, soon after Kovács arrest, the Smallholders entered into negotiations with the left bloc parties. Out of this interparty conference came the so-called March agreement, by which the Smallholders yielded even more ground to the left wing. Under the March agreement, the government adopted a three-year plan for the further rehabilitation of Hungary's economy, whose effect was to advance state control of the economy. The agreement also provided for the resignation from the cabinet of several staunchly anti-Communist Smallholders and their replacement by a member of the pro-Communist National Peasant Party and several Smallholders willing to work closely with the Communists.

Although the March agreement left the Smallholders badly weakened, it did not destroy them. But no one could be sure how long the new political truce might last.[25]

* * * * *

Soon after the March settlement, Prime Minister Nagy decided to take a three-week vacation in Switzerland, to begin on 14 May. Exactly what motivated him to do this is disputable. According to his memoirs, he felt a "keen and very natural craving for a rest" following the exhaustion of his "year-long struggle in the Prime Ministry."[26] On the other hand, an Associated Press despatch of 14 May quoted unnamed "private informants" as saying that Nagy's vacation might last longer than the scheduled three weeks and might in fact continue until the Hungarian peace treaty took effect and Soviet forces left Hungary.[27] The apparent implication was that the premier was seeking to avoid Communist political pressure. In any case, Nagy's planned journey abroad did not attract noteworthy attention in diplomatic circles at the time. Nagy and other government and political party leaders agreed that Mátyás Rákosi, head of the Communist Party and a deputy prime minister, would serve as acting prime minister during his absence.

A foreboding situation sprang up on 9 May, when the Communists began agitating for the nationalization of Hungary's three largest banks. Since these banks owned or controlled well over half of all Hungarian industry, this was a very serious issue. The ramifications of their nationalization would extend well beyond the banks themselves and go a long way toward nationalizing the entire economy. So important was this new problem that Helm and Schoenfeld believed the Communists had put the demand forward not only to advance their goal of socializing the Hungarian economy, but also as a pretext for reopening the political offensive suspended by the March agreement.[28]

Whatever the Communists' motives may have been, their new demand unnreved Nagy considerably.[29] Still, in an unusual act of defiance, the Smallholders made clear to the Communists their adamant opposition to the nationalization of the banks. The demand also jolted the Social Democrats, especially their right-wing, and they too opposed such a radical measure, at least for the moment. The question produced the first significant, though still subterranean, rupture between the Communists and the Social Democrats, and between the two wings of the Social Democratic Party. The Communists may not have anticipated such concerted resistance to their proposal, and it is possible that this surprising opposition may have convinced them that the time had finally arrived to follow up

their sustained assault on the Smallholders with the coup de grace.[30] Whatever the merits of such speculation, the Communists backed off on their
nationalization demand for the time being.

Meanwhile, though the political atmosphere had become somewhat
clouded, Nagy left for Switzerland as scheduled on 14 May. He would
never return to Hungary. Before the month was out, the Communists
and the Russians would force his resignation and that of his coalition
cabinet.

The crisis, played out in a flurry of dramatic and sensational incidents,
began on 28 May, by which time Nagy had been in Switzerland nearly
two weeks. On the evening of that day, Smallholder associates of the
prime minister informed him by telephone that General Sviridov had produced a document, alleged to be a confession by Béla Kovács, which implicated Nagy in the anti-republican conspiracy.[31] Nagy learned that the
political police had arrested his private secretary, and he was urged to return to Budapest at once. The next day, as Nagy was about to leave
Switzerland, his associates told him to stay there for the time being. It
is commonly assumed that Communist and Soviet pressure forced them to
change their advice. On 30 May, they telephoned again to tell him that
the Russians would arrest him if he returned to Hungary, and that he
should therefore resign. Nagy agreed to do so provided that his five-year
old son be sent to him from Hungary. Later that day, the official Hungarian press agency carried a report that Nagy had resigned, though in
fact he had not yet done so.

Also on 30 May, the Communists demanded that the Smallholder
Party leadership agree to replace Nagy and the Smallholder Foreign
Minister János Gyöngyösy, with two Communist-backed Smallholder
ministers who had entered the Nagy cabinet as a result of the March
agreement. The Smallholder leadership was very reluctant to sanction
the Communists' proposal—which would have sealed the coup—and remained non-committal. However, President Tildy, who was under Communist pressure to approve the cabinet change or resign, chose the former
and gave his approval to the reorganization on 31 May. On 1 June, the
cabinet formally resigned and reconstituted itself. From Nagy's viewpoint,
the change was made on 2 June, when he acquired custody of his son and
signed a letter of resignation, which he presented to an emissary of the
Hungarian government.[32]

An extraordinary feature of the May-June coup d'état was its facade of legality. Since the Communists, in league with the Soviet occupation authorities, obtained Premier Nagy's resignation without an outward show of force, they could claim that the change in government was carried out within the framework of constitutional continuity. This was especially so because the coup did not appear to have produced any dramatic changes in terms of party alignment. The distribution of cabinet seats among the parties remained the same, and Smallholders continued to hold very prominent positions. The president, who remained in office, and the new premier, Lajos Dinnyés, as well as the new foreign minister, Ernő Mihályfi, were all Smallholders.

Nevertheless, these facts should not obscure the main point: the coup broke the back of the Smallholders Party decisively and destroyed its ability to obstruct the Communist will. That result had been produced through a process begun in December 1946, when the Communists swept away hundreds of Smallholders and other rightists in a wave of arrests, and it peaked momentarily when the Russians intervened directly and arrested the secretary general of the Smallholders Party. At that point it was clear that anyone who resisted the Communists did so at their certain peril. Had Nagy returned to Hungary to face Soviet accusations, he would have played a more heroic role but with disastrous consequences to himself. His only accomplishment would have been to compel the Communists to grasp for power blatantly rather than with a measure of subtlety. But this would not have deterred them, for their actions throughout 1947 had made it plain that they would use force to attain a desired objective. Nagy's resignation capped the process, for it demonstrated that the Communists could remove at will any recalcitrant Hungarian, even the prime minister.

After the coup, the Smallholders Party rapidly shed a number of members, some of whom fled into exile while others fought on to the bitter end. And there the Party stood—a mere rump of its former self, containing only those willing to cooperate with the Communists. The Smallholders became, in effect, a party of the left bloc, or at most a loyal opposition.[33]

But it must also be added that the coup brought to power, not the Communists, but the left bloc, of which the Communists were only one element, albeit the leading and most influential one. The left bloc was not monolithic. There were fissures within the structure, though these had remained mainly below the surface as long as the rightist, Smallholder challenge persisted. Up to the time of the coup, the Communists had cooperated quite closely with the Social Democrats, their main partners in the left bloc, in promoting social reforms and fighting the Smallholders. With victory, disagreements burst into the open and ruptured what so far had been the outward unity of the bloc.

The rift essentially involved the degree of social radicalism shared by the Communists and the Social Democrats. Although the two parties agreed on the need to reorganize Hungarian society, the Social Democrats, who tended toward moderation and pragmatism, preferred that social change be more limited and implemented more slowly than did the Communists. The Social Democratic opposition to the immediate nationalization of the largest Hungarian banks was a case in point. Once the coup had eliminated the obstructive power of the Smallholders, the Social Democrats became the next impediment to unrivalled Communist power. But before the Communists could set to work on subduing the Social Democrats—assuming that they intended to do so at all—they first had to consolidate the left bloc's position and their own position within it in the wake of the coup. This required finishing off the last vestiges of the rightist opposition, which was accomplished during the next four months.

The Hungarian coup d'état sent momentary shock waves through Europe, but it jolted the American government more forcefully than it did the British. Washington was stunned and angered as it observed the Communists sweep the Smallholders away and make Hungary the most recent gain for pro-Soviet forces. The State Department now feared that the Russians might push their political influence still farther westward. Noting that the Soviet Union as a result of events in Hungary had acquired "virtually complete control throughout the Danube Basin," American policy makers concluded that Moscow, "unless checked," might "threaten an independent Austria"—already under partial Soviet occupation and the focal point of a serious four-power deadlock—and influence to a "possibly determining extent" the "precarious political conditions in Italy and France."[34] American involvement in the Hungarian question reached an unprecendentedly high level of attention when President Truman, having been briefed by the State Department on recent developments, declared at a press conference on 5 June that the Hungarian situation was an "outrage" and that the United States would not stand by idly, though he did not recommend any specific action.[35]

It was precisely such bravado that the British wanted to avoid. Although the Hungarian coup disquieted the British by confirming the intention of the Soviet Union to establish its control throughout Eastern Europe, they had long since concluded that the Western powers were unable to prevent this process. Whenever feasible, the British were willing to attempt to slow it down, but they remained convinced that Moscow could force it at will. The Foreign Office saw the Hungarian coup as part and parcel of a general Soviet thrust in Eastern Europe, and Orme Sargent, for example, found no reason to become entangled in a public controversy with the Soviet Union over this latest development.[36]

The British were especially anxious to avoid the continued public protests in which the Americans had engaged over the Kovács affair. Michael S. Williams thought the Americans had made "fools" of themselves by their actions.[37] The Foreign Office attitude was that a new public protest over the coup would "simply court a [similar] rebuff from the Russians" and "demonstrate how impotent we are to influence the course of events in Hungary."[38] Foreign Secretary Bevin, in a rare instance of direct involvement in the Hungarian problem (he even referred the matter to the cabinet),[39] summed up the Foreign Office view on what not to do about the coup when he said that "we should not do any protesting."[40] The British felt so strongly about this matter that when the State Department a few days later asked for London's support for precisely such a protest, the Foreign Office not only declined but also advised the United States to abandon the plan.[41]

Although the British were willing to accept the Hungarian coup as an accomplished fact, they were quite concerned about what the coup might portend regarding future Soviet action in Hungary. In particular, they wondered whether the Russians intended to exclude Great Britain from all influence there. Seeking an answer to this question, the Foreign Office instructed Ambassador Sir Maurice Peterson in Moscow to discuss the Hungarian situation with Molotov and, "if possible, to provoke Mr. Molotov to argument and to obtain a clarification of Soviet policy towards Hungary." Peterson was to criticize the Russians for not showing Béla Kovács' alleged confession—which purportedly implicated Nagy in the anti-government conspiracy—to the British and Americans, who, as members of the Allied Control Commission, were entitled to see it. He was also to say that the United Kingdom could not "but harbour grave doubts as to the activities of the Soviet authorities in Hungary." The Soviet government seemed determined to "undo step by step the results of the free Parliamentary elections" of 1945, "bring about the dissolution of the Smallholders Party," and "establish in power a Government entirely subservient to the Hungarian Communists." Peterson was directed to declare that his government "would welcome assurances" that the Soviet government did "not intend to prevent or hinder the development of normal relations between Hungary and the United Kingdom."[42]

Thus, London was prepared to raise very provocative issues with Moscow, but the purpose was merely to determine Moscow's intentions, not to counter or obstruct them. Also significant was the British insistence on a confidential rather than a public approach. The Foreign Office tried to convince the State Department that this provided the opportunity "to pursue the matter at greater length and more fully with the Soviet Government" and did not expose the British and Americans to open "rebuffs from the Russians."[43] No doubt the British also considered such a quiet approach to be less offensive to the Russians than a public one.

The British démarche, though made behind closed doors, quickly and unexpectedly degenerated into a bitter Anglo-Soviet squabble. Amabassador Peterson saw Molotov on 9 June. The Soviet foreign minister flatly denied that there had been any Soviet intrusion into Hungarian politics. Turning the British charge around, he even reproached Great Britain for its intervention. This confounded the Foreign Office, and Peterson was directed to see Molotov again, challenge his allegation concerning British interference, and repeat the British assertion about Soviet meddling. This time Peterson was also instructed to join in the renewed call by the Americans for a tripartite investigation of the Hungarian situation.[44] Peterson left an aide-mémoire to this effect with Molotov on 17 June.[45]

The Soviet response, delivered by note a few days later, was extremely caustic: "The new British statement . . . is devoted mainly to repetition of the slanderous fabrications about pressure exerted by Soviet organs on the Hungarian Government and the Smallholders' Party, which are being systematically spread by certain organs of the reactionary press hostile to the Soviet Union."[46] Bevin's only comment was: "I do not see what I can do more."[47] In fact, all the Foreign Office did do was to inform Moscow on 25 June of its rejection of the comments contained in the Soviet note.[48] Clearly, the British démarche had turned sour, and London had not even come close to entering into a serious discussion with Moscow over the future of Hungary.

In the meantime, the Americans still maintained, though with a rapidly diminishing vigor, the far more ambitious hope of at least partially nullifying the effects of the Hungarian coup. Against British advice, the Americans responded to Nagy's overthrow by filing a formal and publicized protest with the Allied Control Commission. The Foreign Office, this time, was informed in advance, and the advice of the American envoys in Budapest and Moscow was also sought. Taking the solicited recommendations into account, the State Department toned down its protest somewhat. In its first draft, the protest letter would have censured the Russians for those instances of intervention in Hungarian politics which had led to the "formation of a government dominated by the minority parties." It would also have renewed the call for a tripartite commission of investigation and threatened to refer the Hungarian question to the United Nations if the Russians refused.[49]

The final version of the note, delivered to the Russians on 11 June, downplayed particular references to Soviet interference in Hungarian affairs, which the Budapest and Moscow missions considered difficult to prove. Instead, the note emphasized the Soviet refusal to show Kovács' alleged confession to the British and American Allied Control Commissioners. In response to British advice, it did not castigate the "minority parties" but only the Communist Party. In consequence of Premier Nagy's resignation, it was pointed out, there had been a "realignment of political authority in Hungary so that" the Communist minority, which had won only 17 percent of the vote in the 1945 elections, had "nullified the expressed will of the majority of the Hungarian people," who had voted for the Smallholders Party. The note did call for the establishment of an investigatory commission, but there was no unqualified threat to take the issue up before the United Nations. There was only the ambiguous statement that, if the Russians did not agree to such a commission, the United States, "conscious of its obligations" as a United Nations member, would "consider such further action as may be appropriate."[50]

The American protest had no apparent impact on the Russians. In his reply of 14 June, General Sviridov denied that there had been any shift in political power in Hungary or that the will of the majority of the Hungarian people had been nullified. He asserted that the refusal of Nagy to return to Hungary had caused the recent crisis, which had been "solved through the efforts of all parties of the coalition government in strict conformity with constitutional standards." Sviridov again refused to hand over a copy of Kovács' alleged confession, claiming that it was of no concern to the British and American section of the control commission. He also rejected the call for a three-party investigatory commission as a "rude interference in Hungarian internal affairs, which is not permissible."[51]

The only possibility left for challenging Nagy's overthrow was to bring the matter up before the United Nations. Political pressure on behalf of such action was in fact brought to bear both in Washington and in London. Senator Arthur Vandenberg, in a Senate speech on 3 June, proposed that the Hungarian situation be referred to the United Nations,[52] and a Labour Member of Parliament, John M. Martin, made the same plea ten days later in a letter to Hector McNeill, Minister of State in the Foreign Office.[53]

A major debate on whether to bring the Hungarian issue before the United Nations soon "rocked" the State Department, as Harold C. Vedeler of the Division of Central European Affairs put it.[54] Robert McClintock of the Office of Special Political Affairs argued that the United States "could make a fairly good case" condemning the Soviet Union for Nagy's overthrow.[55] But H. Freeman Matthews, director of the Office of European Affairs opposed a United Nations protest. One reason was that the Security Council was at that time discussing the Greek question, an issue with which the United States and Great Britain were vitally concerned, and he feared that the Hungarian question might "deflect attention" from Greece. There was also the recently announced European Recovery Program, on which the Soviet reaction was not yet in. Moreover, the Hungarian problem, if brought before the United Nations, would necessarily produce a Soviet-American dispute, and Matthews did not want to "risk a major test" in the United Nations over a debatable case involving the occupation of an ex-enemy state by a former ally. In fact, the United States might not even receive sufficient support from other United Nations members, including Great Britain, to win such a confrontation. Finally, Matthews doubted that a United Nations initiative would have much of a chance of success in view of the Soviet domination of the Balkans. "Even if. . . the Soviets might in the face of world condemnation be disposed to recede to some extent in Hungary," as Matthews noted some officials in the Division of Eastern European Affairs were "inclined to hope," there was "little likelihood" that the Russians "would equally compromise in Rumania or Bulgaria where their domination [was] further advanced."[56] Both Secretary of State Marshall and the newly appointed Under Secretary Robert A. Lovett backed up Matthews,[57] and thus the State Department tentatively abandoned the idea of a United Nations protest. But it instructed the London embassy to sound out British views.[58]

The British were solidly opposed to a United Nations protest on the Hungarian situation, and for mostly similar reasons. The Foreign Office did not believe there was a sufficiently convincing case to bring the issue before the United Nations. Since Hungary was a former enemy controlled by a legitimate armistice regime, it would be very difficult to prove Soviet interference in Hungarian affairs. To raise the matter in the United Nations Security Council would require proof of the dubious contention that the Hungarian situation was a threat to peace. It would be better, so Assistant Under-Secretary Gladwyn Jebb urged, to go before the General Assembly, where a simple representation of the case would do and no proof was required. But neither Jebb nor the Foreign Office as a whole favored even a General Assembly initiative, since it would "inevitably. . . lead to a serious clash with the Soviet Union."[59]

As it happened, the question of whether to admit Hungary—as well as Rumania, Bulgaria, and Albania—to membership in the United Nations was already scheduled to come up in the Security Council in August. The British, though opposed to raising the Hungarian problem as a special item, saw the membership debate as an opportunity "to call in question the fitness of these countries to be received into the comity of nations."[60] The British seemed to feel that the debate on membership was a less obtrusive forum, not only because they and the Americans were going to participate in it anyway, but also because the debate would not concentrate exclusively on Hungary but cover several nations.[61]

The Americans agreed with this strategy. Consequently, from mid-August to early October, the Security Council intermittently debated the status of the nations of Southeastern Europe, with particular reference to the membership qualifications of the applicants. The long debate continually focused on the question of whether the Balkan governments were representative of the majority of the people or were minority regimes forcibly imposed on the majority. The latter view prevailed, and the three Balkan states therefore failed to attain United Nations membership in 1947. Britain and the United States abstained on the final Security Council vote,[62] clearly in order not to upset the chances for their own candidates, such as Italy, to be admitted.[63]

The failure to reach agreement on the question of United Nations membership was both a consequence and a symbol of the growing East-West discord over Hungary and the rest of Southeastern Europe. The Security Council debate made it plain that the two sides had not settled their differences over the Danube region. Their conflict persisted, which made it likely that a continued deterioration of the Hungarian situation would also lead to further friction between the Soviet Union and its two Western adversaries.

* * * * *

Until the Hungarian coup of May 1947, the main East European trouble spots in East-West relations had been elsewhere. From Poland to Bulgaria, manipulated elections and political purges, combined with Communist-directed economic reconstruction, had placed the Soviet-supported left firmly in power, although nowhere did a Communist party as yet rule alone. Now the Hungarian situation had been brought into line with that already prevailing elsewhere in Soviet-occupied Eastern Europe. And Hungary would remain a key point of friction in East-West relations for several more months as its Communists, with Soviet backing, made their final bid for total power.

VII

SOVIETIZATION ACCOMPLISHED

After the overthrow of Ferenc Nagy and the evisceration of the Small-holders Party, only two more obstacles stood in the way of the complete sovietization of Hungary. The Communists still had to eliminate the residual power of scattered bourgeois parties and politicians, and they had to break the independent strength of the Social Democratic Party, now a potential rival within the Hungarian labor movement. Within a year, both tasks had been accomplished.

* * * * *

Early in June 1947, the new, leftist-dominated Hungarian government announced its intention to hold a general election in the near future. The date was eventually set for the last day of August. Parliament was dissolved on 25 July, signalling the start of the election campaign.

It was clear to observers that the leftists had called for a premature election—constitutionally, none was required until 1949—in order to consolidate their recent gains. As Minister Helm and his staff suggested in despatches to the Foreign Office, the two labor parties wanted to attain a combined leftist parliamentary majority in order to bolster their mandate and stifle all potential opposition. A leftist victory would also make it possible to dispense altogether with the Smallholders Party.

Actually, while the Communists and Social Democrats continued to work together against non-leftists, unmistakable friction had emerged

112

between them. Having acceded to power through the ouster of Ferenc Nagy, they now began to fight each other for dominance. Behind a "front of amicable relations," so the new American Minister Selden Chapin reported to Washington, an "embittered fight for supremacy" raged between the two leftist parties.[1] Until the election, they would continue to direct most of their energy against their common enemies on the right, but the period of smooth Communist-Social Democratic cooperation had come to an end.

From the outset of the election campaign, the bourgeois parties were at a disadvantage. The Smallholders Party had already been reduced to a mere facade and was in reality a tool of the leftists. On the far right of the political spectrum, the Freedom Party remained a relatively minor factor, although it increased its membership somewhat by absorbing expelled rightist Smallholders. Other parties, some of which had been too insignificant to play any role in Hungarian politics before, also entered the election campaign. One of these was the Democratic People's Party, a progressive Catholic party led by István Baránkovics, a journalist whose moderate stance earned him the disfavor of Hungary's extremely conservative Roman Catholic hierarchy. Also contesting the election was the Hungarian Radical Party, a middle-class grouping now led by a former Social Democrat Károly Peyer who sharply disagreed with that party's long-standing cooperation with the Communists. Still other parties, newly formed and with little support, entered the campaign.

The proliferation of bourgeois parties was perhaps a natural—if not unavoidable—development under the circumstances. British and American observers in Budapest decried the inability of the Hungarian non-leftists to unite, but they also believed that the Communists, precisely in order to divide the opposition, deliberately encouraged new parties to enter the election.[2]

The Communist tactic was indeed successful, for not only did the large number of parties split the non-leftist vote, it also rendered each party vulnerable to physical attack. This was the fate of the Freedom Party, which the Communist-dominated political police cracked down on violently in June and July, forcibly breaking up party meetings, beating up members, and carting many off into custody. Fearing more of the same, its leaders dissolved the Freedom Party in late July. Some of its members escaped to the West.[3] The Russians then permitted adherents of the defunct party to set up a new group, the Hungarian Independence Party, with the same general political program, and authorized its participation in the August election.[4] Thus, violence had reduced the ranks of the far right, although it retained organizational form and thus remained capable of drawing votes away from other bourgeois parties.

It should be noted that the violent treatment of the Freedom Party was the exception, not the rule, in this election campaign, which on the whole was conducted very peacefully.[5] The Communists, in their attempts to influence the election, relied less on overt violence than on disfranchisement. The electoral law of 1947 stipulated various grounds beyond those stated in the 1945 electoral law for disfranchising former members of "Fascist" organizations. This made possible the disfranchisement of many voters whose alleged association with fascist activity was quite dubious.

From the outset, the main concern of the British and American governments had been that the Hungarian election would not be free or fair, and that the leftists, especially the Communists, would manipulate it in their own favor.

The Americans especially feared that the 1947 electoral law would lead to serious abuses. The British, on the other hand, believed that the law, if equitably applied, might actually facilitate a free and fair election. As it turned out, the Communist-dominated electoral committees which drew up the voter registration lists used their power to disfranchise a broad spectrum of known anti-Communists. British and American estimates variously placed the number of disfranchised at from 500,000 to a million persons, or roughly ten to twenty percent of all eligible voters.[6]

Hoping to halt or minimize the disfranchisement abuses threatening to mar the elections, the British and Americans decided to intervene in the situation. After consulting each other, they issued parallel, but not identical, statements on 17 August, condemning irregularities in the voter registration lists. These irregularities, it was argued, violated the Hungarian peace treaty, which guaranteed to all persons under Hungarian jurisdiction the "enjoyment of human rights and fundamental freedoms, including freedom of political opinion." The American statement also explicitly castigated the "minority Communist Party" for its "unwarranted interference" by difranchising voters in a way "obviously intended" to assure it and "its collaborators" control of the new parliament "regardless of

the outcome of the balloting."[7] The Foreign Office made no direct criticism of the Hungarian Communist Party. It was concerned, as G. T. C.
Campbell noted, that any attempt to influence the Hungarian government would "incur the Soviet charge of interference in Hungarian internal
affairs."[8]

The British and American governments ordered their envoys in Budapest to seek a joint interview with Prime Minister Lajos Dinnyés to discuss
the charges of pre-election irregularities. According to their reports on this
interview, Dinnyés readily admitted that there had been improprieties,
though not on the scale suggested. He blamed the abuses that had occurred
on the inefficiency of the new administrative machine and on the "megalo-
mania" of petty officials on the voter registration committees. He also
assured the two envoys that the Hungarian government was taking energetic measures to punish those responsible for such abuses, and to review
and correct all injustices that might have occurred.[9]

In London and Washington, foreign policy makers doubted that the
Hungarian government would refranchise voters on any appreciable scale.
Typically, John H. Watson, assistant head of the Foreign Office's Southern
Department, feared that Dinnyés' assurances amounted to little more
than a "delaying action."[10] In fact, tens of thousands of voters may have
been refranchised following Dinnyés interview. Just before election day,
however, the electoral committees reintroduced fresh batches of dis-
franchisements, affecting an equivalent number of people and thus essentially nullifying any refranchisements that had occurred.[11]

Another issue also arose, one which not only strained relations between
the Hungarian government and the Western powers, but also reflected a
persistent Anglo-American discord which was especially marked during
the election campaign. On election day, so-called "flying voter squads"
of Communist Party workers or their close allies, who had acquired numerous voter registration forms from government officials, travelled around
the country casting multiple votes. Stories circulated that some had cast
as many as twenty or more votes. It was clear that many instances of
plural voting occurred, and that this increased the Communists' share of
the vote, but the extent of the damage done could not, under the circumstances, be determined. Since no authorized electoral observers independent of those associated with the Hungarian government were present,
it was virtually impossible to come up with reliable voting figures, a state

of affairs which gave rise to considerable speculation. Thus, Chapin claimed that as many as 600,000 to a million votes were cast fradulently.[12]
Helm scoffed at these estimates. Chapin's figures, he thought, might "be
right or too high or too low," but there was "no solid basis" for them.[13]
After the election, the British legation was to put the number of multiple
votes at 100,000 to 200,000, or roughly two to four percent of the
electorate.[14] Several years later, Antal Bán, a prominent Hungarian Social
Democrat who fled the country in 1948, claimed that the Communists
had cast "about 300,000 false votes."[15]

The day following the election, but before the official results were announced, Helm suggested to the Foreign Office that, while the precise
figure [of plural voting] may never be known," the Communists, in a
free and fair election, would achieve just about the same vote in 1947 as
they had in 1945—that is, 17 percent.[16] If Helm's estimate was near the
mark, the 1947 election was fradulent, but not overwhelmingly so, for
the Communists received 22 percent of the vote. This was not a substantial
increase though it was enough to make them the single largest party. Of
their allies, the Social Democrats won 15 percent of the vote, down from
17 percent in 1945, and the National Peasant Party increased it share from
six percent to eight. The Smallholders suffered a stunning defeat, winning
less than 16 percent of the vote as compared to 57 percent two years
before. But the *total* bourgeois vote, now dispersed among seven different
parties, was comparable at 55 percent. The largest of the non-government
bourgeois parties was the Catholic progressive party (Democratic People's
Party), with almost 17 percent of the vote, and the extreme rightist Hungarian Independence Party, with 14 percent.[17]

The British and Americans disagreed not only on the extent of multiple
voting, they also evaluated in markedly different terms the overall character of the election. Chapin desribed it as a "carefully planned fraud"
and an "obvious" scandal; quoting an unnamed Smallholder politician, he
called it the "most corrupt . . . in Hungarian history."[18] Helm, while not
denying that electoral abuses had taken place, minimized them. He ex-
pectedly emphasized instead that the election proceedings had been
unexpectedly "fair, free and secret," with "no sign of intimidation" or
pressure by the Hungarian or Soviet authorities.[19]

Neither Chapin's nor Helm's view of the 1947 election—views with
which their respective governments essentially agreed—was wholly accurate

for both contained a good deal of exaggeration. That election fraud occurred was not in doubt, but the Americans made too much of it. As the
Foreign Office pointed out to the State Department a week after the
election: "There is a difference between electoral frauds such as disfranchisement and plural voting to which the Communists resorted in
order to obtain even one-fifth of the votes, and the organised cooking
of results that has taken place elsewhere,"[20] meaning in Poland, Rumania,
Bulgaria, and Yugoslavia. Chapin certainly overstated the case when he
described the election as the "most corrupt" in Hungarian history, for
the 1947 election was no more fraudulent, and probably less so, than the
extraordinarily dishonest elections that occurred under the Horthy regime
during the interwar period.[21] On the other hand, the British government's
more unconcerned attitude toward the election was also somewhat misplaced. After all, the election was less than scrupulously conducted, and
it permitted the Communists to become the single largest party, a status
to which they were not arithmetically entitled had the election been completely fair.

What motivated British and American analyses of the election was, it
would seem, their perception of the general political situation as it already
existed prior to 31 August. The Americans, who could not—or refused to—
distinguish between shades of leftism, were inclined to believe that the
Communists had virtually acceded to power with Nagy's resignation in
June. Consequently, they saw the August election as little more than a
staged triumph, used by the Communists to consolidate their control. The
British, on the other hand, did not believe that Nagy's ouster had rendered
the Communists dominant—only the leftists, including the Social Democrats. And the British, concentrating their attention on the Communist-
Social Democratic balance of power, contended that the election had
preserved the pre-election, intra-leftist equilibrium. So long as the Social
Democrats remained independent, the Foreign Office believed, they could
prevent, or at least delay, a complete Communist takeover.

* * * * *

While it remained a point of Anglo-American dispute whether the Social
Democrats were a viable source of anti-Communist strength, neither Western government had any confidence that the bourgeois parties were. In
this they were right, for soon after the election the Communists moved
against the remaining bourgeois parties and crushed them easily.

The technique was by now familiar to Western observers. The Communists—still joined by the Social Democrats, though by now less aggressively—engaged in daily press attacks against their new target, the Hungarian Independence Party, led by Zoltán Pfeiffer. The attacks, denouncing Pfeiffer and his adherents as "Fascistic" and "treasonable," began in early November and were soon followed by arrests "for interrogation" of members and supporters of the party. At the same time, demands began for lifting the parliamentary immunity of the party's deputies and cancelling their seats. At that point the party collapsed. Some of its members, including Pfeiffer, escaped to the West, others were incarcerated, and the party was dissolved—all before the month of November was out.[22]

Other bourgeois parties fared no better. One by one they were disbanded and their members either fled, were imprisoned, or submitted to the rising tide of leftism, which by the winter of 1947-48 had become irresistible. By the turn of the year, the only significant non-leftist opposition party still around was the Democratic People's Party, already incapable of any independent, anti-government activity. It too was dissolved toward the end of 1948.[23] It survived that long only at the pleasure of the Communists, who, it seemed, kept it around as a possible counterweight to the ultrarightist Hungarian Catholic hierarchy. The Catholic hierarchy remained an anti-Communist force, albeit one of unproven ability and unconnected with any political party.

The British and the Americans, to whom the Communist crackdown came as no surprise, took no action to save the embattled Hungarian bourgeois parties. Had they been inclined to do so, they could have brought into effect the elaborate machinery laid down in the Hungarian peace treaty to deal with alleged violations of civil rights. Since effective action along these lines required the cooperation of the Soviet and the Hungarian governments, however, London and Washington concluded that such efforts would be futile. On the other hand, the State Department and Foreign Office both sought to make known to the Hungarians and others their disapproval of the suppression of opposition activity, mainly by stepping up their publicity activities. They also decided to deliver periodic protests to the Hungarian government, as the occasion warranted.[24]

Although the British and American governments made virtually no attempt to rescue the Hungarian bourgeois parties, the case of the Social Democrats brought a far different response from the British. In the months following the August election, they concentrated intently on the Communist-Social Democratic confrontation which had finally burst into the open. The Americans, who failed to see much difference between the political aims of Communists and Social Democrats, belittled this British concern. As Chapin noted in July, before the Communist-Social Democratic quarrel had become hot, British diplomacy was "hypnotized by a fantastic hope that somehow the forces of Social Democracy, which is presumed to have a sympathetic link with the British Labour Party, can be galvanized into taking the leadership in the political life in Hungary."[25]

The British, however, took their efforts to bolster the moderate leftists quite seriously, nurturing their relations with the Social Democrats assiduously and encouraging them to resist Communist encroachment. In addition to their envoy in Budapest, who held discussions with representatives of all parties, the main British link with the Hungarian Social Democrats was the Labour Party. The usual method by which the Foreign Office communicated with it was through the party's International Committee, headed by International Secretary Denis Healey, who was also a member of the National Executive Committee.

The Labour Party did all it could to assist its government in the conduct of domestic and foreign affairs. The International Committee frequently sent the Foreign Office reports of the annual congresses of foreign socialist parties, which a British Labour observer traditionally attended.[26] Of even more importance to the Foreign Office was the assistance that the Labour Party, with its historical links to European social democracy, could provide as a courier of information to foreign socialists, in the prsent case Hungarian Social Democrats. A typical example occurred in June 1947, when the International Socialist Conference was meeting in Switzerland. In the wake of Nagy's recent resignation, the Foreign Office wanted to get a message to the Hungarian Social Democratic Party—some of whose members were in Zurich attending the conference—to "stiffen" their stand against the Communists. The Foreign Office cabled the British envoy in Berne, and instructed him to ask Morgan Phillips, head of the British Labour Party and part of its delegation, to pass this message along to the Hungarians.[27] The Labour Party, in order to coordinate its activities in the socialist movement, also sought the advice of the Foreign Office. For example, while the party was preparing for the March 1948 congress of the Hungarian Social Democratic Party, which it was planning to attend, Healey inquired of the Foreign Office's Southern Department whether it wanted the Labour representative to say anything special in his speech. Geoffrey Wallinger and I. F. Porter of the Southern Department offered suggestions.[28] At the same time, to keep the Labour Party leadership informed of events, the Foreign Office sent Healey despatches from British envoys abroad, when these were particularly relevant to developments in the international socialist movement.[29]

Despite Britain's continuous effort to bolster the Social Democrats' anti-Communist resistance, London saw its attempt collapse within a matter of months. In the end, the Foreign Office could not prevent the Communists from purging all right-wing Social Democrats—that is, those Social Democrats who refused to cooperate with the Communists—and, after the purge had been carried out, from fusing the rump Social Democrats with the Communists. The result was the demise of the Social Democratic Party and of a moderate leftist opposition.

The most serious and overt breach in the Communist-Social Democratic leftist front occurred at the very end of the election campaign. The Social Democrats charged—with clear validity—that just before the election the Communists had disfranchised, at Social Democratic expense, tens of thousands of voters to make room for the Communist-dominated "flying voter squads." A crisis ensued when rightist elements of the Social Democrats protested this development to the Communists. Nevertheless, a total rupture between the two parties was averted when the left-wing leader of the Social Democrats, Árpád Szakasits, threatened to resign from the party if his colleagues persisted in their rebellion. A compromise was reached when the dissidents, reluctant to see their party torn apart, backed down, though they also called, ineffectually, for equality with the Communists in public offices and trade unions. Meanwhile, the British, who closely followed this episode, disagreed amongst themselves as to whether the dissidents had acted wisely in allowing the matter to blow over. Helm argued that an open break and the overthrow of Szakasits would have been desirable, and that anti-Communists among the Social Democrats had lost an opportunity.[30] Back in London Wallinger and Christopher

Warner agreed with Helm,[31] but at least one, John Watson of the Southern Department, did not. Watson said that "behind the curtain, discretion is the better part of valour," adding that "he who fights and runs away lives to *fight* another day."[32] In any event, the Foreign Office had no quarrel with Helm's judgment that the Social Democratic showing in the election was rather poor, the last-minute disenfranchisements notwithstanding. Helm blamed the relatively low vote on the electorate's dissatisfaction with the party's long-standing collaboration with the Communists.[33]

The election victory by the Communists enhanced their position. As a result of the election, the Communists acquired five of the fifteen cabinet seats, and their close allies, the National Peasants, two more against four portfolios each for the Smallholders and the Social Democrats. Thus fortified, the Communists proceeded to launch the final offensive against the Social Democrats. The denouement came within a few months, as the Communists applied relentless pressure for a purge of the Social Democratic right-wing and for the fusion of the two labor groups. Since the social Democratic Party itself was already divided over this issue, the continuous Communists blasts served to split it further. By January 1948, the British were beginning to abandon hope that the anti-Communist wing of the Social Democratic Party would be able to maintain itself in the party and hold back the growing demand from both the Communists and pro-Communist Social Democrats for fusion. Wallinger noted on 7 February that the "process of communisation" was proceeding "quickly," adding that Helm was "much more depressed about prospects than he [had been] a few months ago."[34] In late January, Wallinger wrote to Denis Healey that "Hungary is freezing over rather fater than had at one time seemed likely."[35]

February 1948 marked the beginning of the end for the Social Democrats, as the right wing of the party caved in under the continuous barrage from the left. Waves of purges commenced. These affected not only the party, but the government as well, from which right-wing Social Democrats were successively ousted. At first, the purges hit hardest the Ministry of Industry, but soon the process reached into all facets of government administration. It continued until the Communists and their allies had eliminated all Social Democratic anti-Communists as completely as they had eliminated Smallholder anti-Communists before them.[36]

The move that sealed the fate of the Social Democratic Party also came in February. György Marosan, a Social Democrat completely subservient to the Communists, assumed effective leadership of the party, displacing Szakasits. Szakasits had willingly cooperated with the Communists since late 1944, but he was reluctant to preside over his party's dissolution. Marosan's accession ensured that the left-wing rump would vote for fusion with the Communists at the annual congress of the party, to be held in March.[37]

This was precisely what happened at the March congress. Immediately thereafter, the practical work of integrating the two organizations, such as their various committees and their newspapers, proceeded apace. In actual fact, however, integration, or fusion, entailed the absorption of the rump Social Democratic Party by the Communists, who took effective control of the entire structure. Though the task of fusion began following the March congress, it was not made official until June 1948, when, during a weekend of speeches, ceremonies, and mass gatherings, the Hungarian Workers' Party formally came into being. Still faithful to their tactics of gradualism, the Communist founders of the new party permitted its titular head (president) to be Árpád Szakasits, former leader of the Social Democrats; but the real chief was Mátyás Rákosi, its secretary general and leader of the former Communist Party. With the establishment of the new organization, the terms Communist and Communism officially disappeared. "The declared aim of the new party," reported Helm, "is the victory of Socialism." But, he added, "whatever the terms used, Communism is in full control."[38]

* * * * *

While the elimination of the Social Democratic Party was the final event securing the sovietization of Hungary, further developments tightened the Soviet Union's control both in Hungary and throughout Eastern Europe. One of these was the founding of the Cominform in September 1947. In its ranks were included the Communist parties of all the East European countries except Albania as well as the French and Italian parties. With the Soviet Union as its dominant component, the Cominform provided the Kremlin with a central apparatus to direct and coordinate Communist activity throughout much of Europe. Of course, as the subsequent rift with the Yugoslav party demonstrated, there were geographical limitations on the ability of the Cominform to impose its will.

While the Cominform forged a pattern of ideological unity among the increasingly powerful Communist parties of Eastern Europe, the Soviet Union also sought to establish political and military cohesion in this strategic region. It took a step toward that end by concluding a network of pacts throughout Eastern Europe based on treaties of "friendship, cooperation, and mutual assistance." The most important element of these pacts was that they bound the signatories to come to each other's aid in the event of aggression by Germany or any state allied with Germany—a clear reference to the Western powers. Such a treaty already existed, since December 1943, between the Soviet Union and Czechoslovakia. Beginning in 1945, Moscow concluded pacts with other East European nations, including Hungary in February 1948. The East European countries themselves also established ties with each other based on mutual assistance treaties. Besides its pact with Russia, for example, Hungary signed treaties with Rumania in January 1948, with Poland in June, and with Bulgaria in July.

An event greatly strengthening this alliance structure was the Communist coup in Czechoslovakia in February 1948. Hitherto, Czechoslovakia was the least sovietized of the East European nations. Seemingly well entrenched pro-Western forces balanced Czechoslovakia's strong Communist Party, making its ruling coalition more genuine than the sham coalitions elsewhere in Eastern Europe. But following the coup the sovietization process surged forward, and Czechoslovakia was soon completely integrated into the Soviet satellite system. By mid-1948, all of Eastern Europe—save for its northern and southern peripheries in Finland and in Greece—had entered the Soviet bloc. It is true that Yugoslavia, which did not adjoin Soviet territory, was soon to withdraw from the orbit, but others did not follow the Yugoslav example.[39]

From an international viewpoint, the state of affairs developing in Eastern Europe was a major setback for the Western world and its leading powers, the United States and Britain. By 1948, the trend of events in Eastern Europe had become crystal clear, and the British and American governments had to determine their policies towards this region, from which they now had been virtually excluded.

As a result of the breakdown of the Council of Foreign Ministers in December 1947, and the apparent impossibility of reaching a four-power agreement with the Russians on Germany, the Foreign Office concluded that the time had come to review the world situation, including that of Eastern Europe, in the light of Soviet policy. Consequently, between January and March 1948, the Foreign Office prepared for the cabinet a series of papers devoted to this subject.

A principal point emerging from these documents is that, as the Foreign Office perceived it, the Soviet Union posed an unmistakable and grave danger to the Western world. In Eastern Europe, the Soviet threat had already materialized. A paper of January 1948, entitled "Review of Soviet Policy," argued that the Russians had "ruthlessly consolidated" their position throughout Eastern Europe, adding: "Everywhere in Eastern Europe the development has been similar. It is only the pace that has differed." East European governments no longer applied "purely national policies," but instead had "become the administrative agents of the Communist Party both internally and in international affairs." The Soviet Union had established in Eastern Europe a "*bloc* of Communist-administered territory where human rights and freedoms no longer" existed, and where "local needs [were] subordinated to the policy requirements of the Cominform and the Kremlin." Although the "degree of elimination" of opposition parties and leaders varied "from country to country," nowhere did an "effective and active opposition to the Communists (apart from the Roman Catholic Church) still" exist, except in Czechoslovakia.[40] In early March, shortly after the Czechoslovak coup, the Foreign Office noted in another paper that Czechoslovakia also was in the "process of being absorbed into the Soviet Orbit."[41] Thus the Foreign Office believed, as early as January, that the Communists had established virtually complete control, though of varying intensity, throughout Eastern Europe.

By early March, the European crisis had deepened further. Having consolidated its hold on Eastern Europe, the Soviet Union was, so the Foreign Office believed, on the brink of infiltrating Western Europe. Citing the Czechoslovak coup, the collapse of the Hungarian Social Democratic Party, and Soviet demands on Finland for a mutual assistance pact, the Foreign Office declared in another cabinet paper that "western civilization" was in dire peril of succumbing to the "fast increasing threat" posed by Soviet expansion. The Soviet Union not only refused to "co-operate in any real sense with any non-Communist or non-Communist controlled government." Even more than that, it was actively preparing to extend its hold over the remaining part of continental Europe and, subsequently, over the Middle East and no doubt the Far East as well. In other words, physical control of the Eurasian land mass and eventual control of the whole World Island is what the Politburo is aiming at—no less a thing than that. The immensity of the aim should not betray us into believing in its impracticability.

The Foreign Office warned that, "unless positive and vigorous steps [were] shortly taken," the Soviet Union stood to gain—"within the next few months or even weeks"—new "political and strategical advantages."[42]

The Foreign Office had essentially written Eastern Europe off as lost. It believed that the problem now facing the West was to prevent Soviet influence and control from spreading elsewhere. To do this, it took steps to establish a West European alliance, an idea originally put forward by the Belgians in 1944. Churchill rejected the idea on the basis that the continental countries were so weak that an agreement to defend them was not in British interests. Bevin, when he became Foreign Secretary, favored as a long-term goal the establishment of close relations with the countries on the Atlantic and Mediterranean fringes of Europe. But he did not want to ake active steps towards forming a defense alliance with them until he had had time to consider possible Soviet reactions. He would however, seek close political and economic ties.[43]

By 1948, Bevin considered the Soviet threat so serious as to require the earliest possible establishment of a Western Union, "backed by the power and resources of the Commonwealth and the Americas."[44] When he presented the idea to the government, it readily gave approval. He was advised, however, not to place "too much emphasis. . .on its anti-Soviet aspect," lest he "fail to rally the Socialist forces in Western Europe" behind it.[45] When on 22 January he unveiled the plan before Parliament, he was careful, as he later explained to the cabinet,[46] not to frame Western Union as a bloc directed against the Soviet Union. Bevin stated in Parliament that the West had the right to make security arrangements among its "kindred souls," as the Russians did in Eastern Europe among theirs.[47] By March, Bevin's initiative had yielded the Brussels Treaty Organization, itself the basis of the North Atlantic Treaty Organization and of subsequent alliance structures.

The establishment of an alliance system was vitally important to the British, who saw it as the foundation for protecting the Western world. Their attitude toward the European situation had become totally defensive. Their goal was to keep Western Europe out of Soviet hands—Eastern Europe was already lost. While the British intended to maintain the policy of publicizing their disapproval of events in Eastern Europe, they would decline "to encourage subversive movements in Eastern European countries or anti-Russianism, or to lead the anti-Communists to hope for support" which they could not give. This policy, the British noted, they had been "scrupulously careful" to pursue.[48]

It was in this essentially defensive posture that British policy differed from American. The Americans were under no illusions as the sovietized nature of the East European governments. In the case of Hungary, they had come to believe long before the British that its government was Communist-dominated, mainly because the State Department had little faith in the strength of the Social Democratic Party. But rather than direct all of its attention to saving the West from perceived Soviet expansionism, Washington maintained serious hope that it might one day be able to switch to the offensive in Eastern Europe and drive the Russians back. Thus a State Department Policy Planning Staff paper of August 1948 stated as American goals:

> ...the gradual retraction of undue Russian power and influence from the present satellite area and the emergence of the respective eastern-European countries as independent factors on the international scene;

as well as,

> ...the development in the Soviet Union of institutions of federalism which would permit a revival of the national life of the Baltic peoples.[49]

In fact, the State Department believed it probable that internal forces would some day develop to bring their own challenge to the Russians. According to another Policy Planning Staff paper written months before, in

November 1947, the Russians would "probably" be able to "maintain their position" behind the iron curtain "for some time by sheer police methods." Nevertheless, the paper continued,

> . . . the problem will become an increasingly difficult one for them. It is unlikely that approximately one hundred million Russians will succeed in holding down permanently, in addition to their own minorities, some ninety millions of European with a higher cultural level and with long experience in resistance to foreign rule.

While no anti-Russian uprising was anticipated "in the immediate future," the State Department foresaw the probability of such an occurrence eventually.[50]

To the British, such speculation would doubtlessly have been sheer fantasy at worst, and at best very wishful thinking. That later events, such as those in Hungary in 1956, might lend credence to the American view would not have made it any more plausible in the late 1940s.

* * * * *

Although by mid-1948 the Communists had succeeded in eliminating all political party opposition, religious opposition remained, especially from the Roman Catholic Church. Relations between the increasingly left-leaning Hungarian government and religious organizations were never cordial. In July 1946, the government restricted the activities of the Catholic Youth Organizations, and in March 1947 it prepared plans for the substitution of voluntary for compulsory religious instruction. All harmony broke down in 1948, as the Communists, having eliminated all other opposition, finally turned on the churches. The dispute centered on the important issue of control of religious schools, which in May 1948 the government revealed its intention to nationalize. Though two principal Protestant churches, the Reformed and the Lutheran, were split on whether to reach accommodation with the government, both eventually agreed to do so. They promised loyalty to the state in exchange for such concessions as guaranteed religious liberty, financial grants, and exemption from nationalization for a few schools. But the Roman Catholic Church, led by Jószef Cardinal Mindszenty, Prince Primate of Hungary, refused to compromise at all, insisting that school nationalization be dropped, controls on Roman Catholic organizations lifted, and a Catholic newspaper allowed to appear. The upshot of this conflict between church and state was the Cardinal's arrest in late 1948; in February 1949 he was sentenced to life imprisonment. The Roman Catholic Church, like the Protestant, was allowed to exist, but not to challenge the authority of the state.[51]

The church-state conflict, intensified by the school nationalization issue, simmered throughout 1948. When the Cardinal asked the British and Americans for assistance in his dispute with the government over the schools, they declined. Chapin, with State Department approval, explained to Mindszenty that American backing was unlikely in view of the "well-known traditional American attitude of refusing state support to secretarian or private schools."[52] A "somewhat controversial business," was how J. C. Petersen of the Foreign Office referred to the nationalization question, noting that there was a difference between the right to denominational schools and freedom of religion.[53]

On the broader question of how to deal with the outspoken Cardinal Mindszenty, Western policy makers were of two minds. On the one hand, they supported his anti-Communist objective, and his resolute and even courageous stance against the Communist-dominated government won widespread recognition. On the other hand, his attitude was rigidly unyielding, which invited confrontation and made an eventual showdown—which the Cardinal would certainly lose—ever more likely. Typifying the mixed opinion of the Western governments towards Mindszenty was the somewhat grudging concession by John Watson of the Southern Department: "One cannot help feeling some sympathy with the Prince Primate . . . [whose] tactics are refreshing, if suicidal."[54] Such conflicting attitudes on the part of the two Western governments continued in 1949, when the church-state conflict in the wake of Mindszenty's imprisonment erupted into a conflict which attracted international attention and brought British and American statements of condemnation.[55] Though the initial clamor attending the Mindszenty affair subsided within two or three months, the episode soured even further the already strained relations between the Western powers and the Hungarian government.

Before the sovietization of Hungary was complete, the Communists not only had to eliminate anti-government opposition from the churches, they also had to remodel the form of the Hungarian republic itself. In large measure, such a move was more symbolic than substantive, for Hungary had already become an integral component of the Soviet bloc, where anti-Communist parties were forbidden and indeed had ceased to exist. Nevertheless, the Hungarian government remained theoretically a coalition of several different parties, which formed in late 1948 as the National Independence Front. In February 1949, the ruling coalition changed its name to the People's Independence Front. In the May general election, the front offered a single, unopposed slate of candidates, for which, according to official returns, more than 90 percent of the electorate voted.[56]

Following the establishment of the Hungarian Workers' Party in June 1948, the nature of the Communist movement itself underwent a transformation. Until mid-1948, the Communists had presented themselves as a more or less monolithic group. Thereafter, however, the semblance of unity broke down. An intra-Communist crisis ensued not only in Hungary but throughout Eastern Europe, a crisis which was to have major ramifications for the world Communist movement.The schism was made public in June 1948, when the Cominform expelled from its ranks the Yugoslav Communist Party, led by President Tito, on the grounds of anti-Soviet behavior and political deviation from Cominform policies.

The emergence of Titoism as a political force independent of and directed against the Kremlin presented a serious problem to those East European Communists whose orientation remained fixed on Russia. Pro-Soviet Communists tied the welfare of their own countries to that of the Soviet Union. In doing so they sought to rise above the petty, destructive nationalism of recent decades and advance the cause of internationalism, which they believed the Soviet Union represented. Titoism cast their constant support of Moscow in sharp relief. Those like Mátyás Rákosi who backed the Kremlin—and at this point it it proper to speak of them as Stalinists—faced a threat from Titoism. For the Stalinists could maintain power only if no anti-Soviet, nationalist force arose to challenge their reliance upon Russia. Those, sometimes called national communists, who sympathized with Tito's non-Soviet model of economic organization, presented such a challenge. The Stalinists thus felt compelled to root out the Titoist virus, and to do so quickly before the infection spread.

Ministers Helm and Chapin believed that the Tito problem forced the pace of Hungarian Stalinists. The issue of the peasantry is instructive. Within less than a week of the Cominform expulsion of Tito, the Hungarian government initiated sharp economic measures mainly in the form of severe taxation, against property-owning peasants, whom it simultaneously denounced as kulak exploiters. The British and American ministers had no doubts that this move—which seemed to herald the collectivization of agriculture, though not necessarily in the immediate future—was directly related to the rift with Tito. They noted that the

Cominform resolution expelling Tito denounced the Yugoslav agricultural system as one in which "an individual peasant economy prevails" and "considerable land is concentrated in the hands of kulaks." Helm, expanding on this perceived relationship, contended that the Stalinist leaders had collectivization of agriculture as their ultimate goal. But, he argued, the customarily cautious Stalinists would not have moved against the land-holding peasants when they did, had it not been for the urgency born of the Tito schism. Since the schism took place, however, the Stalinists, who could not afford any charge of backsliding, moved rapidly ahead in the rural sector.

On the heels of the agricultural taxation action, purges began in the government, the party, and all facets of social life. The governmental purges commenced in the Agriculture Ministry (apparently in connection with the rural economic developments), but soon spread to numerous administrative agencies such as the Ministries of Foreign Affairs, Justice, and Education, and also the universities and the professions. Meanwhile, the anti-Tito campaign opened up in the Hungarian Workers' Party in September 1948, when the ruling Political Committee announced that it would freeze new membership applications for a period of six months, during which time it would also scrutinize the current party list to weed out undesirable elements.[57]

This entire process of Stalinist-oriented purges was symptomatic of the anti-Tito drive, which climaxed at various times in various East European countries. The sensation of the Hungarian anti-Titoist measures occurred in June 1949, when László Rajk, a high-ranking official of both the Communist Party and the government and one of the few leading Communists in Hungary whose political education had been in the West rather than the Soviet Union, was arrested and tried on charges of being a pro-Tito nationalist and an imperialist agent. In October 1949, Rajk and several alleged collaborators were executed.[58]

As far as Yugoslavia was concerned, the emergence of Titoism played a profound role in the conduct of East-West affairs. Both the British and the Americans believed that the existence of the nationalist heresy, embodied in the Yugoslav government, placed stress on the Soviet bloc, and London and Washington both sought to bolster the Tito regime.[59]

Apart from Yugoslavia, however, the Tito schism had little direct impact on international relations. The question revolved around whether anti-Stalinists had any chance of overthrowing the Moscow-oriented governments elsewhere in Eastern Europe. If anti-Stalinist forces could successfully challenge pro-Soviet governments, then the Anglo-Americans could use those forces as an internal opposition to the Stalinist rulers. This would complement Western efforts to sustain Yugoslavia as a base of opposition to the Soviet Union. If the anti-Stalinists could not challenge the governments, and instead were crushed by them, then the status quo—which meant pro-Soviet regimes throughout Eastern Europe, except Yugoslavia—would be maintained.

The prevailing belief in the West in 1949 was that the status quo in Eastern Europe was likely to endure for the time being. A State Department review of the situation explicitly stated that there was "no prospect at this juncture of a successful attempt to emulate Tito's action" elsewhere in Eastern Europe because of those nations' geographical position on the Soviet border and the "lack of any organized opposition." The British attitude was similar. The Foreign Office certainly showed no indication in 1948 that it anticipated the overthrow of Stalinist rule. In short, for the British and Americans to rely upon an internal, anti-Stalinist opposition would not have been a realisitic policy, because whatever opposition existed was powerless. It may be noted, however, that in 1949 the United States decided to launch an information campaign in the Soviet bloc countries, such as through the Voice of America, stressing the "independence from Kremlin domination that Yugoslavia" had attained and the "exploitation of the satellite countries by the Soviet Union." "Titoism as a disintegrating force" in the Soviet bloc, said the State Department, "should be stimulated and encouraged by all devices of propaganda."[60] Whether Britain endorsed this aggressive propaganda effort, and if so to what extent, is unclear.

Notwithstanding any pro-Tito, anti-Soviet propaganda campaign that the Western Powers may have inaugurated, the fact remained that of all the Eastern European governments only the Yugoslav adopted an anti-Soviet policy. In the long run, it is true, the same nationalist and anti-Stalinist forces that had arisen in Yugoslavia also came to the fore in other countries, and led to such events as the 1956 uprising in Hungary. But those events were still years away. In the short run, Titoism did not weaken the hold of the pro-Soviet Communists in Hungary. By prodding them to consolidate their power rapidly, Titoism, if anything, strengthened the Stalinists, who retained full control and ruled over a sovietized Hungary.

* * * * *

Sovietization signified the establishment of regimes stronag and stable enough to continue without an immediate Soviet presence. The East European nations, having become sovietized, assumed control over their own affairs. But they did so only if they followed the Kremlin's lead. The Russians viewed deviation from it as a threat to Soviet political and military security. If the deviation became flagrant, Moscow was prepared to reestablish direct control over Eastern Europe, and would restore autonomy only when loyal elements had regained power. The Eastern European nations were therefore free agents, as long as they defined freedom in Soviet terms.

* * * * *

Contemporary Hungarian historiography refers to the twelve-month period from Ferenc Nagy's ouster as premier to the establishment of the Hungarian Workers' Party as the "year of change."[61] This it certainly was. In mid-1947, Hungary's government contained a powerful left wing of Communists and Social Democrats, but also an influential if embattled center which was considerably stronger than centrist forces in most other East European states. By mid-1948, Hungary was completely Communist-controlled, and all bourgeois elements as well as the Social Democrats had been reduced. Hungary had become as sovietized as any other East European country. Any difference in political structure were by that time insignificant, for political similarities for outweighed any dissimilarities. Hungary had also become a fully integrated component of the Soviet bloc. Thus, the steady movement to the left from June 1947 to June 1948 had strengthened a crucial part of the Soviet Union's strategic western wall.

In March 1945, Sir Orme Sargent, then deputy under-secretary of state at the Foreign Office, had said that the Russians were creating in Eastern Europe a "cordon sanitaire et strategique against Germanism." He had raised the question as to whether Stalin would "be satisfied that it should remain solely a line of defense, or whether he [would] try to transform it eventually into a forward base from which to operate into Central and Western Europe."[62] Sargent's question was still relevant three years later. It was also more pressing, for the sovietization of Hungary and Czechoslovakia had solidified the central portion of the "cordon sanitaire." The Russians could use this "cordon" as a buffer zone to help absorb the shock of any future anti-Soviet attack from Europe, but they could also deploy it as a springboard for further westward forays, to the eastern shores of the North Atlantic Ocean or even beyond. In that a sovietized Hungary was an essential element of this defensive—and possiblly offensive—Soviet alliance structure, the Hungarian "year of change" had European-wide and worldwide significance.

VIII

ANGLO-AMERICAN POLICY AND
THE TACTICS OF ANTI-SOVIETISM

This study has sought to trace British and American policy toward Hungary as a case history of their evolving policy toward one Eastern European country from the closing months of the Second World War to 1948, by which time a pro-Soviet leadership had become paramount in the political life of the Eastern European nations. The purpose underlying the inquiry has been to compare and contrast the British and American responses to the sovietization of Eastern Europe, and to explain in what ways and for what reasons those responses converged or diverged.

* * * * *

It is useful to examine the Anglo-American response to the sovietization of Hungary, and more broadly Eastern Europe, on two levels—strategic and tactical.

As a long-term, strategic consideration, both Washington and London opposed the Communist political, social, and economic system as practised by the Soviet Union. This opposition had been a consistent aspect of British and American foreign policy ever since the October Revolution. Western governments greeted that momentous event with hostility, and soon they intervened against the Bolsheviks during the Russian Civil War.[1] Their belligerent reaction was instinctive, for with the ascent to power of the Bolsheviks came the territorial realization of what previously had

5811043678901

been only the idea of communism. The implementation of the idea produced a powerful and terrifying shock on propertied classes throughout the world, because it brought to the surface the worst fears of mass unrest and social turmoil which the European and American elites had entertained since at least the time of the French Revolution.[2]

Ideology was not the sole factor behind the East-West schism. An equally important ingredient was great-power—and especially Anglo-Russian—rivalry, into which the United States eventually was drawn on Britain's side. The Anglo-Russian conflict, which preceded the Bolshevik Revolution, provided the geopolitical framework for what developed after 1917 into the Soviet-Western conflict. Discord between the Soviet Union and the Western powers was territorial as well as ideological. In the words of one historian,

> The Cold War has its origins in the struggle for power in Central Asia between the rival imperialisms of Britain and Russia in the nineteenth century. . . . So the struggle was there—and so was the traditional doctrine of mutual suspicion—even before the Red Flag floated over the Winter Palace on that cataclysmic day in 1917.[3]

Thus, the Bolshevik seizure of power introduced ideology into the equation of Anglo-Russian rivalry.

The Soviet regime's survival through the Civil War forced the British and American governments to come to terms with it. This was never a smooth affair. Soviet-Western relations proceeded on a basis of official non-recognition, recognition mixed with antagonism, or at best mutually suspicious accommodation.[4]

A major improvement in East-West relations occurred with the onset of the world war and the forging of the Grand Alliance in the effort to defeat Nazi Germany. Yet, so unstable was the alliance that victory over the common enemy—in fact, the mere approach of victory as the Axis powers waned—rocked and shattered the thin basis of Soviet-Western accord. East-West relations again became embittered, as the opposing forces became locked in what came to be known universally as the Cold War. The deterioration in the state of affairs signified in large measure a reversion to the prewar status of essentially unbridled animosity between the Soviet Union and the Western powers.[5]

But in the postwar period this animosity was directed not only against the Soviet Union itself, but also against the extension of Soviet power and the Soviet system into Eastern Europe. Just as the Western governmnts had opposed the Soviet Union since 1917, they also opposed the sovietization of Eastern Europe in the late 1940s. Whether they believed that they were tactically capable of preventing that process is another matter.

One factor behind British and American opposition to the sovietization of Eastern Europe was economic. If the region fell under the domination of the Soviet Union and became absorbed into the Soviet system, its potential value to the West as an economic sphere of interest would be lost. The British and Americans wanted to keep Eastern Europe open as an area of investment.[6] This was the reason behind their persistent efforts at the Paris Peace Conference to write into the peace treaties provisions guaranteeing most-favored-nation status to all powers. For the same reason London and Washington sought to forestall ratification of the Soviet-Hungarian and Soviet-Rumanian economic collaboration agreements, which promised to bind those countries tightly to the Soviet Union and exclude the West.

Although the British and Americans regarded Eastern Europe as a possible economic sphere of interest, their existing investments in and trade with the region were limited, amounting to only a small percentage of their total foreign holdings and commerce.[7] True, British and American nationals had investments in certain Eastern European-based industries and private investors stood to lose from their expropriation. The British and American governments often intervened on behalf of those private investors. For example, they raised the issue of Rumanian oil at the Potsdam Conference with a view to halting the Soviet seizure of Allied-owned oil property and obtaining compensation for lost property. Still, concern over these relatively insubstantial investments did not usually motivate the thinking of Western foreign policy makers toward Eastern Europe.

The motivating factor behind their Eastern European policy was the region's geopolitical importance. British and American policy makers had feared since before the end of the war that the Russians would not stop with Eastern Europe but would go on, by means of political subversion or military intervention, to extend their spheres of control even further. This notion later became known as the domino theory.[8]

Averell Harriman, for example, put forward such an argument in September 1944 in a cable to the State Department on the Polish question. "What frightens me . . . is that when a country begins to extend its influence by strong arm methods beyond its borders under the guise of security it is difficult to see how a line can be drawn. If the policy is accepted that the Soviet Union has a right to penetrate her immediate neighbors for security, penetration of the next immediate neighbor becomes at a certain time equally logical."[9] In March 1945, Deputy Under-Secretary Sir Orme Sargent of the Foreign Office pondered whether Stalin intended Eastern Europe to "remain solely a line of defense," or whether he would "try to transform it eventually into a forward base from which to operate into Central and Western Europe."[10] A year later in his famous Fulton, Missouri speech, from which Ernest Bevin refused to dissociate himself, Winston Churchill declared that "nobody knows what Soviet Russia and its Communist international organization intends to do in the near future, or what are the limits, if any, to their expansive and proselytizing tendencies." Churchill went on to assert that they desired the "indefinite expansion of their power and doctrines."[11] When the Hungarian left maneuvered Nagy out of office in mid-1947, fears were heightened in the State Department that Austria was immediately threatened.[12] The dread of Soviet power spreading throughout the Middle East permeated British and American thinking on the Greek problem.[13] By March 1948, the Foreign Office was warning the cabinet that stemming Soviet expansionism had "really become a matter of the defence of western civilisation, or everyone will be swamped by this Soviet method of infiltration."[14]

The Western powers believed, therefore, that the chief danger posed by a sovietized Eastern Europe was its role as a potential springboard for Soviet forays into crucial regions. From the Lübeck-Trieste line, the Russians could strike into the Western zones of Germany and move on into France as well, especially if Austria were to fall under Soviet control. From France they would be in a position to threaten the British Isles and, eventually, even North America. From Eastern Europe, moreover, the Russians threatened Greece and, again if Austria came into Russia's grasp, Italy. These latter countries guarded the Mediterranean line of communication to the oil-rich Middle East, the Indian subcontinent, and the Far East. And, of course, Germany, France, Italy, and Greece were important in themselves for political, economic, and military reasons.

The loss of any one of them would be catastrophic for Western interests. In short, Eastern Europe *per se* was not indispensable. But if Soviet power advanced beyond the positions reached by 1948 and broke into the Western and Southern European rimland, then the West would be in serious difficulty.[15]

In the immediate postwar period, therefore, before the political situation had crystalized and Soviet control in Eastern Europe had solidified, the Western powers had a clear reason to try to keep the region from falling into Soviet hands. If the effort succeeded, it would keep Soviet power far behind the danger point.

However, millions of Soviet troops stood on or next to the territories of the Eastern European states, and the Soviet government by its actions and statements left no doubt that it wanted the area. An attempt by the West to prevent the sovietization of Eastern Europe might well lead to a bitter diplomatic struggle with the Russians, and if the Russians refused to retreat, the West would have to admit defeat and abandon all efforts to influence events there. The only alternative would be to oppose the Russians with military force. However, as the American Joint Chiefs of Staff noted in late 1945, "it is apparent that the United States could not fight Russia successfully in the Balkans."[16] Neither could Britain, of course.

In sum, Eastern Europe was important enough to the Western powers to tempt them to challenge the Russians there—but not militarily. Given this ambivalence of political temptation and military impotence, the Western powers differed over tactics as they approached the problem.

The tactical difference revolved around the extent to which the British and the Americans should accept or resist by diplomatic and political means the growing Soviet control in Eastern Europe. Here the two Western governments diverged considerably. The United States conducted its Eastern European policy with little if any concern for reaching a settlement with its Soviet rival. Of course, since the Soviet Union was in military occupation of the region and the United States had no intention of offering an armed challenge, the only practical solution was to accept the region's sovietization as an inevitable fact. But far from resigning itself to inaction, the United States tried to counter every Soviet move by diplomatic démarche or public confrontation. Even after the Russians had consolidated their control and eliminated virtually all Western influence in

Eastern Europe, the American government nourished hopes that it might one day recover its lost position there in the wake of an anti-Soviet uprising.

This American policy of bluster and relentless opposition was in marked contrast to Britain's defensive approach to the Eastern European problem. The outline of that approach had begun to emerge as early as October 1944, when Churchill and Stalin concluded their famous percentages agreement. According to this, the Russians would acquire equal influence with that of the West in two Eastern European countries, including Hungary, and the lion's share of influence in two others; Greece was to be a Western preserve. This spheres-of-influence agreement amounted to a partition of Europe, and characteristically the Americans, who refused to concede anything to the Russians, would not be bound by it. Nonetheless, the British retreat from Eastern Europe proceeded apace. In March 1945, Sir Orme Sargent urged the Foreign Office to abandon an "untenable" position and "tacitly" and "without further protest or argument" accept the existing Balkan governments "no matter what their political colour" might be. Eastern Europe, he argued, was "not vital" to British interests in Europe, whereas it was to the Russians, constituting an "essential part of their security system."[17]

The Foreign Office never formally endorsed Sargent's proposal, but its actions clearly coincided with it. British policy toward Eastern Europe, and its divergence from American policy, was highlighted during the Hungarian crises of 1947, following the arrest of Béla Kovács and the ouster of Prime Minister Nagy. In this critical period, the Americans, to the annoyance and over the objections of the British, publicly issued a series of strongly worded condemnations of Soviet and Communist activity, which aggravated an already tense situation. The British consistently maintained a low profile, discussing the Hungarian situation with the Russians behind closed doors and doing their best to mollify American assertiveness.

Of course, the British had no desire to see the Soviet Union establish unrivalled control in Eastern Europe, and they were willing to make efforts to slow down the sovietization process if such attempts required no more than minimal diplomatic intervention. But they also believed that the West could do nothing if the Russians insisted on controlling the region, as they were likely to do. Thus, the British avoided whenever possible a direct clash with the Russians over the fate of Eastern Europe. The Americans, on the other hand, had no qualms about engaging in such non-military clashes and got involved in quite a few of them. Nonetheless, they, like the British, lost all political influence in Eastern Europe. Virtually driven out of the region, they still refused, however, to accept Soviet control as a durable reality of the postwar European balance of power, while the British recognized it as a fact. Believing that an attempt to maintain political influence in Eastern Europe was certain to fail, the British voluntarily if grudgingly withdrew.

* * * * *

Of the fact that the aggressive Americans adopted a tactical approach toward the Eastern European situation different from that of the defensive British, there is no doubt. The question that must be answered is why this was the case.

The answer must be sought in the factors of power and geography. Whichever country was weaker and less capable of thwarting Soviet ambitions, and whichever lay closer to a possible Soviet spearhead, had to be the more cautious about provoking the Russians. Both conditions describe Great Britain's dilemma.

For half a century before the Second World War, Britain already had been in a state of relative decline as an international power. At the end of the war, it was greatly weakened and overextended. The Labour government was aware of this fact and recognized that Britain could not maintain itself in such a situation for any length of time. Britain had to retrench and reduce its foreign commitments, and to carry out such a retreat, as in the case of India, was a high-priority objective of postwar British diplomacy.[18]

Nevertheless, Britain could not rush headlong into a policy of withdrawal without regard to the consequences. The Labour Party leadership made this point quite clearly in the pamphlet *Cards on the Table,* written by Hugh Dalton and Denis Healey. The pamphlet stated,

> . . . this reduction [in foreign commitments] must be carried out in an orderly way so that at no point [will] we lose our power of initiative and our ability to control the process. Above all, we must avoid creating by our withdrawal, vacuums into which the other Great Powers might surge in irresistible and world-shattering conflict.[19]

The concern that other great powers—meaning the Soviet Union—might expand into power vacuums left behind by Britain's retreat is significant. The Labour government sought to exert a balance of power against what it perceived to be Soviet expansionism. In doing so, it pursued a foreign policy objective that preceding British governments had practised for some two-and-a-half centuries.

"The general character of England's foreign policy is determined by the immutable conditions of her geographical situation on the ocean flank of Europe as an island State with vast overseas colonies and dependencies." Thus wrote Sir Eyre Crowe, chief clerk at the British Foreign Office, who later rose to become its permanent under-secretary, in an important Foreign Office memorandum of 1907. He also spoke of the necessity for open sea lanes, the need to keep unbroken the so-called imperial lifeline, through the Mediterranean and into the Middle East. Finally, Crowe noted the remaining strategic requirement for Britain's security, and this was the necessity of preventing any single European power from establishing hegemony over the continent. The "only check" on such a threat "always consisted" in the establishment of an equilibrium, "technically known as the balance of power."[20]

Crowe wrote this memorandum in the context of the threat to the European balance of power posed by Wilhelmine Germany. In the 1930s and early 1940s it was Hitlerian Germany that endangered the European balance. Then as before, British statesmen saw the need to oppose the would-be hegemonist, for otherwise the crucial balance of power would be lost. But in no case did Great Britain attempt to confront the European conqueror singlehandedly. Instead it always sought to establish itself as the pivot of an international alliance.

In its end-of-the-war and postwar relations with Soviet Russia, Great Britain once again faced an expansionist power that threatened the European balance, and once again it met the threat by forming an alliance to oppose the hegemonic power. But in the late 1940s, for the first time in centuries—indeed, since its establishment as a nation-state—Great Britain had to form and guide an anti-hegemonic alliance working from a position of severe weakness. Though still a great power, it had become the least of the Big Three. Such circumstances obliged Britain to engage in a policy of withdrawal, while simultaneously organizing the alliance. As far as Europe was concerned, London had to abandon all but the most essential areas and to draw back its defense perimeter dangerously close to the continent's indispensable rimland, which prevented the Soviet Union from breaking out into the non-Arctic high seas or the Mediterranean. The weakest point in the European rimland was Greece, and Britain therefore had to devote enormous attention to that region, from which it could not retreat, financially burdensome though its intervention was. As disconcerting for Britain was the fact that it was desperately dependent upon American financial and military backing, without which London had little hope of maintaining even limited objectives for long.

This was the state of affairs which Ernest Bevin faced when he took up the reins of the British Foreign Office in July 1945. What was Bevin's policy towards the international crisis? According to his sympathetic biographer, Francis Williams, a collaborator of Bevin since trade-union days, Bevin believed that he had to hold the line against the Soviet Union until he was able to draw America into the active defense of Europe. He judged that the time and the issue had arrived in February 1947 in Greece. At that time, Bevin informed the State Department that Britain could no longer continue to provide the main reserve of financial and military support for Greece or Turkey. After initial shock (the Americans demanded to know if this move indicated a fundamental change in British policy), the Americans soon promulgated the so-called Truman Doctrine, by which the United States committed itself to the defense of the Eastern Mediterranean. Satisfied that the inevitable British withdrawal from this region of traditional British influence would no longer leave a power vacuum that the Russians might be tempted to exploit, Bevin maintained the initiative. Seeking to widen and consolidate the anti-Soviet alliance, Bevin turned his attention to Western Europe. In March 1947, Britain signed the Treaty of Dunkirk with France, the "first substantial brick" in a structure of Western European alliances, as Williams noted. A year later Britain bolstered that structure when it, France, and the Benelux nations signed a treaty of mutual assistance binding them together. Eventually, in April 1949, the "climax of Bevin's efforts," the North Atlantic Treaty Organization was founded, thereby establishing a massive, anti-Soviet alliance system.[21] Thus, once again, Great Britain had preserved the European balance of power.

But Britain did not preserve the European balance of power intact, and it could not have done so. Stretched to the limit, Britain had to abandon all but the essential regions of Europe, of which Eastern Europe was not one. Britain was willing, through diplomatic action, to place obstacles in the way of those forces seeking to draw Eastern Europe into the Soviet camp. But at no time did London seriously expect such efforts to halt, and certainly not to reverse, Soviet political gains in the region. Moreover, on those occasions when Great Britain undertook diplomatic representations, it often did so to pacify its aggressive American ally. Had it been left to itself, London would have let events take their own course, unnoticed and unprotested, so that it could tend to more important matters, namely the European rimland.

The United States was historically and strategically in a totally different situation from that of Great Britain. Unlike the latter, which had been in a state of decline long before World War Two, the United States did not yet have within its historical consciousness the experience of a forced retreat (although following the First World War it had voluntarily withdrawn from European affairs). Moreover, the United States had emerged from the recent war a stronger power militarily and economically, quite the reverse of its British ally. Under such circumstances, Washington was scarcely inclined submissively to write off Eastern Europe as lost and abandon it to Soviet Communism. On the contrary, the United States government's inclination was to hold its position stubbornly, even in the face of several million Red Army soldiers. Of course, as we have noted, the United States was not prepared to challenge those soldiers militarily, and thus the American government, for all of its persistent and indeed obstinate diplomatic efforts, was forced out of the region and ended up with as little influence—in other words, no influence—in Eastern Europe as did Great Britain. But there the difference lay: London, backed to the wall, realistically recognized the futility of resistance in Eastern Europe and voluntarily withdrew; America, the awakened giant (but not an omnipotent one) had to be driven out, and even then it maintained hopes of someday returning.

Along these lines, it is useful to add that the international situation in the postwar period was very dangerous for both Western powers (as well as for the Soviet Union). But it was far more dangerous for Britain than for America. Not long after the Second World War had ended, it became clear that the main confrontation in any new, Soviet-Western war would come along the Lübeck-Trieste line,[22] which was then in the process of solidifying. Though certainly not an inconsequential matter for the United States, Lübeck-Trieste was nonetheless a long distance from the ocean-protected shorelines of the United States, whose national territory had emerged unscathed in the recent war, with the sole exception of Pearl Harbor. The American government, in its relatively safe environment, had few security qualms about playing a policy of open bluster against the Russians. But the British did, because for them the Lübeck-Trieste was not remote. If indeed the Russians were to break through that line, only the narrow English Channel would stand in the way of yet a further Soviet advance. And clearly, the British national experience of the German air attacks and rocket bombs was much too recent for that to be of much consolation, especially when a new European war might be of the nuclear type.[23]

For England, therefore a policy of anti-Soviet bravado, over a non-crucial region, was not only impractical; it was unjustifiably hazardous. Britain wanted to avoid yet another war in Europe, and it certainly did not want to get involved in one over Eastern Europe. According to one political scientist, it was a common belief in British public opinion that "the United States regarded Britain primarily as an unsinkable aircraft carrier and as a more or less expendable site from which to launch an attack on the Soviet Union."[24] Whether such an attitude was a fair appraisal of the strategic outlook of the United States may be debateable. But without question the Americans were mindful that a clash across the Lübeck-Trieste line would hit the British Isles well before it reached the United States; the British Isles were an advance line of defense for America.[25] To serve as such was surely no comfort to the British government, which remained convinced that a policy of restraint toward the sovietization of Eastern Europe was the safest and wisest path to follow. As long as the Russians proceeded no farther than Eastern Europe, Britain did not want to become entangled in what British Minister A. K. Helm once called "America's anti-Russia game."[26] To engage in the anti-Soviet game was, for exhausted Britain, an adventure it could not afford. For powerful America, however, it was a temptation it could not resist.

* * * * *

Did not the United States consume a great deal of diplomatic effort uselessly by its policy of unyielding resistance to the sovietization of Eastern Europe? No doubt it did, for the effort failed. By the same token,

Great Britain's passive role toward Eastern Europe was more realistic, since it did not compete with far more pressing requirements for British security and defense.

Great Britain's realism stemmed from its role as a declining power, for it had learned the need to make strategic retreats and to draw back its defense perimeter to more manageable proportions. It had sustained enough blows to its national ego and strategic position that, by the late 1940s, it could undertake further retreats—though they were now becoming drastic—without too serious a psychological or material shock.

The United States, by contrast, had never experienced anything but successful expansion. And, having emerged from World War II as the victor in all theaters, it had not yet been compelled to determine the limits of its strength. It saw no reason to stage a withdrawal from any region, even a non-crucial one like Eastern Europe. Such an attitude was quite unrealistic, of course, for the United States did not, in fact, have the military capability to challenge the Soviet hold on that area. It was unable to influence the situation in Eastern Europe, yet it remained unwilling to accept the existing situation there. The United States placed itself in a dilemma, which it could not possible resolve on favorable terms. Thus, it sought to prevent any resolution at all, and maintained a state of continuous diplomatic tension over Eastern Europe. Such an uncompromising stand gained the United States nothing, and even interfered with its own priorities. American policy makers had long concluded that the United States should not risk war for the sake of Eastern Europe. Yet, by its stubborn behavior, its refusal to cede Eastern Europe to the Soviet Union, this is precisely what the United States did risk. The legacy to the world had been the threat to peace.

* * * * *

For Stalin, Rákosi, and their followers, postwar developments in Eastern Europe must have been welcome. There had not been a successful advance in world Communism since the Bolshevik revolution. Following that tumult the Soviet Union settled down to the grim task of forced collectivization, much of whose results the colossal destruction of World War II wiped away, along with some 20 million Soviet citizens. For their part the Hungarian Communists had only the debacle of 1919 to look back upon. They then had to endure a quarter century of reaction followed by the brief but bloody fighting of 1944-1945, which devastated regions of Hungary.

But finally events began to take a positive turn. Postwar chaos and the presence of the Red Army created ideal conditions for the Hungarian Communists to take power. Often they moved unobtrusively, almost with stealth, tipping their hand only when they had set the stage to snatch up easily some new political prize; on other occasions they struck openly and violently. Step by step they assumed unrivalled control over virtually every facet of Hungarian politics and government.

In the long run the material consequences of the Soviet era on Eastern Europe have been favorable in many respects. Although this issue cannot be pursued at length here, it may suffice to note that not only Marxist economists but some non-Marxists as well acknowledge the "economic benefits for Eastern Europe in the close association with the Soviet Union." The non-Marxists are quick to argue that such advances were purchased at the price of national independence[27] or individual sacrifice,[28] but significant economic gains are difficult to deny.[29]

In the ideological sphere as well the Communists had much genuine success. In the Hungarian election of 1945, by all accounts a fair one, the left bloc achieved 43 percent of the vote, an impressive minority. Of that the Communists obtained 17 percent and their rural allies, the National Peasants, nine percent. The election two years later, though less scrupulously conducted, produced similar results. Even the 1956 uprising did not indicate a complete repudiation of the Soviet system. True, most Hungarians were vexed at the subservience their country had to show Russia, and the nationality problem persists. Before the uprising, moreover, all politically interested Hungarians, except the most orthodox of Communists, chafed under Rákosi's rigidity. Nonetheless, even writers critical of the Soviet role in postwar Hungary observe that among the industrial workers at least there was little sympathy in 1956 for a restoration of the prewar semifeudal, capitalist system. Most workers wanted to maintain the social and economic gains made since 1945, although many wanted to modify and "liberalize" the political features of the system.[30] But the revolutionary changes brought to Hungary in the postwar period were not imposed upon a completely unwilling or alienated mass.

Of course, as we have seen, such revolutionary changes were not ushered in peacefully. They never are. The Communists preferred to avoid force, but had no qualms about its use when they perceived it necessary. Politicos like Rákosi and Stalin had no reason to be ambivalent. Both men suffered hardship at the hands of the old regimes, especially Rákosi who endured many years of harsh imprisonment. They had learned by experience alone that the exercise of political power involves the use of force, and they would not have considered it unreasonable to employ strong-arm methods against their own enemies. Their final justification for using force was that in their hands, it had a higher morality since it was intended to serve a progressive cause—the achievement of working-class rule in Hungary and simultaneously the protection of the Soviet Union, the first socialist state. In fact the only immorality would have been to shrink from violent means when they were necessary to attain power.

It cannot be doubted that the Soviet and Hungarian Communist leaders earnestly wanted to take control of Hungary and transform it into a workers' state. This, Rákosi stated quite candidly in 1952, was their "final aim."[31] American conservatives did not simply misread Soviet intentions, as much of liberal revisionist historiography suggests. The Communists actively sought to extend their sphere of control to Eastern Europe. That relentless drive placed them at loggerheads with the ruling, capitalist forces of the West, who gave up Eastern Europe only with the utmost unwillingness.

Thus, it may be said that the Communists also posed a threat to world peace. True enough, the pro-Soviet elements could have accepted peace, but it would have been peace at the price of subjection to the Western powers, which regarded collectivism with repugnance. It was better to make a principled stand in defense of social revolution, the Communists reasoned, and risk the peace than to cave in to the forces of Western reaction and have to suffer the restoration of the old regimes once again. As it turned out, the worldwide correlation of forces in the postwar period greatly favored East over West, and the East European Communists won this battle on both fronts: they kept the peace and transformed Hungary.

NOTES

Key to abbreviations

C	Central Department, Foreign Office
CAB	Cabinet Office
C.M.	Cabinet conclusions
C.P.	Cabinet memoranda
D/S	Department of State
FO	Foreign Office
FRUS	*Foreign Relations of the United States: Diplomatic Papers* (before 1932, *Papers Relating to the Foreign Relations of the United States*)
JCS	Joint Chiefs of Staff
NARS	National Archives and Records Service, Washington, D.C.
OIR	Office of Intelligence Research, Department of State
OSS	Office of Strategic Services
PPS	Policy Planning Staff, Department of State
PRO	Public Record Office, Kew, England
R	Southern Department, Foreign Office
R & A	Research and Analysis
RG	Record Group
S/S	Secretary of State
UR	Supply and Relief Department, Foreign Office
UR	Supply and Relief Department, Foreign Office

Notes to Chapter I

1. For a recent study of American relations with Turkey, concentrating on the twentieth century, see Harry N. Howard, *Turkey, the Straits, and U.S. Policy* (Baltimore, 1974). On the Eastern Question in general, see, for example M. S. Anderson, *The Eastern Quetion, 1774-1923* (New York, 1966).

2. For the pre-1918 history of Hungary, see C. A. Macartney, *Hungary: A Short History* (Edinburgh, 1962) and for a brief discussion, Stephen D. Kertesz, *Diplomacy in a Whirlpool: Hungary between Nazi Germany and Soviet Russia* (Notre Dame, 1953), pp. 3-10.

3. Rudolf L. Tölkés, *Béla Kun and the Hungarian Soviet Republic: The Origins and Role of the Communist Party of Hungary in the Revolutions of 1918-1919* (New York, 1967); Sándor Szilassy, *Revolutionary Hungary, 1918-1921* (Astor Park, Fla., 1971); Iván Völges, ed., *Hungary in Revolution, 1918-19: Nine Essays* (Lincoln, Neb., 1971).

4. For an in-depth analysis of Trianon, see C. A. Macartney, *Hungary and Her Successors: The Treaty of Trianon and Its Consequences* (London, 1937).

5. For the United States attitude at the Conference to Hungarian claims, see Robert H. Ferrell, "The United States and East Central Europe before 1941," in *The Fate of East Central Europe: Hopes and Failures of American Foreign Policy,* ed. Stephen D. Kertesz (Notre Dame, 1956), p. 43; for British reactions, C. A. Macartney, *A History of Hungary, 1929-1945,* 2 vols. (New York, 1956-57), I, 82; and for both nations, Francis Deák, *Hungary at the Paris Peace Conference: The Diplomatic History of the Treaty of Trianon* (New York, 1942), passim. Deák also provides a long discussion of the complex French role at the Conference relative to Hungary (pp. 253 ff.).

6. But until stability returned, they were deeply concerned with Hungary and Central Europe generally. The American and British delegations at the Paris Peace Conference participated in the frequent discussions of the Central European upheavals of 1919. And both nations, directly involved in East European affairs due to their participation in the Russian Civil War, maintained close contact with the situation throughout 1920 via their diplomatic offices. See *FRUS: The Paris Peace Conference, 1919,* vols. IV, VII, VIII, IX, XI, and XII, passim; *FRUS, 1918:*

Russia, 3 vols; *FRUS, 1919: Russia; FRUS, 1920,* III, 436 ff.; and *FRUS: The Lansing Papers, 1914-1920,* II, 343 ff. Also Great Britain, Foreign Office, *Documents on British Foreign Policy, 1919-1939,* ed. E. L. Woodward and Rohan Butler (London, 1947 ff.), first series, vols. I and II, passim, and especially VI, chap. 1, and XII, chap. 2.

7.   For American diplomatic correspondence on matters of trade and finance with Hungary in the interwar period, see *FRUS, 1924,* II, 325-32; *FRUS, 1925,* II, 341-57; and *FRUS, 1931,* II, 593-96.

8.   Macartney, *History of Hungary,* I, 42-44.

9.   Ibid., 63 and 65.

10.   On the Arrow Cross and other Right Radical movements, see Nicholas M. Nagy-Talavera, *The Green Shirts and the Others: A History of Fascism in Hungary and Rumania* (Stanford, 1970).

11.   For a discussion of Hungarian politics in the 1930s, see Macartney, *History of Hungary,* I, 114 ff., and Kertesz, *Diplomacy in a Whirlpool,* pp. 27-47.

12.   But this decision was a disappointment to Churchill, who had repeatedly argued—and continued to do so even into 1944—for an Anglo-American invasion of the Balkans. See Elisabeth Barker, *British Polcy in South-East Europe in the Second World War* (London, 1976), pp. 101-17, passim; John A. Lukacs, *The Great Powers and Eastern Europe* (New York, 1953), pp. 678-81 and passim; and Trumbull Higgins, *Winston Churchill and the Second Front, 1940-1943* (New York, 1957). On the other hand, there is not universal agreement that the British Prime Minister favored a Balkan move; see Richard M. Leighton, "OVERLORD Revisited: An Interpretation of American Strategy in the European War, 1942-1944," *American Historical Review* 68:4 (1963), 919-37.

13.   On Hungarian wartime diplomacy, see Mario D. Fenyo, *Hitler, Horthy, and Hungary: German-American Relations, 1941-1944* (New Haven, 1972). For the American-Hungarian connection, see Paul Rupprecht, "The Image of Hungary's International Position in American Foreign Policy-Making, 1937-1947," (Ph.D. dissertation, University of Minnesota, 1967), which, it should be noted, lacks useful documentation for the years after 1944. Nandor A. F. Dreisziger, *Hungary's Way to World War II* (Toronto, 1968) concentrates on the 1930s and the early war years, and John Flournoy Montgomery, *Hungary: The Unwilling Satellite* (New York, 1947), carries the story to the end of the war. See

also Macartney, *History of Hungary,* II, 3 ff., and Kertesz, *Diplomacy in a Whirlpool,* 48-85.

14. Miklós Molnár, *A Short History of the Hungarian Communist Party* (Boulder, Col., 1978), pp. 24-33.

15. *Current Biography, 1949: New York Times,* 7 January 1947, 31 December 1948, 6 February 1971.

16. Bennett Kovrig, *Communism in Hungary: From Kun to Kádár* (Stanford, 1979), pp. 154 ff.

17. William O. McCagg, Jr., *Stalin Embattled, 1943-1948* (Detroit, 1978), passim.

18. Macartney, *History of Hungary,* I and II, passim.

19. Ibid., I, pp. 12, 23-27, 41-46; C. A. Macartney and A. W. Palmer, *Independent Eastern Europe: A History* (London, 1962), pp. 208-9; George Schopflin, "Hungary," in *Communist Power in Europe, 1944-1949,* ed. Martin McCauley (New York, 1977), pp. 95-110.

20. Ference Nagy, *The Struggle behind the Iron Curtain,* trans. Stephen K. Swift (New York, 1948), pp. 3-22.

21. On the formation of the Debrecen goverment, and later events, see H. F. Arthur Schoenfeld, "Soviet Imperialism in Hungary," *Foreign Affairs* 26:3 (1948), 554-67; Stephen D. Kertesz, "The Methods of Communist Conquest: Hungary, 1944-1947," *World Politics* 3:1 (1950), 20-54; Sydney Lowery's article in *Survey of International Affairs, 1939-1946,* VI (London, 1955), 317-32; Hugh Seton-Watson, *The East European Revolution,* 3rd ed. (New York, 1956), pp. 190-93.

22. Matthews memorandum to S/S, 28 December 1944, Matthews-Hickerson Files, RG 59, NARS. For a similar analysis (perhaps the foundation for Matthews' view), see OSS, R & A Report No. 2797, "The Soviet Sponsored Hungarian Government," 28 December 1944, NARS.

23. Michael S. Williams, Acting First Secretary, minute, 28 December 1944, FO 371/39267 [C 18010/10/21]; see also FO to Madrid, No. 1416, 31 December 1944, FO 371/39267 [C 18107/10/21], PRO.

24. *FRUS, 1944,* III, especially 943-44, 952-53, 965-66, and 973-75, and *FRUS: The Conferences at Malta and Yalta, 1945* [hereafter cited as *Yalta*], pp. 238-40 and 513-14. Williams minute, 29 December 1944; FO to Moscow, 31 December 1944, FO 371/ 39256 [C 18564/10/21]; Sir John Balfour, chargé d'affaires in Moscow, to FO, 31 December 1944, FO 371/39256 [C 18564/10/21]; Balfour to FO, 15 January 1945; Williams

minute, 17 January 1945, FO 371/48474 [R 1170/82/21]; unsigned
memorandum to the War Cabinet, 9 January 1945, FO 371/48474 [R
223/82/21]; unsigned FO memorandum, 17 January 1945, FO 371/
48474 [R 1350/82/21], PRO.

25.   *FRUS, 1945,* IV, 800-2.

26.   FO to Moscow, 19 November 1944, FO 371/39256 [C 15963/
10/21]. When the Russians proved not to be forthcoming on the British
demand, the British insisted as a minimum that the price level be explicitly stipulated; on this pont the Russians acquiesced. FO to Washington, 5
January 1945, FO 371/48474 [R 212/82/21]; unsigned FO memorandum,
FO 371/48474 [R 1350/82/21], PRO.

27.   *FRUS, 1944,* III, 908-9.

28.   Ibid., 922.

29.   Ward minute, 10 November 1944, FO 371/39255 [C 15321/10/
21], PRO.

30.   Chaplin minute. 10 November 1944, ibid.; see also FO to Moscow,
19 November 1944, FO 371/39256 [C 15963/10/21], PRO.

31.   The text of the armistice is in United States, Department of State,
United States Statutes at Large, 1945, 59 (pt. 2), 1304.

Notes to Chapter II

1.   H. C. Allen, *Great Britain and the United States: A History of
Anglo-American Relations (1783-1952)* (New York, 1955), p. 870.

2.   For the American and British views on the question of dividing
Southeastern Europe, see Lynn Etheridge Davis, *The Cold War Begins:
Soviet-American Conflict over Eastern Europe* (Princeton, 1974), pp.
140-71, and Sir Llewellyn Woodward, *British Foreign Policy in the Second
World War,* 5 vols. (London, 1970-76), III, 115-23 and 146-53. Churchill
described his meeting with Stalin in *The Second World War,* 6 vols. (Boston 1945-53), vol. VI: *Triumph and Tragedy,* pp. 227-28. For Eden's
views on Eastern Europe, see, besides Woodward, *The Reckoning: The
Memoirs of Anthony Eden, Earl of Avon* (Boston, 1965), pp. 370-71. A
useful source on the American position is the Yalta Briefing Book Paper,
entitled "American Policy toward Spheres of Influence," *FRUS: Yalta,*
pp. 103-6; see also the Policy Committee report of 25 October 1944, num-
bered PC-8 (Revised), Matthews-Hickerson Files, RG 59, NARS.

3.   Adam B. Ulman, *Expansion and Coexistence: Soviet Foreign Policy, 1917-73,* 2nd ed. (New York, 1974), pp. 364-65.

4.   Charles E. Bohlen, *The Transformation of American Foreign Policy* (New York, 1969), p. 33.

5.   Albert Resis, "The Churchill-Stalin Secret 'Percentages' Agreement on the Balkans, Moscow, October 1944," *American Historical Review* 83:2 (1978), 368-87.

6.   William Taubman, *Stalin's American Policy: From Entente to Detente to Cold War* (New York, 1982), p. 91.

7.   This claim is sometimes made relative to other countries. But, according to Elisabeth Baker, *British Policy in South-East Europein the Second World War,* pp. 146-47, "it is wrong to think" that Churchill abandoned any country in Southeastern Europe with the percentages proposal. She notes that "the Red Army was already in military control" of much of the area before he concluded the agreement, "which merely formalised an already existing situation."

8.   Vojtech Mastny, *Russia's Road to the Cold War: Diplomacy, Warfare, and the Politics of Communism, 1941-1945* (New York, 1979), p. 211.

9.   The declaration is in *FRUS: Yalta,* pp. 971-73.

10.   Athan G. Theoharis, *The Yalta Myths: An Issue in U.S. Politics, 1945-1955* (Columbia, Mo., 1970).

11.   Bohlen letter to Samuel I. Rosenman, 11 July 1949, Bohlen Records, RG 59, NARS. For further defenses by Bohlen against this claim, see his *The Transformation of American Foreign Policy,* p. 46, and *Witness to History, 1929-1969* (New York, 1970), pp. 350-52.

12.   Edward R. Stettinius, *Roosevelt and the Russians: The Yalta Conference* (Garden City, N.Y., 1949), pp. 295, 303-4, 306.

13.   Sargent memorandum, 13 March 1945, FO 371/48219 [R 5063/5063/67]; for a minute by Sargent along similar lines, written on 6 March 1945, see FO 371/48217 [R 3459/3168/67], PRO.

14.   *FRUS, 1945.* V, 822-24. For a virtually identical view by Gen. John Deane, head of the United States Military Mission in Moscow, who discussed Soviet-American relations with Harriman, and between whom (Harriman states) there was agreement, see "Revision of Policy with Relation to Russia," JCS 1313, 16 April 1945, especially p. 3, RG 218, NARS.

15.   Oral History Interview with H. Freeman Matthews by Richard D. McKinzie, Harry S Truman Library, 7 June 1973, Washington, D.C., pp. 29-32.

16.   George F. Kennan, *Memoirs, 1925-1967* (Boston, 1967), p. 427.

17.   Kennan to Bohlen, 26 January 1945, Bohlen records, RG 59, NARS.

18.   *FRUS, 1945*, V, especially 859-60.

19.   Ministry of Foreign Affairs of the U.S.S.R., *Correspondence between the Chairman of the Council of Ministers of the U.S.S.R. and the Presidents of the U.S.A. and the Prime Ministers of Great Britain during the Great Patriotic War of 1941-1945*, 2 vols. (Moscow, 1957), I, 361, and II, 239. One can only speculate as to why Stalin wanted to delay Western recognition of Hungary, but it seems fair to assume that he did not want to strengthen its government—which at the time was not firmly in Soviet hands—by recognition from the West.

20.   *FRUS: The Conference of Berlin (The Potsdam Conference)*, 1945 [hereafter cited as *Potsdam*], I, 357-59.

21.   Stewart minute, 21 June 1945, FO 371/48476 [R 10492/82/21]; see also his minute of 25 July 1945, FO 371/48464 [R 12081/26/21], PRO.

22.   On this, see Woodward, *British Foreign Policy*, III, 587-95, and V, 352-53. Also *FRUS: Potsdam*, I, 393-94 and 409-10.

23.   *FRUS: Potsdam*, II, 643-44.

24.   On Soviet efforts to split the British and Americans, see McCagg, *Stalin Embattled*, passim.

25.   *FRUS: Potsdam*, II, 698 and 1044.

26.   Ibid., 150-55. For Potsdam Conference discussions on Balkan problems—as well as for later discussions during the September Council of Foreign Ministers session and the December Conference of Foreign Ministers—see also the treatment by Davis, *Cold War Begins*, pp. 288-96, 314-19, and 327-31.

27.   *FRUS: Potsdam*, II, 363.

28.   Ibid.

29.   Ibid., 1509-10.

30.   See also Davis, *Cold War Begins*, pp. 296-97.

31.   James F. Byrnes, *Speaking Frankly* (New York, 1947), p. 79.

32.   *Hansard's Parliamentary Debates* (Commons), 5th series, 313 (20 August 1945), 291.

33.   *FRUS: Potsdam,* I, 212-18, and II, 1500-1.

34.   *FRUS, 1945,* II, 147-50.

35.   Ibid., 182-85.

36.   Ibid., 219-22, 263-67, and 311-12.

37.   William G. Hayter, Acting Counsellor, minute, 12 September 1945, FO 371/48224 [R 15122/15122/67], PRO. As at Potsdam, the British and Americans chose not to attack the Hungarian government.

38.   *FRUS, 1945,* II, 194-202, 243-47, 288-98, and 300-10.

39.   *FRUS, 1945,* IV, 886-87; also ibid., 867 ff.

40.   Ibid., 313-15 and 331-33. The Big Five, largely a figment of Roosevelt's imagination, never really functioned. China rarely took part in Council of Foreign Ministers meetings, and Molotov ignored it.

41.   For Byrnes' account of the London session of the Council of Foreign Ministers, see his *Speaking Frankly,* pp. 91-109.

42.   Gascoigne despatch to Bevin, No. 362, 20 September 1945; Stewart minute, 8 October 1945, FO 371/48469 [R 170008/26/21]; Hayter minute, 24 October 1945, FO 371/48470 [R 18149/26/21]; Williams minute, 26 October 1945, ibid. [R 18155/26/21]; Gascoigne to FO, No. 518, 26 October 1945, ibid. [R 18229/26/21]; minutes by Stewart and Williams, 8 November 1945, FO 371/48471 [R 18894/26/21], PRO.

43.   This synthesis is drawn from the sizable body of diplomatic correspondence accumulated as the British and Americans closely monitored the elections situation. On the British side, see especially Gascoigne despatch to Churchill, No. 166, 19 July 1945, FO 371/48464 [R 12156/26/21]; FO to Budapest, No. 305, 23 August 1945, FO 371/48465 [R 14053/26/21]; Gascoigne despatch to Bevin, No. 357, 25 September 1945; Stewart minute, 10 October 1945, FO 371/48468 [R 16960/26/21]; minutes by Stewart and Hayter, 9 October 1945, FO 371/48469 [R 17137/26/21]; Gascoigne to FO, No. 475, 17 October 1945; Hayter minute, 21 October 1945, ibid. [R 17718/26/21]; Gascoigne despatch to Bevin, No. 441, 8 November 1945; Stewart minute, 10 November 1945, FO 371/48471 [R 18924/26/21]; Gascoigne to FO, No. 598, 15 November 1945; minutes by Williams and Sargent, 16 November 1945, FO 371/48471 [R 19368/26/21], PRO. For American correspondence, see *FRUS,*

1945, IV, 851 ff., passim; Schoenfeld to S/S, No. 467, 22 August 1945, 864.00/8-2245; No. 780, 17 October 1945, 864.00/10-1745; No. 786, 18 October 1945, 864.00/10-1845; No. 792, 19 October 1945, 864.00/ 10-1945; No. 900, 13 November 1945, 868.00/11-1345, RG 59, NARS.

44.   John M. Addis, Second Secretary, minute, 15 August 1945, FO 371/48465 [R 13208/26/21]; H. M. Hedley minute, 19 October 1945, FO 371/48467 [R 151313/26/21], PRO.

45.   Addis minute, 10 September 1945, FO 371/48466 [R 14673/ 26/21], PRO.

46.   Steward minute, 5 October 1945, FO 371/48468 [R 16815/26/ 21]; Hayter minute, 21 October 1945, FO 371/48470 [R 17863/26/21], PRO.

47.   *FRUS, 1945,* IV, 891-92; Schoenfeld to S/S, No. 451, 20 August 1945, 864.00/8-2045; No. 467, 22 August 1945, 864.00/8-2245; No. 780, 17 October, 1945, 864.00/10-1745; No. 786, 18 October 1945, 864.00/ 10-1845, RG 59, NARS.

48.   *FRUS, 1945,* IV, 852-53.

49.   Ibid., 854, 863-64, 886-67, and 869-70.

50.   *FRUS, 1945,* II, 581-99, passim. See also Sir John Wheeler-Bennett and Anthony Nicholas, *The Semblance of Peace: The Political Settlement after the Second World War* (London, 1972), pp. 424-26.

51.   The Moscow decision on peace treaty procedure is explained in chapter 5, where the Hungarian peace treaty is discussed. In the meantime, the foreign ministers' agreement on procedure was published as article 1 of the conference communique, *FRUS, 1945,* II, 815-17.

52.   Stewart minute, 26 November 1945, and Williams minute, 27 November 1945, FO 371/48220 [R 19813/5063/67], as well as two memoranda prepared in the Southern Department, dated 12 December 1945, FO 371/48220 [R21263/5063/67], PRO.

53.   British delegation in Moscow to FO, No. 49 WORTHY, 21 December 1945, FO 371/48220 [R 21284/5063/67]; No. 50 WORTHY, 22 December 1945, A. Russell minute, 24 December 1945, FO 371/48220 [R 21392/5063/67], PRO.

54.   *FRUS, 1945,* II, 728-34, and Davis, *Cold War Begins,* pp. 328-29.

55.   *FRUS, 1945,* II, 821-22.

Notes to Chapter III

1.   On the British labor movement, see Henry Pelling, *The British Communist Party: A Historical Profile* (New York, 1958); *The Origins of the Labour Party, 1880-1900,* 2nd ed. (Oxford, 1965); *A Short History of the Labour Party,* 4th ed. (London, 1972); G. D. H. Cole, *A Short History of the British Working Class Movement, 1789-1947,* new ed. (London, 1947); B. C. Roberts, *The Trades Union Congress, 1868-1921* (Cambridge, Mass., 1958); Carl F. Brand, *The British Labour Party: A Short History,* rev. ed. (Stanford, 1974).

2.   The present concern is, of course, solely foreign affairs. The question concerning domestic affairs is whether Labour's nationalization program involved a revolutionary reorganization of British industry. See Earnest Watkins, *The Cautious Revolution: Britain Today and Tomorrow* (New York, 1950); Martin Harrison, *Trade Unions and the Labour Party since 1945* (Detroit, 1960); William A. Robson, *Nationalized Industries and Public Ownership* (Toronto, 1960).

3.   Michael R. Gordon, *Conflict and Concensus in Labour's Foreign Policy, 1914-1965* (Stanford, 1969), pp. 1-44 and 188-52.

4.   M. A. Fitzsimons, *The Foreign Policy of the British Labour Government, 1945-1951* (Notre Dame, 1953), pp. 177-80.

5.   S. Northedge, *British Foreign Policy: The Process of Readjustment* (London, 1962), pp. 31-32.

6.   Elaine Windrich, *British Labour's Foreign Policy* (Stanford, 1952), pp. 258-259.

7.   Anthony Eden, *Full Circle* (Boston, 1960), pp. 5-6.

8.   Two valuable studies on the left-wing rebellion are Eugene J. Meehan, *The British Left Wing and Foreign Policy: A Study of the Influence of Ideology* (New Brunswick, 1960); Gordon, *Conflict and Concensus.* Less useful is Robert J. Jackson, *Rebles and Whips: An Analysis of Dissension, Discipline and Cohesion in British Political Parties* (London and New York, 1968).

9.   *Keep Left* (London, 1947), especially pp. 34-38. See also Meehan, *British Left Wing and Foreign Policy,* pp. 109-12.

10.   *Cards on the Table: An Interpretation of Labour's Foreign Policy* (London, 1947). See also Meehan, *British Left Wing and Foreign Policy,* p. 112; Gordon, *Conflict and Concensus,* pp. 139-40.

11.   See Gordon, *Conflict and Concensus*, pp. 222 ff.

12.   *Report of the 45th Annual Conference, 1946*, pp. 148-49; *Report of the 46th Annual Conference, 1947*, pp. 160-82; *Report of the 47th Annual Conference, 1948*, 184-200.

13.   *FRUS, Potsdam*, II, 155.

14.   J. Samuel Walker, *Henry A. Wallace and American Foreign Policy* (Westport, Conn., 1976), pp. 3, 136-37, 151-53; Richard J. Walton, *Henry Wallace, Harry Truman, and the Cold War* (New York, 1976), pp. 70-80, 87, 91-93, 103-5; Daniel Yergin, *Shattered Peace: The Origins of the Cold War and the National Security State* (Boston, 1978), pp. 247-48.

15.   John Hollister Hedley, *Harry S. Truman: The "Little" Man from Missouri* (Woodbury, N.Y., 1979), p. 67.

16.   Bert Cochran, *Harry Truman and the Crisis Presidency* (New York, 1973), pp. 141-42, 398-99; Daniel Yergin, *Shattered Peace* (Boston, 1978), pp. 82-83. Truman, *Year of Decisions* (Garden City, N.Y., 1955), pp. 79-82, 412; *FRUS, 1945*, V, 256-58.

17.   George Curry, *James F. Byrnes*, v. 14 of *The American Secretaries of State and Their Diplomacy*, advisory ed. Samuel Flagg Bemis (New York, 1965), pp. 87-89, 96-104; Robert J. Donovan, *Conflict and Crisis: The Presidency of Harry S Truman, 1945-1948* (New York, 1977), pp. 13-18; Patricia Dawson Ward, *The Threat of Peace: James F. Byrnes and the Council of Foreign Ministers, 1945-1946* (Kent, Ohio, 1979), p. 2.

18.   Bohlen, *Witness to History*, p. 256.

19.   Charles Mee, Jr., *Meeting at Potsdam* (New York, 1975), p. 308.

20.   Joyce and Gabriel Kolko, *The Limits of Power: The World and United States Foreign Policy, 1945-1954* (New York, 1972), p. 42.

21.   Harold F. Gosnell, *Truman's Crises: A Political Biography of Harry S. Truman* (Westport, Conn., 1980), p. 309; Robert L. Messer, *The End of an Alliance: James F. Byrnes, Roosevelt, Truman, and the Origins of the Cold War* (Chapel Hill, 1982), pp. 10, 187-88, passim.

22.   James F. Byrnes, *Speaking Frankly*, p. 279.

23.   Gar Alperovitz, *Atomic Diplomacy: Hiroshima and Potsdam: The Use of the Atomic Bomb and the American Confrontation with Soviet Power* (New York, 1965), pp. 225-26.

24.   Donovan, *Conflict and Crisis*, pp. 161-62.

25.   Messer, *End of an Alliance*, pp. 156 ff. See also Jonathan Daniels, *The Man of Independence* (Philadelphia, 1950), pp. 309-11; Cochran, *Harry*

Truman, pp. 178-80; Donovan, *Conflict and Crisis,* pp. 159-61; Ward, *Threat of Peace,* pp. 72-77.

26.   Ward, *Threat of Peace,* p. 175; Messer, *End of an Alliance,* pp. 183, 188-94.

27.   See below, chapter 5.

28.   Kolko and Kolko, *Limits of Power,* pp. 178-79, 400-1.

29.   Lawrence S. Wittner, *Cold War America: From Hiroshima to Watergate,* expanded ed. (New York, 1978), pp. 113-15, 130-34.

30.   James Aronson, *The Press and the Cold War* (Indianapolis, 1970), pp. 31 ff.

31.   *Detroit Times,* 5 November 1948.

32.   *New York Times,* 19 April 1951.

33.   See Phelps H. Adams, correspondent for *The Sun* (Washington), letter to Vandenberg, 11 January 1945; Bernard H. Baruch letter to Vandenberg, 16 January 1945, Vandenberg scrapbooks, University of Michigan.

34.   Marshall letter to Vandenberg, 30 July 1947, ibid.

35.   Justus D. Doenecke, *Not to the Swift: The Old Isolationists in the Cold War Era* (Lewisburg, 1979), pp. 73 ff.

36.   Terry H. Anderson, *The United States, Great Britain, and the Cold War, 1944-1947* (Columbia, Mo., 1981), pp. 118 ff.

37.   H. C. Allen, *Great Britain and the United States: A History of Anglo-American Relations (1783-1952),* (New York, 1955), pp. 887, 910-915; H. G.Nicholas, *The United States and Britain* (Chicago, 1975), p. 113; Anderson, *United States, Great Britain, and the Cold War,* pp. 63, 130-31; Robert M. Hathaway, *Ambiguous Partnership: Britain and America, 1944-1947* (New York, 1981), pp. 234-38.

38.   *FRUS, Potsdam,* I, 253-66.

39.   Nicholas, *United States and Britain,* pp. 115-47; Hathaway, *Ambiguous Partnership,* pp. 134-39.

40.   Geir Lundestad, *The American Non-Policy towards Eastern Europe, 1943-1947: Universalism in an Area Not of Essential Interest to the United States* (Tromsö, 1978), p. 41 and passim.

Notes to Chapter IV

1.   For a comprehensive and detailed study of postwar economic development in Eastern Europe, see Nicholas Spulber, *The Economics of*

Communist Eastern Europe (New York, 1957); a more general work, and chiefly concerned with questions of trade, is Margaret Dewar, *Soviet Trade with Eastern Europe, 1945-1949* (London, 1951).

2. Two contemporary, official analyses of Soviet economic policy in Hungary are a British Foreign Office memorandum, dated 31 May 1947, FO 371/67196 [R 16454/85/21], PRO, and a longer, more detailed, and documented study by the State Department, OIR Report No. 4721.1 (PV), 8 September 1948, "Soviet Economic Penetration of Hungary, Rumania, and Bulgaria: I. Hungary: Preliminary Vesrsion," NARS, which is particularly useful. Also consult Spulber, *Economics of Communist Eastern Europe,* pp. 109-19, 159-60, and 185-89; Dewar, *Soviet Trade with Eastern Europe.*

3. The armistice provisions concerning war booty and requisitions are in articles 7 and 11, in *United States Statutes at Large.*

4. An example of the Hungarian hyperinflation comes from two Associated Press despatches in the *New York Times* of 16 and 26 June 1946. At the earlier date, when the inflation was already well-advanced, the *Times* reported that the Hungarian government had issued a one trillion pengoe (the Hungarian currency) note, worth about 35 U.S. cents. Ten days later, Hungary issued a 100 trillion pengoe note, by then worth only 20 cents—"enough for a cup of coffee and a small piece of cake in a Budapest restaurant." On the inflation, also see Spulber, *Economics of Communist Eastern Europe,* pp. 109-12.

The reparation provisions are found in article 12 of the armistice.

5. See especially OIR Report, "Soviet Economic Penetration," pp. 7-11 (above, n. 2).

6. Maurice Pearton, *Oil and the Romanian State* (Oxford, 1971), pp. 295-301. *FRUS: Potsdam,* I, 420-23 and 428-32; *FRUS, 1945,* IV, 921-22.

7. *FRUS, 1945,* IV, 814-16; D/S to Budapest, No. 159, 4 July 1945, 864.6363/7-445, RG 59, NARS.

8. *FRUS: Potsdam,* II, 130 and 234-37.

9. Ibid., 547-48, 743-46, and 1496-98.

10. *FRUS, 1945,* V, 6655 ff.

11. *FRUS: Potsdam,* II, 566-69, 579-80, and 1506.

12. OIR Report, "Soviet Economic Penetration," pp. 12-23, and Foreign Office memorandum, 31 May 1947, pp. 3-4 (see above n. 2)..

13. On the joint companies, see OIR Report, "Soviet Economic Pene-tration," especially pp. 24-27 (above, n. 2), and Spulber, *Economics of Communist Eastern Europe,* pp. 182-89; also *Department of State Bul-letin* 15:378 (1946), 394-98.

14. For the transcription of a cabinet debate on the prospective agreement, see Kertesz, *Diplomacy in a Whirlpool,* pp. 255-60.

15. *FRUS, 1945,* IV, 879-83.

16. Ibid., 888-89; memorandum of conversation, 12 February 1946, 661.6431/2-1246, RG 59, NARS.

17. *FRUS, 1945,* IV, 896-97.

18. Ibid., 901-2.

19. Ibid., 910.

20. *FRUS, 1946,* VI, 265-67 and 285-87. *Department of State Bul-letin* 15:370 (1946), 229-32; 15:379 (1946), 263-65; and 15:384 (1946), 638-39.

21. Stewart minute, 5 September 1945, FO 371/48227 [R 15210/1622/67], PRO.

22. Foreign Office memorandum on East-West trade, 11 August 1948, FO 371/71923 [UR 4225/1841/98], PRO.

23. Coulson minute, 6 November 1945, FO 371/48218 [R 18468/4698/67], PRO.

24. Sargent minute, 6 September 1945, FO 371/48227 [R 15210/1622/67], PRO.

25. Williams minute, 2 November 1945, FO 371/48218 [R 18468/4698/67], PRO.

26. Hayter minute, 25 January 1946, FO 371/59012 [R 1026/325/21]; see also his minute, 2 November 1945, FO 371/48218 [R 18468/4698/67], PRO.

27. Hayter minute, 15 October 1945; Frank K. Roberts, ambassador in Moscow, letter to Vyshinski, 17 October 1945, FO 371/48516 [R 17521/9311/21], PRO.

28. Stewart minute, 31 October 1945, FO 371/48218 [R 18468/4698/67], PRO.

29. Williams minute, 24 January 1946; Hayter minute, 25 January 1946; Sargent minute, 26 January 1946, FO 371/59012 [R 1026/325/21], PRO.

30. Waldemar J. Gallman, chargé d'affaires in London, letter to Chris-topher F. A. Warner, assistant under-secretary of state, 4 March 1946, FO 371/58969 [R 3522/73/21], PRO.

31.   Coulson minute, 9 March 1946, ibid.

32.   Russell minute, 8 March 1946; Williams minute, 8 March 1946; Hayter minute, 8 March 1946; FO to Moscow, No. 735, 9 March 1946; Roberts letter to Molotov, 11 March 1946, ibid.

33.   *FRUS, 1946,* VI, 308-16. Hayter to Gascoigne, No. 451, 6 May 1946, FO 371/59023 [R 6475/1266/21]; FO to Budapest, No. 494, 28 May 1946, FO 371/59023 [R 7904/1266/21], PRO.

34.   Draft minutes of interagency meeting, 25 November 1945, FO 371/48502 [R 20811/4634/21], PRO.

35.   Hall-Patch minute, 21 December 1945, FO 371/48502 [R 21522/4634/21], PRO.

36.   Williams minutes, 18 and 22 December 1945; Hall-Patch minute, 21 December 1945; A. Lincoln minute, 21 December 1945; FO to British delegation in Moscow, No. 70 NEPHEW, 22 December 1945, ibid.

37.   Draft minutes, 25 November 1945 (see above, n. 34).

38.   *FRUS, 1945,* IV, 914-15.

39.   *FRUS, 1945,* IV, 917-20; *FRUS, 1946,* VI, 256-57, 258-60, 293-94.

40.   Ibid., 250-51, 263-64, 287-89, 315-16; *FRUS, 1947,* IV, 268-69. *Department of State Bulletin* 14:365 (1946), 1120; 15:384 (1946), 638; 16:399 (1947), 341-42.

41.   *FRUS, 1946,* VI, 347-50.

Notes to Chapter V

1.   *FRUS, 1945,* II, 815-17.

2.   *New York Times,* 18, 23 April 1946.

3.   C. R. Attlee, *As It Happened* (New York, 1954), pp. 237-38.

4.   *Times* (London), 20, 29 July 1946.

5.   Byrnes, *Speaking Frankly,* pp. 150-54.

6.   *Survey of International Affairs, 1939-1946* (London, 1955), VI, 339-42.

7.   Articles 2, 3, 4, 6, 12, and 22 of the Hungarian treaty; see also *Survey, 1939-1946,* VI, 243-44. For the text of the treaty, see United States, Department of State, *United States Statutes at Large,* LXI, 2109-43.

8.   *FRUS, 1946,* IV, 76-77, 107, 401, 402, and 464.

9.   For a discussion of the most-favored-nation clause, and its usual exceptions, see Richard Carlton Snyder, *The Most-Favored-Nation Clause: An Analysis With Particular Reference to Recent Treaty Practice and Tariffs* (New York, 1948), pp. 156-85 and the concluding chapter, pp. 211-33. Note that the author did not consider the present treaties in his study.

10.   *FRUS, 1946,* IV, 76-77, 107, and 465-66; also *FRUS, 1946,* II, 637-39.

11.   *FRUS, 1946,* III, 10-15 and 213-15.

12.   FO memorandum, 19 June 1946, prepared for the Hungarian Prime Minister's visit to London that month, FO 371/59024 [R 9158/1266/21], PRO. *FRUS, 1946,* VI, 361-73; see also the remarks of Walter Bedell Smith, U.S. ambassador in Moscow, *Department of State Bulletin* 15:386 (1946), 744.

13.   *FRUS, 1946,* III, 375-76.

14.   Ibid., VI, 272-73.

15.   Ibid., IV, 852-53.

16.   Ibid., III, 375-76.

17.   FO memorandum, 19 June 1946, FO 371/59024 [R 9158/1266/21], PRO.

18.   Williams minute, 31 May 1946, FO 371/59024 [R 8085/1266/21]; Frderick A. Warner minute, 20 June 1946; Hayter minute, 20 June 1946, FO 371/59024 [R 8923/1266/21], PRO.

19.   FO to Washington, No. 5640, 7 June 1946, FO 371/59024 [R 8085/1266/21]; also Lord Inverchapel, ambassador in Washington, to FO, No. 3960, 15 June 1946, FO 371/59024 [R 8922/1266/21], PRO.

20.   Some of these points are in William Hardy McNeill, *America, Britain, and Russia: Their Cooperation and Conflict, 1941-1946* (London, 1953, as a volume of *Survey of International Affairs, 1939-1946;* reprint ed., New York, 1970), pp. 722-23.

21.   In accordance with the Anglo-American policy of relaxing Allied military supervision of Italy, the word "control" was dropped on 25 October 1944 from the name of the Allied Control Commission.

22.   On the establishment of the left bloc, see Kertesz, *Diplomacy in a Whirlpool,* p. 147.

23.   Nagy, *Iron Curtain,* pp. 372 and 433-34. Judging from the British and American diplomatic records, Nagy's account of events seems to be an

accurate and trustworthy one, though of course it was written as an apologia for his actions, which ultimately failed to avert the sovietization of Hungary.

24.   On the March crisis, see Schoenfeld to S/S, No. 449, 4 March 1946, 864.00/3-446; No. 483, 8 March 1946, 864.00/8-346; No. 499, 12 March 1946, 864.00/3-1246, RG 59, NARS; *FRUS, 1946,* VI, 271-72. FO to Washington, No. 2268, 9 March 1946, FO 371/59003 [R 3560/256/ 21], PRO.

25.   *FRUS, 1946,* VI, 271-72. W. Mitchell Carse, chargé d'affaires in Budapest, to FO, No. 260, 12 March 1946, FO 371/59004 [R 3869/256/ 21]; Gascoigne to Bevin, No. 205, 8 April 1946, FO 371/59005 [R 5745/ 256/21], PRO.

26.   Russell minute, 13 March 1946, FO 371/59004 [R 3809/256/ 21], PRO.

27.   H. Freeman Matthews memorandum to Acheson (which refers to Ben Cohen), 19 March 1946, 864.00/3-846, RG 59, NARS. Hayter minute, 18 April 1946, FO 371/59005 [R 5745/256/21], PRO.

28.   Matthews memorandum (see above, n. 27).

29.   Warner memorandum to Sargent, 7 March 1946; FO to Washington, No. 2268, 9 March 1946, FO 371/59003 [R 3560/256/21]; Warner minute, 23 April 1946; see also Williams minute, 17 April 1946, FO 371/ 59005 [R 5745/256/21], PRO.

30.   *FRUS, 1946,* VI, 273-74. FO to Budapest, No. 240, 30 March 1946; Earl of Halifax, ambassador in Washington, to FO, No. 1927, 26 March 1946, FO 371/59005 [R 4765/256/21], PRO.

31.   *FRUS, 1946,* VI, 304-6. Carse to FO, No. 624, 5 June 1946, FO 371/59006 [R 8418/256/21]; No. 627, 5 June 1946, ibid. [R 8428/256/ 21], PRO.

32.   A full discussion of the Soviet demands and Nagy's treatment of them is in the telegram from Budapest of 7 July 1946 by Brig. Gen. George H. Weems, U.S. representative on the Allied Control Commission, and of 10 and 11 July 1946 by Schoenfeld, *FRUS, 1946,* VI, 318-22.

General Weems represented the United States on the Allied Control Commission from June 1946 to September 1947, when it went out of existence. He left a collection of personal papers to the Tennesse State Library and Archives. Regrettably, most of that portion of his papers pertaining to the Eastern European situation in the postwar period, which comprises not quite a hundred items, is of a personal nature and of no value to this study.

33. *FRUS: Potsdam*, II, 1494.

34. D/S to Budapest, No. 678, 3 July 1946, 864.00/7-346; W. Averell Harriman, ambassador in London, to S/S, No. 6600, 10 July 1946, 864.00/ 7-1046, RG 59, NARS; *FRUS, 1946*, VI, 322-24. F. A. Warner minute, 8 July 1946; FO to Washington, no. 6796, 10 July 1946, FO 371/59006 [R 9955/256/21]; FO to Budapest, No. 691, 20 July 1946, FO 371/59007 [R 10681/256/21], PRO.

35. *FRUS, 1946*, VI, 326-29.

36. Alexander Knox Helm to FO, No. 891, 13 August 1946, FO 371/ 59007 [R 12025/256/21]. Helm had replaced Gasciogne as head of the British mission in Hungary and Italy.

37. *FRUS, 1946*, VI, 335.

38. Gascoigne to Bevin, No. 165, 18 March 1946; Williams letter to Gascoigne, No. 337, 4 April 1946, FO 371/59005 [R 4786/256/21], PRO. D/S to Budapest, No. 524, 26 April 1946, 864.00/4-2646, RG 59, NARS.

39. *FRUS, 1946*, VI, 336-37 and 339-40.

40. Schoenfeld to S/S, No. 1970, 18 October 1946, 864.00/10-1846, RG 59, NARS. Helm to FO No. 441, 25 November 1946, FO 371/59008 [R 17607/256/21], PRO.

41. Schoenfeld to S/S, No. 2197, 23 November 1946, 864.00/11-2346, RG 59, NARS; *FRUS, 1946*, VI, 344-46. Helm to FO, No. 441, 25 November 1946, FO 371/59008 [R 17607/256/21], PRO. For Nagy's comments on the question of provincial elections, see *Iron Curtain*, pp. 259-60.

42. Paul Ignotus, "The First Two Communist Takeovers of Hungary: 1919 and 1948," in *The Anatomy of Communist Takeovers*, ed. Thomas Hammond (New Haven, 1975), p. 394. Ignotus, who had been a member of the Hungarian Social Democratic Party, was arrested by the Communists in 1948 and sentenced to imprisonment.

Notes to Chapter VI

1. Helm despatch to Attlee, No. 473, 12 December 1946, FO 371/ 59008 [R 18431/256/21], PRO. *FRUS, 1946*, VI, 354-55.

2.   Chancery of British Mission in Budapest letter to Southern Department, 13 December 1946, FO 371/59008 [R 18344/256/21], PRO.

3.   On the conspiracy, see for example, Helm despatch to Bevin, No. 26, 29 January 1947, FO 371/67170 [R 1575/11/21], PRO. Schoenfeld to S/S, No. 2370, 28 December 1946, 864.00/12-2846; No. 2382, 31 December 1946, 864.00/12-3146, RG 59, NARS.

4.   Williams minute, 11 February 1947, FO 371/67170 [R 1756/11/21], PRO. Schoenfeld to S/S, despatch No. 2461, 17 January 1947, 864.00/1-1747; No. 163, 31 January 1947, 864.00/1-3147; OIR Report No. 4306, 19 February 1947, "New Light on the Hungarian Political Crisis," NARS.

5.   Walworth Barbour, Chief of the Division of Southern European Affairs, memoranda to Matthews, 28 January 1947 and 6 February 1947, 864.00/1-2747, RG 59, NARS; *FRUS, 1947,* IV, 264 and 268-69.

6.   John R. Colville minute, 21 February 1947; Williams minute, 21 February 1947; C. Warner minute, 24 February 1947, FO 371/67170 [R 2268/11/21], PRO.

7.   Helm despatch to Bevin, No. 30, 6 February 1947, FO 371/67170 [R 2470/11/21]; Helm to FO, No. 210, 15 February 1947, ibid. [R 2150/11/21]; Colville minutes, 10 February 1947, ibid.[R1756/11/21]; 21 February 1947, ibid. [R 2268/11/21]; Williams minute, 31 March 1947, FO 371/67172 [R 4003/11/21]; FO to Washington, No. 7542, 26 July 1947, FO 371/67179 [R 8942/11/21], PRO.

8.   Williams minute, 11 February 1947, FO 371/67170 [R 1756/11/21], PRO. *FRUS, 1947,* IV, 267-68.

9.   For information on the Kovács case, see Helm to FO, No. 243, 25 February 1947, FO 371/67170 [R 2625/11/21], PRO. Schoenfeld to S/S, No. 198, 7 February 1947, 864.00/2-747; No. 337, 6 March 1947, 864.00/3-647, RG 59, NARS; *FRUS, 1947,* IV, 269-72.

10.   Williams minute, 28 February 1947, FO 371/67170 [R 2625/11/21], PRO.

11.   Hickerson memorandum to Marshall and Acheson, 1 March 1947, 864.00/3-147, RG 59, NARS. On the Kovács question, see *FRUS, 1947,* IV, 271-75.

12.   The text of the note is in *Department of State Bulletin* 16:402 (1947), 495.

13.   Williams minute, 6 March 1947; C. Warner minute, 7 March 1947, FO 371/67171 [R 2940/11/21], PRO. Also, Gallman to S/S, No. 1460, 5 March 1947, 864,00/3-547, RG 59, NARS, for his report on a conversation with Warner.

14.   FO to Moscow, No. 964, 6 March 1947; FO to Budapest, No. 258, 6 March 1947, FO 371/67171 [R 2940/11/21], PRO.

15.   Helm to FO, No. 299, 7 March 1947, FO 371/67171 [R 3113/11/21], PRO.

16.   Schoenfeld to S/S, No. 404, 13 March 1947, 864.00/3-1347, RG 59, NARS.

17.   *FRUS, 1947,* IV, 277-78.

18.   Ibid., 278-81 and 285. The note is in *Department of State Bulletin* 16:404 (1947), 583-84.

19.   Campbell minute, 17 March 1947, FO 371/67172 [R 3592/11/21], PRO.

20.   Helm to FO, No. 344, 17 March 1947, ibid.

21.   Colville minute, 18 March 1947; C. Warner minute, 19 March 1947; FO to Budapest, No. 315, 19 March 1947; FO to Washington, No. 2650, 20 March 1947, ibid. [R 3561/11/21], PRO. Lewis W. Douglas, ambassador in London, to S/S, No. 1704, 18 March 1947, RG 59, NARS, for his report on a discussion with Warner.

22.   *FRUS, 1947,* IV, 285-86.

23.   D/S to Budapest, No. 367, 3 April 1947, 864.00/4-347; *FRUS, 1947,* IV, 288-90.

24.   Inverchapel to FO, No. 1720, 20 March 1947, FO 371/67172 [R 3858/11/21]; No. 1760, 22 March 1947, ibid. [R 4017/11/21], PRO. *FRUS, 1947,* IV, 292-93.

25.   On the March agreement, see Helm despatch to Attlee, No. 71, 15 March 1947, FO 371/67172 [R 4054/11/21], PRO. *FRUS, 1947,* IV, 290-91. Nagy, *Iron Curtain,* pp. 390-91.

26.   Ibid., pp. 398-400.

27.   *New York Times,* 15 May 1947, p. 7. In May, the coming into force of the peace treaty appeared to be very close at hand, became Great Britain had ratified the pact in April, the United States Senate seemed ready to do so, and the Soviet Union had stated that it would ratify the treaty once Britain and America had done so. In July, after the United States had ratified the treaty, the Soviets unexpectedly delayed ratification

for two months. But this could obviously not have been foreseen in May.

28.   Helm to FO, No. 571, 14 May 1947, FO 371/67195 [R 6553/85/21] ; Helm despatch to Bevin, No. 127, 16 May 1947, ibid., [R 6831/85/21] , PRO. Schoenfeld to S/S, No. 780, 12 May 1947, a cable which was sent to and discussed by the Balkan Committee of the Department of State, which coordinated Department treatment of Balkan problems; see CBA D [document] 19 and CBA M [meeting] 20, RG, 43, NARS.

29.   Nagy, *Iron Curtain,* pp. 402-3.

30.   For the comments of one Foreign Office official on the relationship of the bank nationalization crisis to the soon-to-occur coup, see Colville minute, 3 June 1947, FO 371/67174 [R 7321/11/21] , PRO.

31.   As for the charge levelled against Nagy, he certainly had not been involved in the anti-government plot from the start. On the other hand, once the Russians and Communists had uncovered it and began making arrests, he unquestionably had conferred at length with his political allies, including Kovács, as to how to handle the situation, and could therefore be regarded as having abetted the conspirators.

32.   For the events of the coup, see Helm to FO, No. 618, 30 May 1947, FO 371/67174 [R 7300/11/21] , PRO. *FRUS, 1947,* IV, 301-3. Nagy, *Iron Curtain,* pp. 409-26.

33.   Some of the points in this and the preceding two paragraphs are in Helm letter to C. Warner, 24 June 1947, FO 371/67179 [R 8942/11/21] , PRO, a particularly noteworthy and useful summary of events.

34.   D/S to London, No. 2877, 3 July 1947, 864.00/7-347, RG 59, NARS.

35.   *Public Papers of the Presidents of the United States: Harry S. Truman, 1947,* (Washington, D.C., 1963), pp. 265-66. While House files contain a summary of the Hungarian situation dated 2 June 1947, prepared in the State Department for Marshall, who in turn forwarded it to Truman for his information. It also appears that Truman discussed Hungary with Senator Arthur Vandenberg and other congressional leaders, for the While House appointment books show that they met at the White House on 4 June for nearly a hour. The appointment books do not indicate the topic of discussion, but it is a fair guess that the Hungarian crisis was raised, not only because of Vandenberg's foreign policy role, but also because he publicly condemned the Hungarian situation in a Senate speech the day before (*Congressional Record,* 3 June 1947, pp. 6231-32).

36. Sargent minute, 31 May 1947, FO 371/67174 [R 7300/11/21], PRO.

37. Williams minute, 31 May 1947, ibid.

38. FO to Washington, No. 5592, 7 June 1947, ibid. [R 7535/11/21], PRO.

39. C. M. (47) 53rd conclusions, 10 June 1947, CAB 128/10, PRO.

40. Bevin minute, n.d. (but probably either 31 May or 1 June 1947), FO 371/67174 [R 7300/11/21], PRO.

41. FO to Washington, No. 5592, 7 June 1947, FO 371/67174 [R 7535/11/21], PRO.

42. FO to Moscow, No. 1858, 7 June 1947, ibid. [R 7560/11/21]; Peterson aide-mémoire to Molotov, 9 June 1947, FO 371/67175 [R 7840/11/21], PRO.

43. FO to Washington, No. 5592, 7 June 1947, FO 371/67174 [R 7537/11/21], PRO.

44. FO to Moscow, No. 1938, 14 June 1947, FO 371/67175 [R 7840/11/21], PRO.

45. Peterson aide-mémoire to Molotov, 16 June 1947, FO 371/67177 [R 8434/11/21], PRO.

46. Peterson to FO, No. 1394, 22 June 1947, ibid.

47. Bevin minute, n.d., on Peterson to FO, No. 1394, 22 June 1947, ibid.

48. FO to Moscow, No. 2078, , 25 June 1947, ibid.

49. FO to Washington, No. 5592, June 1947, FO 371/67174 [R 7535/11/21], PRO. *FRUS, 1947,* IV, 309-11 and 313-14.

50. *FRUS, 1947,* IV, 317-19.

51. Ibid., 320-21.

52. *Congressional Record,* 3 June 1947, pp. 6231-32.

53. Martin letter to McNeil, 13 June 1947, FO 371/67176 [R 8226/11/21], PRO.

54. Vedeler letter to Laurence A. Steinhardt, ambassador in Prague, 12 August 1947, Laurence A. Steinhardt Papers, Library of Congress, Washington, D.C.

55. Memorandum of conversation between Frederick T. Merrill, Division of Southern European Affairs, and McClintock, prepared by the latter, 5 June 1947, 864.00/6-547, NARS.

56. *FRUS, 1947,* IV, 329-32.

57.   Ibid., IV, 329 n1, 332 n4.

58.   D/S to London, No. 2877, 3 July 1947, 864.00/7-347, RG 59, NARS.

59.   Colville minute, 20 June 1947; Christopher P. Mayhew, Parliamentary Under-Secretary, letter to Martin, 26 August 1947 (Martin letter to McNeil [see above, n. 53] did not call for an immediate reply, and thus the belated Foreign Office should not be regarded as a slight), FO 371/67176 [R 8226/11/21]; Colville minute, 23 June 1947; Sargent minute, 24 June 1947, FO 371/67177 [R8434/11/21]; Jebb minute, 7 July 1947, FO 371/67180 [R 9392/11/21]; FO to Washington, No. 7541, 25 July 1947, FO 371/67179 [R 8941/11/21], PRO, a very important cable, summarizing a Foreign Office-United States Embassy conversation on recommended action for Hungary.

60.   FO to Washington, No. 7541, 25 July 1947, FO 371/67179 [8941/11/21], PRO.

61.   John H. Watson, assistant head of the Southern Department, 17 July 1946, FO 371/67180 [R 9392/11/21], PRO.

62.   United Nations, Security Council, 2nd Year (1947), *Discussion on the admission of new members* (and variations in that title), pp. 2031-55, 2117-41, and 2408-80.

63.   C. Warner minute, 24 June 1947, FO 371/67177 [R 8434/11/21], PRO.

Notes to Chapter VII

1.   Chapin to S/S, No. 1269, 30 July 1947, 864.00/7-3047, RG 59, NARS. Also, Watson minute, 17 July 1947, FO 371/67181 [R 9666/11/21], PRO. Chapin, named U.S. Minister to Hungary on 9 July, had been chargé d'affaires since Schoenfeld relinquished the post on 31 May.

2.   On the pre-election situation, see Helm despatch to Bevin, No. 211, 29 July 1947, FO 371/67181 [R 10667/11/21]; No. 5, 3 January 1948, FO 371/72373 [R 607/53/21], PRO, enclosing a summary of events for 1947, written by secretaries of the Budapest legation. Chapin to S/S, No. 1269, 30 July 1947, 864.00/7-3047, RG 59, NARS.

3.   Watson minute, 18 July 1947, FO 371/67181 [R 10168/11/21], PRO. *FRUS, 1947,* IV, 338-39.

4.   Chapin to S/S, No. 1269, 30 July 1947, 864.00/7-3047, RG 59, NARS.

5. For example, M. D. Hay, Southern Department, minute, 28 August 1947, FO 371/67183 [R 11725/11/21], PRO.

6. James M. Walsh, chargé d'affaires in Budapest to FO, No. 954, 14 August 1947, FO 371/67182 [R 11119/11/21]; Watson minute, 15 August 1947, ibid. [R 10766/11/21], PRO. Lord Pakenham, chancellor of the Duchy of Lancaster, statement on behalf of the government, 5 August 1947, in the *Times,* 6 August 1947. *FRUS, 1947,* IV, 354-58.

7. *Department of State Bulletin* 17:425 (1947), 392-93. The text of the British statement in in the *Times,* 18 August 1947.

8. Campbell minute, 15 August 1947, FO 371/67182 [R 11119/11/21]. For Anglo-American deliberation on possible action, see FO to Washington, No. 8198, 15 August 1947, ibid.,; No. 8239, 16 August 1947; No. 8240, 16 August 1947, ibid. [R 11185/11/21], PRO. *FRUS, 1947,* IV, 354-58.

9. Walsh to FO, No. 967, 19 August 1947, FO 371/67182 [R 11323/11/21]; Walsh letter to Wallinger, 20 August 1947, FO 371/67183 [R 11662/11/21], PRO. *FRUS, 1947,* IV, 360-61.

10. Watson minute, 20 August 1947, FO 371/67182 [R 11323/11/21], PRO.

11. Helm despatch to Bevin, No. 5, 3 January 1948, FO 371/72373 [R 607/53/21], PRO. *FRUS, 1947,* IV, 363-64.

12. *FRUS, 1947,* IV, 363-64.

13. Helm to FO, No. 1035, 1 September 1947, FO 371/67183 [R 12022/11/21], PRO.

14. Helm despatch to Bevin, No. 5, 3 January 1948, FO 371/72373 [R 607/53/21], PRO.

15. Bán, "Hungary," in *The Curtain Falls: The Story of the Socialists in Eastern Europe,* ed. Denis Healey (London, 1951), p. 73.

16. Helm to FO (see above, n. 13).

17. Kertesz, *Diplomacy in a Whirlpool,* p. 101.

18. Chapin to S/S, No. 1469, 1 September 1947, 864.00/9-147, RG 59, NARS; *FRUS, 1947,* IV, 363-64.

19. Helm to FO, No. 1034, 1 September 1947, FO 371/67183 [R 11952/11/21]; No. 1044, 2 September 1947, ibid. [R 12028/11/21]; No. 1045, 2 September 1947, ibid., [R 1292/11/21], PRO.

20. FO to Washington, No. 9200, 7 September 1947, FO 371/66966 [R 11891/268/67], PRO.

21. On the conduct of elections under Horthy, see Macartney, *History of Hungary,* I, 46-49, and Nagy, *Iron Curtain,* pp. 26-32.

22. Helm to FO, No. 1335, 31 October 1947; Watson minute, 4 November 1947, FO 371/67187 [R 14572/11/21]; Helm to FO, No. 1340, 1 November 1947; Campbell minute, 5 November 1947, ibid. [R 14648/11/21]; Helm despatch to Bevin, No. 5, 3 January 1948, FO 371/72373 [R 607/53/21], PRO. *FRUS, 1947,* IV, 396-98.

23. Helm letter to Wallinger, 29 January 1948, FO 371/72373 [R 1591/53/21]; Watson minute, 3 June 1948, FO 371/72390 [R 6278/250/21], PRO.

24. See Foreign Office papers on the "Extinction of Human Rights in Eastern Europe," 24 November 1947, C.P. (47) 313, CAB 129/22, and "Future Foreign Publicity Policy," 4 January 1948, C.P. (48) 8, CAB 129/23. *FRUS, 1947,* IV, 38-41, and *FRUS, 1948,* IV, 357-58.

25. *FRUS, 1947,* IV, 343.

26. See, for example, the report of the 1947 annual congress of the Hungarian Social Democratic Party, held in February. Healey, the Labour observer who prepared the report, sent a copy of it as an enclosure to a 5 June 1947 letter to Under-Secretary Christopher Mayhew, and is in FO 371/67179 [R 9039/11/21], PRO. (According to Healey's letter, he also gave a copy of the report to Minister of State Hector McNeil.) Healey, of course, also deposited a copy of the report in the records of the International Committee, available at Transport House, London.

27. FO to Berne, No. 375, 11 June 1947, FO 371/67174 [R 7663/11/21], PRO.

28. Wallinger minute, 12 February 1948; Porter minute, 23 February 1948, FO 371/72374 [R 2559/53/21], PRO.

29. An example of a despatch shown to Healy is Walsh despatch to Attlee, No. 72, 18 March 1947, FO 371/67172 [R 4003/11/21], PRO, which concerns the situation in the Hungarian Social Democratic Party.

30. Helm to FO, No. 1255, 16 October 1947, FO 371/67186 [R 13160/11/21], PRO.

31. Wallinger minute, n.d. (23 [?] October 1947); C. Warner minute, n.d. (27 [?] October 1947), ibid.

32. Watson minute, 21 October 1947, ibid.

33. Helm to FO, No. 1045, 2 September 1947, FO 371/67183 [R 12092/11/21]; FO memorandum on post-election situation, 21 September 1947, FO 371/67185 [R 12911/11/21], PRO.

34.   Wallinger minute, 7 February 1948, FO 371/72373 [R 1555/53/21]; see also his minute, 22 January 1948, ibid., [R 807/53/21], PRO.

35.   Wallinger letter to Healey, 27 January 1948, ibid. [R 867/53/21]; see also Helm letter to Wallinger, 15 January 1948, ibid.

36.   Helm to FO, No. 101, 12 February 1948; J. C. Petersen minute, 17 February 1948, FO 371/72374 [R 2146/53/21], PRO.

37.   Helm to FO, No. 135, 20 February 1948; Petersen minute, 23 February 1948, ibid. [R 2452/53/21], PRO.

38.   Helm despatch to Bevin, No. 221, 16 June 1948, FO 371/72377 [R 7351/53/21], PRO.

39.   Seton-Watson, *East European Revolution,* pp. 186-90 and 342-43; Wheeler-Bennet and Nicholls, *Semblance of Peace,* pp. 575-76.

40.   "Review of Soviet Policy," 4 January 1948, C.P. (48) 7, CAB 129/23; see also "The First Aim of British Foreign Policy," 4 January 1948, C.P. (48) 6, ibid., PRO.

41.   "The Czechoslovak Crisis," 3 March 1948, C.P. (48), 71, CAB 129/25, PRO.

42.   "The Threat to Western Civilization," 3 March 1948, C.P. (48) 72, ibid.

43.   Woodward, *British Foreign Policy,* III, 103, n. 2, and V, 181-98. Eden favored a Western European alliance. See also his *The Reckoning* (Boston, 1965), pp. 515-18 and 572-73.

44.   "The First Aim of British Foreign Policy" (see above, n. 40); "The Threat to Western Civilization" (see above, n. 42).

45.   C. M. (48) 2nd Conclusions, 8 January 1948, CAB 128/12, PRO.

46.   In "The Threat to Western Civilization" (see above, n. 42).

47.   *Hansard's Parliamentary Debates* (Commons), 5th series, 446 (22 January 1948), 391.

48.   "Extinction of Human Rights in Eastern Europe" (see above, n. 24).

49.   "U.S. Objectives with Respect to Russia," 18 August 1948, PPS-38, NARS.

50.   "Resume of World Situation," 6 November 1947, PPS-13, NARS.

51.   See *Survey of International Affairs, 1939-1946,* VI, 329-30; *Survey, 1947-1948,* (London, 1952), pp. 200-5; *Survey 1949-1950* (London, 1953), pp. 217-19; Seton-Watson, *East European Revolution,* pp. 287-95.

52. *FRUS, 1948,* IV, 336.

53. Petersen minute, 4 June 1948, FO 371/72390 [R 6576/250/21], PRO.

54. Watson minute, 24 June 1948, ibid. [R 6536/250/21], PRO.

55. *New York Times,* 17 January, 20 January, 8 February, and 11 February 1949.

56. Kertesz, *Diplomacy in a Whirlpool,* pp. 112-13.

57. For British reports on the Tito-Cominform rift and its effects in Hungary, see Helm despatch to Bevin, No. 261, 16 July 1948, FO 371/72378 [R 8541/53/21]; No. 306, 25 August 1948, FO 371/72380 [R 10088/53/21]; No. 319, 7 September 1948, ibid. [R 10519/53/21]; No. 389, 26 October 1948, ibid. [R 12268/53/21], PRO. For American reports, Chapin to S/S, No. 1071, 3 July 1948, 864.00/7-348; No. A-457, 21 July 1948, 864.00/7-2148; No. 1277, 9 August 1948, 864.00/8-948, RG 59, NARS. A partial text of the Cominform resolution against Tito in in the *New York Times,* 29 June 1948.

58. Kertesz, *Diplomacy in a Whirlpool,* pp. 118-19.

59. See *FRUS, 1949,* V, 870-71, 941-45, and 947-54.

60. Ibid., 12-13 and 29-31.

61. István Barta et al., *A History of Hungary,* trans. László Boros et al. (London, 1975), pp. 549-51.

62. Sargent minute, 6 March 1945, FO 371/48217 [R 3459/3168/67], PRO.

Notes to Chapter VIII

1. D. F. Fleming, *The Cold War and Its Origins, 1917-1960* (Garden City, 1961), I, 16-35 and passim. But other historians deemphasize the ideological foundations of the intervention. See George F. Kennan, *Soviet-American Relations, 1917-1920,* 2 vols. (Princeton, 1956-1958); Richard H. Ullman, *Anglo-Soviet Relations, 1917-1921,* 3 vols. (Princeton, 1961-1972).

2. I. Deutscher, *The Prophet Armed: Trotsky, 1879-1921* (New York, 1954), pp. 448-50.

3. Desmond Donnelly, *Struggle for the World: The Cold War from Its Origins in 1917* (London, 1965), pp. 10-11.

4. W. P. and Zelda K. Coates, *A History of Anglo-Soviet Relations*

(London, 1943); Sir J. A. R.Marriott, *Anglo-Russian Relations, 1689-1943* (London, 1944), pp. 170 ff; Edward M. Bennett, *Recognition of Russia: An American Foreign Policy Dilemma* (Waltham, Mass., 1970).

5. For discussions of Cold War historiography, see Paul Seabury, *The Rise and Decline of the Cold War* (New York, 1967), pp. 6-10; Charles S. Maier, "Revisionism and the Interpretation of Cold War Origins," *Perspectives in American History* 4 (1970), 313-47; J. L. Richardson, "Cold War Revisionism: A Critique," *World Politics* 24:4 (1972), 579-612.

6. William Appleman Williams, *The Tragedy of American Diplomacy,* rev. ed. (New York, 1962), passim; Gabriel Kolko, *The Politics of War: The World and United States Foreign Policy, 1943-1945* (New York, 1968), passim, and Joyce and Gabiiel Kolko, *The Limits of Power: The World and United States Foreign Policy, 1945-1954* (New York, 1972), passim; David Horowitz, *Free World Colossus: A Critique of American Foreign Policy in the Cold War,* rev. ed. (New York, 1971), passim; Geir Lundestad, *The American Non-Policy Towards Eastern Europe, 1943-1947: Universalism in an Area Not of Essential Interest to the United States* (Tromsö, Norway, 1975), pp. 59-66.

7. American prewar trade and investment figures are in Stephen D. Kertesz, *The Fate of East Central Europe: Hopes and Failures of American Foreign Policy* (Notre Dame, 1956), p. 46, n. 50; Kertesz's sources are from the Department of Commerce and the Treasury. For British prewar trade figures see *South-Eastern Europe: A Political and Economic Survey* (London, 1939).

8. Revisionist historians—those who blame the West, and in particular the United States, for the Cold War—condemn, more or less harshly, Western policy makers for holding this view. See, for example, Kolko and Kolko, *Limits of Power,* passim; Daniel Yergin, *Shattered Peace: The Origins of the Cold War and the National Security State* (Boston, 1978), pp. 198-99, 234, and 279 ff. Traditionalist historians—who blame the East-West conflict on the Soviet Union—argue that Western fears were justified. For example, William H. McNeill, *America, Britain, and Russia: Their Co-operation and Conflict, 1941-1946* (London, 1953), pp. 62-87 and passim; Herbert Feis, *Churchill, Roosevelt, Stalin: The War They Waged and the Peace They Sought,* 2nd ed. (Princeton, 1967), pp. 409 ff. and his *From Trust to Terror: The Onset of the Cold War, 1945-1950* (New York, 1970), pp. 50-52. Lundestad, *American Non-Policy,* pp. 66-73, balances both sides.

9. *FRUS, 1944,* IV, 933.

10. Sargent minute, 6 March 1945, FO 371/48217 [R 3459/3168/ 57], PRO.

11. *New York Times,* 6 March 1946.

12. Department to London, No. 2877, 3 July 1947, 864.00/7-347, RG 59, NARS.

13. For example, Walter Millis, ed., *The Forrestal Diaries* (New York, 1951), pp. 254-97 and passim; Arthur H. Vandenberg, Jr., ed., *The Private Papers of Senator Vandenberg* (Boston, 1952), pp. 346-47; Harry S. Truman, *Memoirs: Years of Trial and Hope* (Garden City, N.Y., 1956), pp. 96 ff.; Hugh Dalton, *High Tide and After: Memoirs, 1945-1960* (London, 1962), pp. 105 and 206-9; Dalton diary, 22 March 1946, London School of Economics; "Review of Soviet Policy," 3 January 1948, C. P. (48) 7, CAB 129/23, PRO.

14. The Threat to Western Civilization," 3 March 1948, C. P. (48) 72, CAB 129/25, PRO.

15. JCS memorandum, 12 May 1947, *FRUS, 1947,* I, 734-50. On the geopolitical function of the European rimland, see also Saul Bernard Cohen, *Geography and Politics in a World Divided,* 2nd ed. (New York, 1973), especially pp. 150-90; Colin S. Gray, *The Geopolitics of the Nuclar Era: Heartland, Rimlands, and the Technological Revolution* (New York, 1977), passim.

16. "Military Position of the United States in the Light of Russian Policy," JCS 1545, 9 October 1945, p. 4, RG 218, NARS.

17. Sargent minute, 13 March 1945, FO 371/48219 [R 5068/5068/ 67], PRO.

18. M. A. Fitzsimons, *The Foreign Policy of the British Labour Government, 1945-1951* (Notre Dame, 1953), pp. 55-86; F. S. Northedge, *British Foreign Policy: The Process of Readjustment* (London, 1962), pp. 1-32 and passim; Joseph Frankel, *British Foreign Policy, 1945-1973* (London, 1975), pp. 151 ff.

19. *Cards on the Table: An Interpretation of Labour's Foreign Policy* (London, 1947), pp. 6-7.

20. Sir Eyre Crowe, "Memorandum on the Present State of British Relations with France and Germany," in *Britain and Europe: Pitt to Churchill, 1793-1940,* ed. James Joll (London, 1961), pp. 204-6.

21. Francis Williams, *Ernest Bevin: Portrait of a Great Englishman*

(London, 1952), pp. 248-70, passim; also Williams' article on Bevin in the *Dictionary of National Biography, 1951-1960,* ed. E. T. Williams and Helen M. Palmer (Oxford, 1971). Alan Bullock, *The Life and Times of Ernest Bevin,* 2 vols. (London, 1960-67), concerns his career prior to becoming Foreign Secretary. On America's role in replacing Britain as the balancer of Europe, see also Paul M. Kennedy, *The Rise and Fall of British Naval Mastery* (London, 1976), pp. 323-46.

22.   Louis J. Halle, *The Cold War as History* (New York, 1967), pp. 5-6; also JCS memorandum (see above, n. 15).

23.   Leon D. Upstein, *Britain—Uneasy Ally* (Chicago, 1954), pp. 265-67.

24.   Ibid., p. 266.

25.   *FRUS: Potsdam,* I, 259.

26.   Helm to FO, No. 689, 9 June 1947, FO 371/67175 [R 7710/11/21], PRO. Helm made this comment in reference to Truman's press conference remarks that Prime Minister Nagy's ouster was an "outrage" and that the United States would not stand by idly.

27.   David Turnock, *Eastern Europe* (Folkestone, Eng., 1978), pp. 233-34.

28.   Stanislaw Wellisz, *The Economics of the Soviet Bloc: A Study of Decision Making and Resource Allocation* (New York, 1964), pp. 235-36.

29.   For a Marxist view, see Egon Kemenes, "The Hungarian Economy, 1945-1969," in *Modern Hungary: Readings from* The New Hungarian Quarterly, ed. Denis Sinor (Bloomington, Ind.).

30.   Tibor Meray, *Thirteen Days That Shook the Kremlin,* trans. Howard L. Katzander (New York, 1959), pp. 212-13; Bennett Kovrig, *The Hungarian People's Republic* (Baltimore, 1970), pp. 121-24.

31.   Mátyás Rákosi, *How We Took over Hungary* (Bombay, 1952), p. 8.

BIBLIOGRAPHY

PRIMARY SOURCES

I. Unpublished material

A. Public Record Office, London

Records of the Cabinet Office

CAB 128 Cabinet conclusions

CAB 129 Cabinet memoranda

Records of the Foreign Office, FO 371

Central Department

Southern Department

Economic Relations Department

Supply and Relief Department

B. National Archives and Records Service, Washington D.C.

RG 43 Records of International Conferences, Commissions, and Expositions: Council of Foreign Ministers Records

RG 59 State Department Decimal File, 1945-1948

Records of the Office of European Affairs, 1935-1947 (Matthews-Hickerson Files)

Records of Charles E. Bohlen, 1942-1952

RG 165 Records of the War Department, General and Special Staffs

RG 218 Records of the United States Joint Chiefs of Staff

C. Private Papers

Hugh Dalton papers, London School of Economics and Political Science, London

Laurence A. Steinhardt papers, Library of Congress, Washington, D.C.
Harry S. Truman papers, Harry S. Truman Library, Independence, Missouri
Arthur H. Vandenberg papers, University of Michigan, Ann Arbor, Michigan
George Hatton Weems papers, Tennessee State Library and Archives, Nashville, Tennessee

II. Published Material

A. Official Documents

Great Britain. Foreign Office. *Documents on British Foreign Policy, 1919-1939.* Ed. E. L. Woodward and Rohan Butler. First Series. Vols. I, II, VI, and XII. London: HMSO, 1947-1962.

Great Britain. Parliament. *Hansard's Parliamentary Debates.* Vols. CCCXIII and CDXLVI.

Public Papers of the Presidents of the United States: Harry S. Truman, 1947. Washington, D.C.: GOP, 1963.

Union of Soviet Socialist Republics. Ministry of Foreign Affairs. *Correspondence between the Chairman of the Council of Ministers of the U.S.S.R and the Presidents of the U.S.A. and the Prime Ministers of Great Britain during the Great Patriotic War of 1941-1945.* 2 vols. Moscow: Foreign Languages Publishing House, 1957.

United Nations. Security Council. 2nd Year (1947). *Discussion on the Admission of New Members.* United Nations: New York, 1964.

United States Congress. *Congressional Record.* Vol. XCIII.

United States. Department of State. *Department of State Bulletin.* Vols. XIV-XVII.

————. *Papers Relating to the Foreign Relations of the United States, 1918: Russia.* 3 vols. Washington, D.C.: GPO, 1931-1932.

————. *Papers Relating to the Foreign Relations of the United States, 1919: Russia.* Washington, D.C.: GPO, 1937.

————. *Papers Relating to the Foreign Relations of the United States: The Paris Peace Conference, 1919.* Vols. IV, VII, VIII, IX, XI, and XII. Washington, D.C.: GPO, 1943-1947.

————. *Papers Relating to the Foreign Relations of the United States, 1920.* Vol. III. Washington, D.C.: GPO, 1936.

————. *Papers Relating to the Foreign Relations of the United States: The Lansing Papers, 1914-1920.* Vol. II. Washington, D.C.: GPO, 1940.

————. *Papers Relating to the Foreign Relations of the United States, 1923.* Vol. II. Washington, D.C.: GPO, 1939.

————. *Papers Relating to the Foreign Relations of the United States, 1925.* Vol. II. Washington, D.C.: GPO, 1940.

————. *Papers Relating to the Foreign Relations of the United States, 1931.* Vol. II. Washington, D.C.: GPO, 1946.

————. *Foreign Relations of the United States: Diplomatic Papers, 1944.* Vol. III; *The British Commonwealth and Europe;* Vol. IV: *Europe.* Washington, D.C.: GPO, 1965-1966.

————. *Foreign Relations of the United States: Diplomatic Papers, 1945.* Vol. II: *General: Political and Economic Matters;* Vol. IV: *Europe.* Washington, D.C.: GPO, 1967-1968.

————. *Foreign Relations of the United States: Diplomatic Papers: The Conferences at Malta and Yalta, 1945.* Washington, D.C.: GPO, 1955.

————. *Foreign Relations of the United States: Diplomatic Papers: The Conference of Berlin (The Potsdam Conference), 1945.* 2 vols. Washington, D.C.: GPO, 1960.

————. *Foreign Relations of the United States: Diplomatic Papers, 1946.* Vol. II: *Council of Foreign Ministers;* Vol. III: *Paris Peace Conference Proceedings;* Vol. IV: *Paris Peace Conference: Documents;* Vol. VI: *Eastern Europe: The Soviet Union.* Washington, D.C.: GPO, 1970.

————. *Foreign Relations of the United States: Diplomatic Papers, 1947.* Vol. I: *General: The United Nations;* Vol. IV: *Eastern Europe: The Soviet Union.* Washington, D.C.: GPO, 1972-1973.

————. *Foreign Relations of the United States: Diplomatic Papers, 1948.* Vol. IV: *Eastern Europe: The Soviet Union.* Washington, D.C.: GPO, 1974.

————. *Foreign Relations of the United States: Diplomatic Papers, 1949.* Vol. V: *Eastern Europe: The Soviet Union.* Washington, D.C.: GPO, 1976.

B. Memoirs and diaries

Attlee, C. R. *As It Happened.* New York: Viking, 1954.

Bohlen, Charles E. *The Transformation of American Foreign Policy.* New York: Norton, 1969.

Byrnes, James F. *Speaking Frankly.* New York: Harper, 1947.

Churchill, Winston S. *Triumph and Tragedy.* Vol. VI of *The Second World War.* Boston: Houghton Mifflin, 1953.

Dalton, Hugh. *High Tide and After: Memoirs, 1945-1960.* London: Frederick Muller, 1962.

Eden, Anthony. *The Reckoning.* Boston: Houghton Mifflin, 1965.

————. *Full Circle.* Boston: Houghton Mifflin, 1960.

Kennan, George F. *Memoirs.* 2 vols. Boston: Little, Brown, 1967-1972.

Millis, Walter, ed. *The Forrestal Diaries.* New York: Viking, 1951.

Nagy, Ferenc. *The Struggle behind the Iron Curtain.* Trans. Stephen K. Swift. New York: Macmillan, 1948.

Stettinius, Edward R., Jr. *Roosevelt and the Russians: The Yalta Conference.* Garden City: Doubleday, 1949.

Truman, Harry S. *Memoirs: Years of Trial and Hope.* Garden City: Doubleday, 1956.

Vandenberg, Arthur H., Jr., ed. *The Private Papers of Senator Vandenberg.* Boston: Houghton Mifflin, 1952.

C. Oral History Interview

H. Freeman Matthews Interview by Richard D. McKinzie, Harry S Truman Library, 7 June 1973, Washington, D.C.

D. British Labour Party documents

Cards on the Table: An Interpretation of Labour's Foreign Policy. London: Transport House, 1947.

Keep Left. London: New Statesman, 1947.

Report of the 45th Annual Conference, 1946. London: Transport House, 1946.

Report of the 46th Annual Conference, 1947. London: Transport House, 1947.

Report of the 47th Annual Conference, 1948. London: Transport House, 1948.

E. Newspapers

Detroit News
New York Times
Times (London)

Secondary Sources

Allen, H. C. *Great Britain and the United States: A History of Anglo-American Relations (1783-1952).* New York: St. Martin's, 1955.

Alperovitz, Gar. *Atomic Diplomacy: Hiroshima and Potsdam: The Use of the Atomic Bomb and the American Confrontation with Soviet Power.* New York: Simon and Schuster, 1965.

Anderson, M. S. *The Eastern Question, 1774-1923: A Study in International Relations.* London: Macmillan: New York: St. Martin's Press, 1966.

Anderson, Terry H. *The United States, Great Britain and the Cold War, 1944-1947.* Columbia, Mo.: University of Missouri Press, 1981.

Aronson, James. *The Press and the Cold War.* Indianapolis: Bobbs-Merrill Company, 1970.

Bán, Antal. "Hungary." In *The Curtain Falls: The Story of the Socialists in Eastern Europe.* Ed. Denis Healey. London: Lincolns-Prager, 1951, pp. 61-82.

Barker, Elisabeth. *British Policy in South-East Europe in the Second World War.* London: Macmillan, 1976.

Barta, István et al. *A History of Hungary.* Trans. László Boros et al. London: Collet's 1975.

Bennett, Edward M. *Recognition of Russia: An American Foreign Policy Dilemma.* Waltham, Mass.: Blaisdell, 1970.

Brand, Carl F. *The British Labour Party: A Short History.* Rev. ed. Stanford: Hoover Institution Press, 1974.

Bullock, Alan. *The Life and Times of Ernest Bevin.* 2 vols. London, Heinemann, 1960-1967.

Calvocoressi, Peter. *Survey of International Affairs, 1947-1948.* London: Oxford University Press, 1952.

————. *Survey of International Affairs, 1949-1950.* London, Oxford University Press, 1953.

Coates, W. P. and Zelda K. *A History of Anglo-Soviet Relations.* London: Lawrence and Wishart, 1943.

Cochran, Bert. *Harry Truman and the Crisis Presidency.* New York: Funk and Wagnalls, 1973.

Cohen, Saul Bernard. *Georgraphy and Politics in a World Divided.* 2nd ed. New York: Oxford University Press, 1973.

Cole, G. D. H. *A Short History of the British Working Class Movement, 1789-1947.* New ed. London: Allen Unwin, 1948.

Crowe, Sir Eyre. "Memorandum on the Present State of British Relations with France and Germany." In *Britain and Europe: Pitt to Churchill, 1793-1940.* Ed. James Joll. London: A. & C. Black, 1961, pp. 204-6.

Curry, George. *James F. Byrnes.* Vol. 14 of *The American Secretaries of State and Their Diplomacy,* ed. Robert H. Ferrell. New York: Cooper Square Publishers, 1965.

Daniels, Jonathan. *The Man of Independence.* Philadelphia: J. B. Lippincott Company, 1950.

Davis, Lynn Etheridge. *The Cold War Begins: Soviet-American Conflict over Eastern Europe.* Princeton: Princeton University Press, 1974.

Deák, Francis. *Hungary at the Paris Peace Conference: The Diplomatic History of the Treaty of Trianon.* New York: Columbia University Press, 1942.

Deutscher, I. *The Prophet Armed: Trotsky, 1879-1921.* New York: Oxford University Press, 1954.

Dewar, Margaret. *Soviet Trade with Eastern Europe, 1945-1949.* London: Royal Institute of International Affairs, 1951.

Doenecke, Justus D. *Not to the Swift: The Old Isolationists in the Cold War Era.* Lewisburg: Bucknell University Press, 1979.

Donnelly, Desmond. *Struggle for the World: The Cold War from Its Origins in 1917.* London: Collins, 1965.

Donovan, Robert S. *Conflict and Crisis: The Presidency of Harry S. Truman, 1945-1948.* New York: W. W. Norton and Company, 1977.

Dreisziger, Nandor A. F. *Hungary's Way to World War II.* Toronto, Hungarian Helicon Society, 1968.

Feis, Herbert. *Churchill, Roosevelt, Stalin: The War They Waged and the Peace They Sought.* 2nd ed. Princeton: Princeton University Press, 1967.

————. *From Trust to Terror: The Onset of the Cold War, 1945-1950.* New York: Norton, 1970.

Fenyo, Mario D. *Hitler, Horthy, and Hungary: German-Hungarian Relations, 1941-1944.* New Haven: Yale University Press, 1972.

Fitzsimons, M. A. *The Foreign Policy of the British Labour Government, 1945-1956.* Notre Dame: University of Notre Dame Press, 1953.

Fleming, D. F. *The Cold War and Its Origins, 1917-1960.* Garden City: Doubleday, 1960.

Frankel, Joseph. *British Foreign Policy, 1945-1973.* London: Oxford University Press, 1975.

Gordon, Michael R. *Conflict and Concensus in Labour's Foreign Policy, 1914-1965.* Stanford: Stanford University Press, 1969.

Gosnell, Harold F. *Truman's Crises: A Political Biography of Harry S. Truman.* Westport, Conn.: Greenwood Press, 1980.

Gray, Colin S. *The Geopolitics of the Nuclear Age: Heartland, Rimlands, and the Technological Revolution.* New York: Crane, Russak, 1977.

Halle, Louis J. *The Cold War as History.* New York: Harper, 1967.

Harrison, Martin. *Trade Unions and the Labour Party since 1945.* Detroit: Wayne State University Press, 1960.

Hathaway, Robert M. *Ambiguous Partnership: Britain and America, 1944-1947.* New York: Columbia University Press, 1981.

Hedley, John Hollister. *Harry S. Truman: The "Little" Man from Missouri.* New York: Barron's Educational Series, 1979.

Higgins, Trumbull. *Winston Churchill and the Second Front, 1940-1943.* New York: Oxford University Press, 1957.

Horowitz, David. *The Free World Colossus: A Critique of American Foreign Policy in the Cold War.* New York: Hill and Wang, 1965.

Howard, Harry N. *Turkey, the Straits, and U.S. Policy.* Baltimore: Johns Hopkins University Press, 1974.

Ignotus, Paul. "The First Two Communist Takeovers of Hungary: 1919 and 1948." In *The Anatomy of Communist Takeovers.* Ed. Thomas T. Hammond. New Haven: Yale University Press, 1975, pp. 385-98.

Jackson, Robert J. *Rebels and Whips: An Analysis of Dissension, Discipline and Cohesion in British Political Parties.* London: Macmillan; New York: St. Martin's, 1968.

Kennan, George F. *Soviet-American Relations, 1917-1920.* 2 vols. Princeton: Princeton University Press, 1956-1958.

Kennedy, Paul M. *The Rise and Fall of British Naval Mastery.* London: Lane, 1976.

Kertesz, Stephen D. *Diplomacy in a Whirlpool: Hungary between Nazi Germany and Soviet Russia.* Notre Dame: University of Notre Dame Press, 1953.

————. ed. *The Fate of East Central Europe: Hopes and Failures of American Foreign Policy.* Notre Dame: University of Notre Dame Press, 1956.

Kolko, Gabriel. *The Politics of War: The World and United States Foreign Policy, 1943-1945.* New York: Random House, 1968.

Kolko, Joyce and Gabriel. *The Limits of Power: The World and United States Foreign Policy, 1945-1954.* New York: Harper, 1972.

Kovrig, Bennett. *Communism in Hungary: From Kun to Kádár.* Stanford: Hoorver Institution Press, 1979.

Kuklick, Bruce. *American Policy and the Division of Germany: The Clash with Russia over Reparations.* Ithaca: Cornell University Press, 1972.

Leighton, Richard M. "OVERLORD Revisited: An Interpretation of American Strategy in the European War, 1942-1944." *American Historical Review,* 68:4 (1963), 919-37.

Lukacs, John A. *The Great Powers and Eastern Europe.* New York: American Book Co., 1953.

Lundestad, Geir. *The American Non-Policy towards Eastern Europe, 1943-1947: Universalism in an Area Not of Essential Interest to the United States.* Tromsö: Universitetsforlaget, 1975.

Macartney, C. A. *Hungary and Her Successors: The Treaty of Trianon and Its Consequences, 1919-1937.* London: Oxford University Press, 1937.

————. *A History of Hungary, 1929-1945.* 2 vols. New York: Praeger, 1956-1957.

————. *Hungary: A Short History.* Edinburgh: Edinburgh University Press, 1962.

————. and A. W. Palmer. *Independent Eastern Europe: A History.* London: Macmillan, 1962.

McCagg, William O., Jr. *Stalin Embattled, 1943-1948.* Detroit: Wayne State University Press, 1978.

McNeill, William H. *America, Britain, and Russia: Their Cooperation and Conflict, 1941-1946.* London: Oxford University Press, 1953.

Maier, Charles S. "Revisionism and the Interpretation of Cold War Origins." *Perspectives in American History,* 4 (1970), 313-47.

Marriott, Sir J. A. R. *Anglo-Russian Relations, 1689-1943.* London: Methuen, 1944.

Mastny, Vojtech. *Russia's Road to the Cold War: Diplomacy, Warfare, and the Politics of Communism, 1941-1945.* New York: Columbia University Press, 1979.

Mee, Charles L., Jr. *Meeting at Potsdam.* New York: M. Evans and Company, 1975.

Messer, Robet L. *The End of an Alliance: James F. Byrnes, Roosevelt, Truman, and the Origins of the Cold War.* Chapel Hill, N.C.: University of North Carolina Press, 1982.

Molnár, Miklós. *A Short History of the Hungarian Communist Party.*
Boulder: Westview; Folkestone, Eng.: Dawson, 1978.

Montgomery, John Flournoy. *Hungary: The Unwilling Satellite.* New
York: Devin Adair, 1947.

Nagy-Talavera, Nicholas M. *The Green Shirts and the Others: A History
of Fascism in Hungary and Rumania.* Stanford: Hoover Institution
Press, 1970.

Nicholas, H. G. *The United States and Britain.* Chicago: University of
Chicago Press, 1975.

Northedge, F. S. *British Foreign Policy: The Process of Readjustment,
1945-1961.* London: Allen Unwin, 1962.

Pearton, Maurice. *Oil and the Rumanian State.* Oxford: Clarendon, 1971.

Pelling, Henry. *The British Communist Party: An Historical Profile.* New
York: Macmillan, 1958.

————. *The Origins of the Labour Party, 1880-1900.* 2nd ed. Oxford:
Clarendon, 1965.

————. *A Short History of the Labour Party.* 4th ed. London: Macmillan; New York: St. Martin's, 1972.

Resis, Albert. "The Churchill-Stalin Secret 'Percentages' Agreement on the
Balkans, Moscow, October 1944." *American Historical Review,* 83:2
(1978), 368-87.

Richardson, J. L. "Cold War Revisionism: A Critique." *World Politics,* 24:
4 (1972), 579-612.

Royal Institute of International Affairs. *South-Eastern Europe: A Political
and Economic Survey.* London: Royal Institute of International Affairs,
1939.

Roberts, B. C. *The Trades Union Congress, 1868-1921.* Cambridge: Har-
vard University Press, 1958.

Robson, William A. *Nationalized Industries and Public Ownership.* Toronto: University of Toronto Press, 1960.

Rupprecht, Paul. "The Image of Hungary's International Position in American Foreign Policy-Making, 1937-1947." Ph.D. dissertation. University
of Minnesota, 1967.

Schoenfeld, H. F. Arthur. "Soviet Imperialism in Hungary." *Foreign Affairs,* 26:3 (1948), 554-67.

Seabury, Paul. *The Rise and Decline of the Cold War.* New York: Basic
Books, 1967.

Seton-Watson, Hugh. *The East European Revolution.* 3rd ed. New York: Praeger, 1956.

Snyder, Richard Carlton. *The Most-Favored-Nation Clause: An Analysis with Particular Reference to Recent Treaty Practice and Tariffs.* New York: King's Crown, 1948.

Spulber, Nicolas. *The Economics of Communist Eastern Europe.* Cambridge, Mass.: Technology Press of Massachusetts Institute of Technology, 1957.

Szilassy, Sándor. *Revolutionary Hungary, 1918-1921.* Astor Park, Fla.: Danubian Press, 1971.

Taubman, William. *Stalin's American Policy: From Entente to Detente to Cold War.* New York: Norton, 1982.

Theoharis, Athan G. *The Yalta Myths: An Issue in U.S. Politics, 1945-1955.* Columbia, Mo.: University of Missouri Press, 1970.

Tőkés, Rudolf L. *Bela Kun and the Hungarian Soviet Republic: The Origins and Role of the Communist Party of Hungary in the Revolutions of 1918-1919.* New York: Praeger, 1967.

Toynbee, Arnold, and Veronica Toynbee, eds. *The Realignment of Europe.* Vol. VI of *Survey of International Affairs, 1939-1946.* London: Oxford University Press, 1955.

Ulam, Adam B. *Expansion and Coexistence: Soviet Foreign Policy, 1917-1973.* 2nd ed. New York: Praeger, 1974.

Ullman, Richard H. *Anglo-Soviet Relations, 1917-1921.* 3 vols. Princeton: Princeton University Press, 1961-1972.

Upstein, Leon D. *Britain–Uneasy Ally.* Chicago: University of Chicago Press, 1954.

Völgyes, Iván. *Hungary in Revolution, 1918-1919: Nine Essays.* Lincoln: University of Nebraska Press, 1971.

Ward, Patricia Dawson. *The Threat of Peace: James F. Byrnes and the Council of Foreign Ministers, 1945-1946.* Kent, Ohio: Kent State University Press, 1979.

Watkins, Ernest. *The Cautious Revolution: Britain Today and Tomorrow.* New York: Farrar, 1950.

Wheeler-Bennett, Sir John, and Anthony Nicholls. *The Semblance of Peace: The Political Settlement after the Second World War.* London: Macmillan, 1972.

Williams, Francis. *Ernest Bevin: Portrait of a Great Englishman.* London: Hutchinson, 1952.

————. "Bevin, Ernest." *The Dictionary of National Biography, 1951-1960.* London: Oxford University Press, 1971.

Williams, William Appleman. *The Tragedy of American Diplomacy.* Rev. ed. New York: Dell, 1962.

Windrich, Elaine. *British Labour's Foreign Policy.* Stanford: Stanford University Press, 1952.

Wittner, Lawrence S. *Cold War America: From Hiroshima to Watergate.* Expanded ed. New York: Holt, Rinehart and Winston, 1978.

Woodward, Sir Llewellyn. *British Foreign Policy in the Second World War.* Vols. III and V. London: HMSO, 1971 and 1976.

Yergin, Daniel. *Shattered Peace: The Origins of the Cold War and the National Security State.* Boston: Houghton Mifflin, 1977.

INDEX

Acheson, Dean, 24, 90, 99, 101
Addis, John M., 35
A.F.L.-C.I.O., 47
Albania, 100, 122
Allen, H. C., 19
Allied Commission, Italian, 13, 162n21
Allied Control Commission, Bulgarian, 13, 83
Allied Control Commission, Finnish, 13
Allied Control Commission, Hungarian: establishment of, 13; and reparations, 15; and 1945 Hungarian elections, 35; and Great Britain, 69; termination of, 83; and political events of 1946, 88-91; and political events of 1947, 97-100, 108-9
Allied Control Commission, Rumanian, 13, 83
Anschluss, 6
Anti-Comintern Pact, 6
Armistice, Hungarian, 61-63, 89
Armistice with German satellites, 78
Arrow Cross Party, 5, 6, 8
Atomic bomb, 53, 55
Attlee, Clement, 29, 78
Austria, 5-6, 63, 83, 105, 136
Austro-Hungarian Empire, 2
Azerbaijan, 54

Balance of power, 139-42
Balkans, question of invading, 7-8, 149n12
Baltic nations, 126

Bán, Antal, 116
Banks, 102-3, 105, 167n30
Baránkovics, István, 113
Bárdossy, László, 7
Belgium, 125
Benelux, 141
Beneš, Eduard, 85
Berlin crisis, 48, 55
Bethlen, István, 4
Bevin, Ernest: foreign policy of, 29, 42-49, 141; on Eastern Europe, 29-30; and Council of Foreign Ministers (London, 1945), 31-32; and Conference of Foreign Ministers (Moscow, 1945), 37-38; Labour rebels on, 45, 48; and peace conference, 78; on Hungarian coup, 106, 107-8; and West European Union, 125; and Churchill's "Iron Curtain" speech, 136
Bipartisanship, 56-57, 78
Bohlen, Charles, 20, 21, 24-25, 51-52
Boy Scouts, 88-89
British Commonwealth, 125
British Isles, 136
Brussels Treaty Organization, 125
Bulgaria: and "percentages" agreement, 20; and Yalta Conference, 21; Sargent on, 22-23; and question of Western recognition, 26-29, 31-32, 36-38, 53; Bevin on, 30; electoral law of 1945, 33; German assets in, 65; Soviet control of, 76; and United Nations, 110

189